VISIONS OF HOPE

RUNNING TOWARDS MY OWN TRUTH

JASON DUNKERLEY

YORKLAND PUBLISHING

Yorkland Publishing

Copyright © 2024 by Jason Dunkerley

All rights reserved. No part of this publication may be reproduced, stored in a retrieval system, or transmitted, in any form or by any means, electronic, mechanical, photocopying, recording or otherwise, without the written prior permission of the publisher.

Published by
Yorkland Publishing
12 Tepee Court
Toronto, Ontario M2J 3A9
Canada
www.yorklandpublishing.com

ISBN: 978-1-7390044-2-2

Book Design by Rosemary Shiller

Printed and bound by IngramSpark

To my beautiful mother, Rae, a ray of sunshine who gave me life, love, self-belief and a vision of hope. Your light guides me forward.

Foreword

By Bruce Kidd, OC, OLY, PhD, LLD

I've experienced nothing as moving and courageous in sport as running blind – runners with no or limited eyesight charging into the void with speed and determination. I still remember witnessing my first blind race at the Toronto Telegram Indoor Games at Maple Leaf Gardens. As the crowd sat deathly silent, five sprinters hurled themselves down the wooden track with only the shouts of their helpers at the finish to direct them. As a fully sighted runner, I had had my share of slips and falls and was always conscious about stepping carefully. And here were sightless runners up on their toes, going full blast with confidence and elan. I cried.

Jason Dunkerley is a blind runner who charges into the void over distances as long as 10,000 metres or 25 laps on a 400-metre track and in marathons on the road – far longer than the 50-yard straightaway sprint I saw long ago at Maple Leaf Gardens. He runs and trains hard – his times would be competitive in most able-bodied meets, but he can only do so with a guide to whom a 25-centimetre rope attaches him. While greatly reducing the risk of crashing, the guiding arrangement requires them to interact as one unit. They must be united on strategy and tactics and navigate the twists and turns of the track, the jostling, and other runners' bursts in constant contact. To achieve such inseparable coordination, Jason and his guide train together, which requires them to schedule a big part of their lives in sync and deal with the inevitable injuries and disappointments as a couple, necessitating a close, personal partnership. Pair figure skating requires similar emotional, tactical, and embodied coordination. Still, few other sports put quite the premium on building and maintaining a strong personal relationship. It's a big part of the sport.

Jason has had a storied athletic career, representing Canada at five Paralympic Games and many other international events and winning five Paralympic medals. He's also completed a degree in International Development, donated a kidney, travelled extensively, and contributed to the development of Paralympic sport in Canada and internationally. Now in his mid-40s, he's lived a remarkable life – with ambition, imagination, and accomplishment, and he's still going strong.

Visions of Hope is an insightful, at times poetic, account of the life of a Canadian Paralympian. You'd never know from the emotions expressed in these pages that Jason is sightless. He tells you in the introduction that while he can only make out vague shapes, he's always loved to run fast. He tells his story engagingly, with honesty and gusto. Right off the top, you're caught up in the stresses and adventures of the sport and the efforts he had to make to manage the relationships and environment around him. I learned a lot and developed tremendous admiration for Jason and his teammates. It's a moving and courageous story.

Bruce Kidd is Professor Emeritus of Sport Politics and Policy at the University of Toronto. Twice elected Canada's Male Athlete of the Year by Canadian Press, he competed in athletics at the 1964 Olympics in Tokyo.

Preface

Listening to the sound of dogs barking, birds singing, and trees breathing in the warm air, feeling stillness, being touched by sunshine on your upturned face and letting it hold you in its light and hug you with its warmth, floating fast and light on a long run where it seems you barely touch the ground – these are gifts from God.

Feeling your essential I Am, connecting with your soul force, that intangible, vital part of you, is surely the key to simple, brilliant living, to survival itself. When we spend time alone listening to our heart rhythm, we become inspired by the powerful realization that by honouring our natural state of being, we empower ourselves to overcome life's hurdles and lead truly fulfilling lives. This book is the story of my journey.

As a boy, I ran with my brothers in the garden of our childhood in Northern Ireland. As an émigré to Canada, I ran to silence the echoes of my homesickness, to ease my loneliness, to be accepted, and to set down roots. I ran for my adopted country. Eventually, I ran for me.

Sometimes, I ran away from, sometimes towards, and other times in circles. I knew that progress in running was not linear. It was attained through lessons learned from failure as well as success. Each cycle of my life has brought new insights, enabling me to navigate the often-unanticipated bumps along the way. I hope this book encourages others to discover and follow their own true path.

1 Remembering

One of my first memories is riding a children's go-cart down our street with my mother frantically chasing me. I was three years old, and my parents, older sister, younger twin brothers, and I lived in a council house in a housing estate whose streets were named after World War II British fighter planes. We lived on Lizander Park. I had somehow managed to escape through the gate in our backyard and was propelling my go-cart towards the busy crossroad at the end of our street at top speed. In a way, it could have been my first run.

This was in Newtownards, Northern Ireland, in the early 1980s. At that time, it had a population of around twenty thousand. Located in County Down on the Ards Peninsula, Newtownards is about fifteen kilometres east of Belfast, overlooked by Scrabo Tower, a historic hill fort that we climbed for picnics or to roll eggs down at Easter. On a clear day, people could look out from Scrabo to the north and east across the Irish Sea and glimpse the Scottish coast.

As I scootered helter-skelter down the street in my go-cart, my mother knew I couldn't see what might have been in front of me. I'd been born with Leber's congenital amaurosis (LCA), a condition that affects the retina at the back of the eye. My younger twin brothers, Jonathan and Christopher, were also born with the same condition; my half-sister Nicki, nearly four years older than I, was unaffected.

LCA is characterized by a dysfunction of the photoreceptor cells in the retina that make vision possible. Normally, photoreceptor cells convert light into electrical signals that are then communicated to the brain and interpreted as visual images.

That I had LCA hadn't been apparent at first, but when I was three months old, my mother noticed I had rapid eye movements and wasn't responding to visual cues. A visit to an optometrist quickly led to a diagnosis.

In children with LCA, both parents typically transmit one mutated copy of the LCA gene along with a normal copy of the gene. Although my parents were unaffected carriers, each of their children had a 25% likelihood of inheriting the two LCA gene copies.

Being born with LCA, I grew up never knowing what it was like to see. Never having had sight, I've never missed it. People who lose their vision later in life have a very different experience because they need to adapt to functioning without the eyesight they previously had. Of course, part of me wishes I could better relate to the visual world. What does a sunrise look like? What does my loved one look like?

I had some light perception, as did my brothers, allowing me to see sunshine or a light on in a room. I could also see shadows that helped me avoid objects in my way, though I couldn't distinguish them. Sometimes, I could tell whether a TV newsreader had on a tie or determine which Nintendo figures were on the screen. Over the years, however, the little bit of light perception I had diminished so that now, although I can still see sunlight, I'm unable to tell whether a light in a room is on or off.

Of course, my brothers and I did have our share of bumps, bruises, and stitches. When I was seven, I fell off my bike while following Nicki on hers. Blood poured out of a deep cut on my knee that led to a trip to the hospital for stitches under general anesthesia.

Unlike many parents of children with disabilities, my parents didn't shelter us. We spent hours playing outside with our cousins and other sighted children in our neighbourhood. My father taught me to ride a bicycle. He started me with stabilizers, which were soon removed when I learned to use speed and forward movement to maintain balance. My brothers were not far behind.

1 Remembering

My father ran a taxi business, and my mother worked with him. My maternal grandmother, my aunts Betty and Karen, and our neighbours created a close web of support and love so that we were well looked after; we never went without.

I have warm memories of my grandmother. She had separated from my grandfather a few years earlier and lived alone in a small house nearby, where my mother had been raised. Occasionally, I would sleep over, just me. Warm and cozy, with good things to eat, an open coal fire, and granny's stories trailing into the embers in a voice made gravelly by years of smoking, I'd climb the spiral stairs to bed and wake to the aroma of breakfast cooking on the gas stove. In those moments, I knew that I belonged somewhere, that I was cared for, and in the future, my past would always matter.

Despite the fond memories of my childhood, living with blindness wasn't always easy. While most kids had our backs and stuck up for us, others sometimes teased us by calling us "blindies" or poked fun at us because we couldn't see them. One incident at school involved a visually impaired kid who had more vision than I. He frequently tapped me on the shoulder and then ran away laughing. He never expected that I might catch him, but when I finally did, I threw him to the ground and beat him up. Both of us received short suspensions from school for fighting. Despite the reproaches of teachers and my mother, I never regretted fighting back against a bully who thought he was being funny.

In the world of adults, bias is usually more nuanced. People sometimes speak more slowly and louder, as though my blindness would prevent me from hearing or understanding them. Potential employers have gone through the motions of interviewing me for jobs I was well qualified for, though it was clear they weren't serious about hiring me. I've even felt it from those closest to me. I often need to remind myself that being around a blind person isn't something people are used to or comfortable with. Sighted people commonly underestimate what a blind person is capable of.

My father, Peter Dunkerley, had arrived in Northern Ireland from Lancashire, England, in the mid-1970s as part of the British Royal Navy.

He met and married my mother, Rae Pollock, leaving the Navy shortly after and started driving taxis. He was about six feet three inches, taller than my brothers or I would become. He was a sportsman, a footballer, a weekend warrior who headed to the pub or the slots right after a match. Sometimes, he took me with him. "Things are looking up, son; we're going to be eating well tonight," he would say when he won. There was abject silence when he lost, which was most often the case.

People who knew my dad painted a picture of him as self-contained and remote, a man who sat and drank alone in a crowded bar. There have been moments in my life when I've felt the shadow of remoteness, too, but knowing its origin, I've pushed back so that it wouldn't claim me as its prisoner.

My father gave my mother very little money, but there was always enough for the pub. He also drank at home. One evening, when my mother was out, he gave me a beer. I must have been about six. It tasted terrible. My head was swimming, and I went shakily up the stairs to bed. The next day, when my mother found out, she was furious with him.

I have poignant memories of my parents fighting late at night. I'd bury my head and try not to hear, but the yelling was impossible to ignore. In the morning, life seemed to go on as normal. My mother got us up, made us breakfast, and the school bus picked us up at ten minutes to eight.

Jon, Chris, and I attended the Jordanstown School for the Blind, the only school of its kind in Northern Ireland. It took in visually impaired and blind children from around the country from nursery age to the sixth form when they were sixteen. We were taught to use a white cane, enabling us to walk independently – when we weren't racing each other down the halls and corridors.

Teachers with specialized training taught classes where Braille, a system in which each letter has a unique combination of raised dots on a six-dot grid, was the *lingua franca* of instruction. A single dot represents the letter A; two vertical dots signify a B; two horizontal dots are a C; and so on. I learned to write Braille using a manual machine – not unlike a typewriter – at the age of five from Mrs. Gibson, my first-year teacher. She challenged us to think and problem-solve. She also had a great sense of humour. Once, she sent me out of class to ask another teacher for the long weight. It ended

1 Remembering

up being a very long wait – I hadn't realized it was April Fool's Day.

As any other child learns to read and write, we absorbed Braille like sponges. Today, Braille is sadly a dying art, as the prevalence of computer screen reading software, smartphones, e-texts, and audiobooks has opened new avenues to education and communication for those with a visual disability.

My brothers and I took a daily hour-long minibus to school through east Belfast into County Antrim and back. In the 1980s, Belfast was a breeding ground for sectarian violence that pitted pro-British Protestant Ulster Unionists against pro-Irish nationalist Roman Catholics. While the latter aspired for a unified Ireland, the former wished to guard Northern Ireland's place within the United Kingdom.

In Northern Ireland, you were born on one side or the other. We were Protestants, as were the other people living on our street. My best friend, Joseph, was Roman Catholic, but for us, friendship stood far above religion. Yet at home, we still celebrated the archetypes of the pro-British Orange movement: the marching bands, Eleventh of July bonfire nights, and Twelfth of July celebrations.

People ventured into Belfast only when necessary because of the threat of violence. Aside from a single bomb scare at my school, the Troubles, which dated back to the late 1960s when Northern Ireland, like much of the world, was caught in the vortex of political upheaval, had little impact on me.

My uncle Alan, however, who served in the British army and patrolled the streets of Belfast in the late 1960s, saw up close the ravages of indiscriminate violence. He hardly ever talked about it, but to this day, he and his wife, Alma, remain steadfast supporters of the Protestant cause.

If my brothers and I had lived any further away from our school, we would have boarded there and returned home only on the weekends, as many of our friends did, much to our envy. It seemed to us that all the fun was to be had in the evenings.

When I was seven, we moved from our house on Lizander Park to a house a couple of streets away on Valetta, still within the same housing estate. It had a coal-burning fireplace that was warm and comforting during the damp, cool evenings. Fewer people use coal now, but it's a smell of home

I'll never forget.

Our house on Valetta was bigger, though small, compared to many North American homes. My twin brothers still shared a room, but I now had one of my own, as did my sister. Perhaps most exciting, at least for my brothers and me, was the big, fenced backyard.

Moving, however, was not enough to save my parents' marriage. I remember the day I realized how bad things had become. My mother had gone out. My father was downstairs, and I was upstairs in my bedroom. I had devised a system to communicate between the two floors by tuning the downstairs radio to an FM frequency that would pick up transmissions from our walkie-talkies. My father was supposed to yell upstairs when he heard my voice. I chattered into the walky-talky for about ten minutes, but he never called out from below. Finally, I went downstairs, only to find him sitting with the hiss of the FM radio filling the room. My voice hadn't come through, but he had remained there, inert and without turning down the static or giving me any indication that my transmission had failed. At that moment, even as a child of seven, the extent of his detachment and depression was achingly apparent. He moved out a short time after that into an apartment my mother helped him set up.

I wanted my parents to get back together so badly. But my father met another woman and quickly moved in with her, and they remained together for about two years. I saw him on weekends at the nearby house they were renting. It was hard feeling close to him, but his presence was reassuring. We would play football in their backyard; he played goalkeeper, and we would try to score on him.

Eventually, he moved back to England and faded out of our lives. He sent us a Christmas card that first year, with ten pounds for each of us. That was the last we heard from him. I was ten. I can only guess that his failed taxi business and the pressure of trying to support a wife and four kids, three of them blind, contributed to his leaving, though I wish I knew why he never kept in touch.

His departure from our lives was jarring in its finality. I often thought about looking for him but never did. He died in England in the spring of 2023 at seventy-five. His obituary, found through a Google search, provided

1 Remembering

few details about his life but enough for me to know without a doubt that it was him. I choose to believe he never forgot us.

After my father left, more responsibility fell on my sister Nicki's shoulders, and my mother had little choice but to lean on her for help. She had given birth to Nicki when she was just nineteen, and Nicki's biological father never played a significant part in her life. My father also hadn't accepted Nicki as his own. She carried this pain with her throughout our childhood, and it saddens me now, thinking back, I had not fully appreciated the depth of pain she internalized and the responsibility that fell on her shoulders.

Jon, Chris and I would listen to football on the radio on the weekends and ride our bicycles around the neighbourhood block. We knew the turns well enough and rode without fear, not venturing beyond our habitual loop. Would I do it now? Probably not, but back then, I never thought twice.

We developed our own adapted games. We played football by tying a plastic grocery bag around a soccer ball so we could hear it moving and a modified version of cricket using the same soccer ball.

At school, my brothers and I formed close friendships with kids from around Northern Ireland. Joseph Kenny and Bronah O'Neill boarded at school, and Neil McCullough, like us, took a daily bus. We sometimes spent weekends at each other's houses, eating everything, staying up late, and listening to mixed tapes of songs by Guns and Roses, Iron Maiden, and Bon Jovi. These friendships were unconditional and uninhibited; anything went, and we were nothing if not irreverent and at complete ease with one another; such is the authenticity of adolescent boys.

A few years ago, Neil told me of an early exchange he had with my mother during a weekend visit. In retrospect, I can envision the scenario, but it's all the more poignant to see your loved ones mirrored back to you through the recollection of others. He asked my mother whether he could use my new CB radio, used for short-distance, two-way communication, to which she responded, "Well, you'll have to ask Jason!" He told me that if it had been his parents and I'd asked to use his radio, they would have almost certainly said yes immediately.

It was important to my mother that we grow up feeling independent and empowered to make our own choices; she wanted us to be able to stand on our own feet. She taught me how to make a peanut butter sandwich, something simple but taught with love, good humour and patience. Today, I enjoy cooking, and I have my mother to thank for introducing me to the basics, as she did with so many things in her own understated, practical way.

She enrolled my brothers and me in the Boys Brigade, or BB as we called it, a precursor to Boy Scouts. Each Monday evening, our group met for organized games and physical activity led by a program leader, who always found ways to include us by pairing us with a partner or modifying the rules so we could participate.

Our mother also involved us in tandem cycling – hugely popular in Northern Ireland. I did weekly time trials with a local cyclist, Gary Crawford, who piloted our tandem. He was an aggressive rider, taking the downhills and corners fast to gain a competitive advantage, given that tandems lose ground to solo cyclists on uphill climbs.

Gary rode a tandem bike to our house on weekends or weekday evenings to do training rides with me of up to 45 kilometres. He introduced me to pushing through pain.

In addition to the local time trial races, I once travelled to England with Gary and my brothers to compete with other tandem teams. Through our club, we also went on a week-long training tour in Austria when I was twelve. Over time, Gary and I eventually increased our training volume to be able to participate that same year in the Mara Cycle, held every June. Riders peddle 100 miles from Belfast to Dublin in one day and return the next.

I had diverse interests growing up. I have always been drawn to music and was fortunate, as were my brothers, to be born with perfect pitch, meaning that we could differentiate notes without the benefit of a reference tone. I started taking piano lessons, then switched to the violin, reaching grade four in the Royal Conservatory of Music system. But the instrument I was most eager to learn was the guitar. My mother bought me a guitar for Christmas one year, a Fender Mustang electric, and I eventually learned to play well enough to be in a band a few of us had formed at school.

When we were kids in the late 1980s, we were glued to the radio, hearing about the famous sports stars of that era, such as the footballers Gary

1 Remembering

Lineker and Chris Waddle as well as Steve Cram, Sebastian Coe, Peter Elliott, and Steve Ovett in British middle-distance running. Although I was always fascinated by running, I wasn't naturally good at it. Nonetheless, I had plenty of self-confidence.

When I was eleven, I travelled with fellow students to another school to run in a cross-country race. On the morning of the race, I confidently told my mother I would win. When it came down to it, I couldn't keep up, I dropped from the main pack and ended up walking. It was a sober lesson in humility, but it also left me with an important insight: I would have to work to get better; it wouldn't happen otherwise. That applied to running, but it would be the same in other areas of my life.

I persuaded my uncle Gary, who had competed in track and marathons when he was younger, to take me out for jogs. Now in his late sixties, he covers fourteen miles daily delivering mail, and he and his wife, our aunt Betty, are regular gym-goers. I also met a local runner, Eddie Johnston, in his early sixties then, whose passion for running and stories of past races while representing Northern Ireland inspired me to keep up with him, although the truth is that he let me.

When I didn't have a guide who could run beside me, I jogged around the perimeter of our backyard. We estimated that sixteen laps added up to a mile. It was monotonous, but I didn't mind because I could do it without a guide.

I also ran at school, guided by teachers. Our best runner was Terence Carlin. A few years older than I, he had partial vision, didn't require a guide, and could run 800 metres on the track in 1:59, which seemed incredible.

Life had its familiar rhythms, routines, and patterns woven around the friends and family with whom we were interconnected. For years, our mother raised us alone, swearing she would never have another man in her life. We didn't have a lot of extras, but I never felt deprived.

She had a good friend, Diane, who lived nearby in Comber. On one occasion, Diane took my mother to Dublin for a Tina Turner concert, eventually reintroducing her to evenings out. On one of those nights out, my mother met Diane's brother, Maurice. He was on vacation from Canada and visiting his family in Northern Ireland.

Maurice was full of stories about living in Canada, having immigrated there ten years earlier. It seemed so far away; my only point of reference was through knowing people who had relatives there. I knew the winters were cold. He talked of big houses, hot summer night pool parties, frigid February mornings driving a Bobcat to move snow, and drinking coffee laced with whiskey. He seemed exotic and not quite real, like a movie star from another world, an actor.

He played guitar. He was smooth, romantic, and unlike anyone I had ever known. I woke up one morning in November 1990 to find him in our house. He had woven his way into my mother's heart. I was thirteen.

In the weeks and months that followed, life would change fundamentally. Maurice returned to spend Christmas with us, and my mother visited him in Canada in January 1991. On that trip, they decided to share their lives. My sister, who by then was seventeen, didn't want to go and moved in with our grandmother.

It happened so quickly that my brothers and I had little time to absorb the magnitude of our impending move. There was scarcely time to say goodbye to the friends who had shaped the contours of our childhood. We left with promises to keep in touch that, sadly, mostly fell by the wayside over time.

A few days before our flight to Toronto, I visited a friend's house for a goodbye lunch. During the meal, my friend's dad made an offhanded remark about Canadians being fat with big mouths, a casual comment, but it planted a strong preconception of Canada in my young mind.

My friend's dad wasn't alone in his way of thinking. Many Northern Irish considered North America a place of excess. People crossed the Atlantic to pursue bigger and better, leaving histories of division and scarcity, such as the Irish potato famine of the mid-1840s. This and the subsequent world wars and Northern Ireland's Troubles contributed to a rising tide of fatalism on the one hand and austerity on the other. People loved to have fun and were hospitable. Still, they could also be guarded, suspicious, and resentful of anybody who seemed to be getting ahead, especially when they appeared to take too much.

Scarcity was a daily reality when I was growing up. Most of us lived modestly and simply. Our homes were tiny compared to those in North America. We paid for electricity by feeding a meter with coins collected monthly by the local council. We heated our homes with coal fires. We shopped daily for groceries because homes had only small refrigerators. Food was rarely thrown away. As kids, we shared our bath water. We had each other. Anything more than that would have felt superfluous.

I didn't realize then how difficult it would be to leave all that behind.

In March 1991, we packed the last of our things, said our tearful farewells, and boarded a plane bound for Toronto with our mother and her friend Diane.

We entered Canada as visitors, and only then did Maurice begin the formal immigration process. At first, Citizenship and Immigration Canada denied our application because they determined my brothers and I were medically inadmissible due to our visual impairment. After teachers and friends wrote letters of support to our local Member of Parliament, and after some local media coverage, we were finally granted Minister's Permits a year later. Eventually, we became permanent residents and, finally, Canadian citizens.

2 Emigre

There was thick snow on the ground when we landed at Pearson International Airport. In Northern Ireland, snow rarely stays for more than a day, whereas winter was a different story in Ontario.

As Maurice drove us from the airport across the Burlington Skyway into Hamilton, the anticipation I'd felt at having crossed an ocean and arriving on new soil so far away from home was tempered by how vast and remote this place seemed.

That first night, we ordered pizza for dinner. This must be Canada, I thought. I had eaten pizza only a few times before as it had barely made its way to Northern Ireland, where fast food was typically fish and chips or Indian takeaway.

Maurice had purchased a three-bedroom bungalow-style house on Hamilton's East Mountain. Jon and Chris once again shared a bedroom, and Maurice's daughter Rachel, who lived with us when she wasn't with her mother, Maurice's ex-wife, slept in the room adjacent to the main bedroom where our mother and Maurice slept.

Maurice set up a room for me in the basement. We didn't have basements in Northern Ireland, so sleeping in one was a novelty for me. I became achingly homesick after the initial excitement of our move wore off, so the basement aptly mirrored my desire to take my feelings underground and bury them there.

2 Emigre

Within a month, my brothers and I started school in Brantford, a 30-minute drive west of Hamilton. The W. Ross Macdonald School for the Blind had 250 blind, visually impaired, and deafblind students aged five to twenty-one coming from across Ontario. As students, my brothers and I once again had access to Braille textbooks; it was an environment where blindness and low vision were the norm, not the exception.

Kids at school were intrigued by our Northern Irish accents. We soon met another family of three siblings, the Swerdfigers, with whom we quickly connected. Rich and Ron were twins, a year older than Jon and Chris. Their sister, Phyllis, was just a few months older than I. In the Swerdfigers, we found allies and kindred spirits manifested in our parallel lives in a place where, until then, we had felt like outsiders.

I was placed in a grade 8 class; my brothers were in grade 5. Despite living relatively close to the school, we fulfilled a wish from back home, becoming residential students. We returned to Hamilton on weekends.

I felt sorry for the day students who were picked up from school each afternoon at four. They got to have dinner at home and spend the evening with their families, but I felt they were missing out on what made my experience at school so special: the after-school and evening sports and music, the togetherness and spontaneity that fed the creation of friendships, and the interdependencies that developed within our close-knit, yet eclectic, community.

And yet, despite making friends quickly, I was desperately homesick in those first weeks.

I was thirteen, an age of transition, with all the angst and identity crises of early adolescence. I was excited and ready to embrace the possibility of bigger and better things ahead, yet terrified, resentful, and yearning to remain rooted in the place and with the people who had formed the bedrock of my life experience. I see in retrospect how impressionable, susceptible, and vulnerable I was.

In Northern Ireland, people looked to Canada as a magical place, which, in my young mind, gave it a special mystery. Yet when we emigrated there, it was as though an imagined narrative was playing out, one I should have been able to embrace, only I couldn't, because it felt as though it had been forced on us. In leaving as we had, we had relinquished the treasured intimacy of familiarity, disentangled from the rhythms and routines of the life that had felt like our birthright, propelled without any say, out of the innocence of childhood, disconnected from the source.

My brothers lived this too, and our mother certainly did as well, but for me, the homesickness felt almost like a physical pain. Perhaps because Jon and Chris were twins and practically inseparable, they might have been better able to lean on one another and absorb our transition during those first weeks and months.

Our mother eventually buried her homesickness in the seams of the present, but I don't believe she ever let go of the feeling that Northern Ireland was where she belonged.

Maurice had a complicated relationship with his birth country. He hated the gossip and the family fighting that seemed to haunt him every time he went back, preferring to head south for the sunshine of Cuba or the Dominican Republic for vacations.

During my first weeks at school, I joined the small track team. It was April 1991. A few teachers guided us in runs and workouts on the school's paved outdoor track. The track was a little more than 300 metres and had a metal railing we could hold onto, meaning we could run on our own when no guides were available. In addition, there was a 105-metre indoor track overlooking our gym where we could do the same.

This was where I caught the running bug, running alone for hours around the outdoor track and completing countless laps on the indoor track.

I could keep up with most of the kids at school, even the older ones, and push the staff who guided us, but the problem was that I wasn't eating. We ate our meals in a cafeteria. What they fed us was not like my mother's home cooking. I barely ate a thing. I also didn't want to become an overweight Canadian with a big mouth, as my friend's dad had implanted in my mind. To signal their desire to have seconds or sometimes thirds, kids raised their hands, and the kitchen staff would bring another plate of food to them. This wasn't what I had been used to, and it only reinforced my preconceptions.

I ran but barely ate and inevitably grew thinner and thinner as the weeks

2 Emigre

passed. My teachers, residence counsellors, and eventually, my mother and Maurice began to notice. Refusing to eat was my immature way of protesting and trying to reclaim a vestige of control I felt had been taken away.

In those first months, all I wanted was to return home. I missed my friends, our house, and everything that had been so familiar growing up. In Canada, I felt like a stranger, even to myself. I felt lost. As spring led into summer, with the unbearable humidity so characteristic of Southern Ontario, I felt frozen, inside and out. I was also hungry and so thin that I avoided our neighbour's cold swimming pool.

The sunshine did nothing to alleviate my misery. I longed for cooler weather and the warmth of our familiar lives. At one point, my brothers, mother, and I even contrived a secret plan to go home.

My mother and Maurice took me to a family doctor that summer. He encouraged me to eat more, but this made little difference. I was a resentful, homesick thirteen-year-old. Eventually, hearing my mother's anguished cries led me to turn the corner. Knowing my actions were hurting those who loved me was probably what saved me in the end.

Eventually, September arrived with its cool temperatures, a return to school, and the prospect of new perspectives. I was fourteen and starting grade 9.

I sat out the first month of cross-country practices. I met with the school psychologist, verbalizing the feelings welling inside me. I started eating again and returned to training with the cross-country team in mid-October. My new roots began to find traction; I began to accept my new reality.

This acceptance set me free to embrace my new homeland. My new friends and teachers became my second family. Those early years provided the impetus for me to learn and develop into whom I would become: a healthy human being first and foremost, a runner, musician, writer, friend, somebody with diverse interests and passions, somebody finding his way on a circuitous path.

Looking back so many years ago to that first summer in Canada and the pain I had internalized as a resentful, homesick thirteen-year-old, I faced two choices: either give up or survive. I chose survival.

Each of us harbours pain, none of us is immune to it. That recognition empowers us to plant seeds of wellness and healing around us. Vulnerability invites vulnerability and creates a greater space for the empathy our world badly needs.

By learning to acknowledge the sources of our inner pain, we can refocus our energy towards building an empowered, resilient life. After that first difficult summer, I realized it was okay to be homesick and that Canada was a welcoming place with lots to offer me. I learned to eat to live. I learned to open up to what was new.

3 High School

I started grade 9 in the fall of 1991. The school followed the mainstream Ontario curriculum, in addition to classes in orientation and mobility, or O&M as we called it, where we were taught how to safely navigate around the school and within the city of Brantford using a white cane.

The first lesson I had from Mrs. Blackford, my first O&M instructor, was practicing the route to Mr. Mugs, a local coffee shop. She emphasized the importance of knowing the way to a coffee shop because, as she emphasized, that's where people meet.

I was a good student, particularly in the social sciences and humanities, but I was most passionate about the daily after-school sports. In the fall, teachers and staff ran beside us as guides during cross-country practices, directing us by the elbow or a short tether that enabled us to run in sync. We raced in local competitions right up to the regional high school championships. We could not compete with sighted rivals because of the undulating terrain, which made it challenging to run fast. But the training made us fit. In the winter, my physical education teacher, Mr. Howe, led daily wrestling practices after school. A teacher there since the early '70s, he has been a revered figure even among non-athletes. He became a catalyzing force in my athletic development.

As blind wrestlers, we could compete at the same level as sighted rivals by beginning on our feet at the centre of the mat with our arms intertwined in a locked position. From there, the dance began as we circled and pushed-pulled, feeling one another out and looking for an opportunity to go for the legs or to throw our opponent.

Our school produced some top wrestlers over the years, including my two brothers, each of whom went on to compete at provincial championships in the Ontario Federation of Secondary Schools Association. In their final year of high school, Jon placed second and Chris fourth in their respective weight classes against the province's top-sighted wrestlers. This was a highly prestigious level of wrestling that we took in stride at the time. In retrospect, I realize it was a monumental achievement for two blind wrestlers merely to participate, let alone place as highly as they did against sighted wrestlers of that calibre. I was and remain deeply proud of them.

I wrestled throughout high school but never at the level of my brothers, who dominated local competitions; still, I enjoyed the physical training, the team element of wrestling, and, when I could, contributing to our school's success at tournaments.

In the evenings, we played intramural sports organized by our residence counsellors. We played a version of floor hockey using a large plastic juice container instead of a puck. We also played goalball, a sport comprising two teams of three blindfolded players who faced off at opposing ends of a court. Using a soccer ball with a bell inside, the objective was to score on the opposing team by throwing the ball at high speed along the ground.

I participated in each of these sports, but running was what I truly enjoyed and where I felt I could excel the most. I found an enabling force in the person who led our track workouts each spring. Mr. Rollings, or Nick as I later called him, was an educational assistant who worked with special needs students in the Special Individualized Program. Having competed in track in high school, Nick wanted to share his passion for running. Shortly after I arrived at school, we struck up a conversation. I told him of my hopes to improve in running. Nick ultimately devoted hundreds of hours, much of it on his own time, to guiding me in training runs, workouts, and races throughout high school.

I also loved music and sang with our school choir, but it was the guitar I was most drawn to. I studied classical guitar throughout high school with

Mr. Rondeau, one of our music teachers, who moonlighted as a jazz bass guitar player. He introduced me to many music genres, from jazz to hip-hop to blues, and he persuaded a few of us to form a music ensemble comprising guitar, piano, bass, drums, and vocals. He showed us the rudiments of such songs as "Low Rider" by War and Tom Petty's "I'm Free," then stood back and let the music happen.

Maurice sparked my growing interest in music. I tried to emulate his fingerpicking folk-rock style, inspired by The Beatles, The Eagles, Simon and Garfunkel, and James Taylor. Years later, whenever we got together, one of us would pick up a guitar, and in a short time, the other joined in, resurrecting our usual repertoire, The Eagles' "Hotel California" or The Beatles' "Yesterday," finding connection through those timeless melodies. Music was a way to unpack my inner thoughts and feelings and to open up to my internal rhythms; running would enable me to do the same.

Over the years, running helped me cope with pent-up emotions, providing me a path of escape. It disrupted the inertia and sense of numbness that sometimes threatened to overtake me. Running protected me from the rough edges of reality, but as I learned over time, running was also a metaphor for reality. I understood, even then, that pain was a rite of passage. I wanted to feel the rawness of my pain and to discover what lay beyond it.

Athletes can be haunted by the races that got away from them. Hindsight often leads us to second-guess ourselves, and I haven't been immune to this self-interrogation over the years. At different moments following a competition, I've been confronted by the difficult question: did I give it my all today? Sometimes, the honest answer has been no.

Sometimes, I knew my mindset had lost me a race, even when I was well prepared physically. Lapses in concentration are not unusual among athletes in distance races. To run well at a sustained fast pace, you must be fully present, confident but not overly so, relaxed, intentional, patient at points and aggressive at others, positive, and committed – in addition to your physical readiness, which, of course, is also crucial.

There are so many justifiable excuses – justifiable to non-runners, that is – that we can turn to when we lose the mental struggle: "I was tired," "I thought I might get hurt," "I was afraid," or any number of other reasons.

I've been in races where athletes have thrown up or even passed out after crossing the line, such was their capacity to push to their limit. I've also seen untrained athletes complete incredible workouts or races that, in theory, should have been far beyond their reach.

Where does this ability to dig deep come from? What is lost when you leave your birthplace at such an impressionable age? Even then, I had a sense of what felt solid and true to me. I knew the pathway to commitment and determination needed to be nurtured from within, and I resolved, and have re-resolved over the years, to stay true to this mission in my running.

In a collection of his essays entitled *A Thousand Small Sanities*, American author Adam Gopnik wrote: "Trees have roots. Human beings don't. What they have instead are histories, and histories are ways of thinking about the past and the present which allow us to imagine new futures."

In high school, I felt that the future was bright. We were in an enabling environment that helped us believe in the power of possibility. The school's motto, "The impossible is only the untried," captured this sentiment.

When it came to running, I was making steady improvements. Nick reached out to Doug Whistance for coaching help. A retired teacher originally from northeast England, Doug coached with the Brantford Track Club. He also oversaw the training of Kevin Sullivan, who became a three-time Olympian and is still the Canadian 1500-metre record holder.

Under Doug's coaching, Nick and I did workouts I never imagined possible, such as kilometre repeats in three minutes and 20 seconds and 200-metre sprints on the track in 34 seconds.

One or two evenings a week during the winter of my final year in high school, Nick drove me to the indoor track at York University, where we joined Doug's training group for track sessions. I had been running consistently around 4:52 for 1500 metres, the fastest at my school but not quick by high school standards. Doug said, "Jason, we'll get you down to 4:30 this spring." It was hard to imagine how that might happen, but it planted a seed in my mind.

Another person instrumental in my athletic development in high school was Brian Rattray. He had studied physical education and, in addition to coaching the swim team, led the Outdoor Education program. Brian, who had coached two swimmers to the 1992 Barcelona Paralympics, encouraged me to believe that with consistent, hard training, the sky was the limit. He introduced me to stair workouts that I could do by myself when no guides were around: plyometric, rapid, repeated exercises to improve my speed and power. They made me stronger.

Brian encouraged me to think big. On our end-of-year canoe trip in grade 12, a conversation with him precipitated an ambitious fundraising idea to coincide with our school's 125th anniversary. The idea was for me to run 25 kilometres a day for five successive days, following five distinct routes in and around the Brantford area, with help from guide runners. The event took place in November 1996. Called Jason's Journey, our fundraising efforts supported the Canadian National Institute for the Blind (CNIB) via the annual United Way Charitable Campaign.

Back then, I hadn't yet completed a single 25-kilometre run, let alone 25 kilometres for five consecutive days, but I was excited to train for it, crazy as it seemed. Brian also might have been unsure of the plan, but the genie was out of the bottle – we were committed. That fall, I increased my running volume, and by early November 1996, everything was in place for me to run the first of the five 25-kilometre legs with Brian as my guide.

It quickly became apparent that it would not be easy. I might have caught a bug or not eaten enough, but shortly after finishing the first day, I threw up and couldn't keep food down; I spent the night in the school infirmary. Some thought it a bad idea to continue, but I wanted to keep going, and Brian understood and encouraged me to do so.

The next morning, we set out again. I was running with Nick, followed by a support van with signs promoting our initiative. I felt the space around us. We were running on quiet country roads, just two people marking off miles in anonymity, feeling the ground pass under our feet and the wind on our faces. I appreciated what it meant to run free, moving under my own power. I knew intuitively that this experience was seminal.

We weren't going for pace as the goal was to make it through to the end. We often ran at five minutes per kilometre or slower. Still, at other points, particularly as we got further along, we sped up, probably dropping close to

4:20 per kilometre or faster – such was the galvanizing energy of adrenalin and the sense that we were getting closer to the finish. The van following behind us was driven either by one of the other running guides or our school principal, Mr. Bethune, who had taken a keen interest in what we were doing. The van contained some food and water, and every few kilometres, the driver pulled up to give us a drink or a quick snack.

Four guide runners helped me over the five days: Nick; Clay Eaton, another educational assistant at our school; a local runner named Ben Van Dyk; and Brian, who had been a swimmer and not a long-distance runner. Brian guided me through two of the legs, subjecting his body to unaccustomed discomfort to be there for me. With the help of this wonderfully committed team of guide runners, I ultimately completed the 125 kilometres, raising close to $3,000 to support the CNIB.

While I had done some longer runs in the weeks leading up to Jason's Journey, I wasn't optimally prepared to run 125 kilometres in just five days. One of the key lessons I took away from this experience was the knowledge that it was possible to keep going even when it seemed unthinkable.

Mr. Bethune, my high school principal who had been one of our van drivers during Jason's Journey, became a mentor. He sometimes pulled you into his office when walking down the hallway, and you'd think you were in trouble, but he just wanted to ask how you were doing. He loved to join us on our outdoor education canoe trips and sit with us at night, relating his backpacking world travels as a young man before returning to Canada, attending teacher's college, and settling down.

Our relationship didn't end when I left high school; if anything, it deepened. He stayed in regular touch and took a keen interest in what I was studying and how I was doing. He made me eligible for a bursary, a welcome financial boost during my lean first year in university. When he passed away in the spring of 2000 following a short, aggressive illness, the earth shook for me. It was like losing a father.

More than two decades later, I'm still absorbing the lessons he taught me. He encouraged me to regard my time in high school as an essential part of the inner core of my life experience and never to stop believing in the value of my past. He helped me realize that my formative years in Northern

3 High School

Ireland, our move to Canada, and everything that had taken place to bring me to where I now was, were crucial to the larger arc of my life experience.

Despite the steady improvement in my running, it was only in the last weeks of high school that I truly began to believe in my potential. Heading into my final high school track season, with a 1500-metre personal best of just 4:52, I couldn't have dreamed of approaching a qualifying standard for international competitions against other blind runners, which required running in the 4:20s. Track running is a sport where athletes often plateau and then leap forward, especially in high school when they're still growing.

Although running was a significant part of my life then, as it still is, there was more to me than being an athlete. Years later, runner friends and I would joke about other athletes who lived and breathed their sport seemingly to the exclusion of everything else. Even in high school, I wanted to be multi-dimensional. As much as I hoped to do well in running, I never wanted to compromise the other parts of me. I always strived to find a balance. I wanted to be known in running circles as a fast runner, and I wanted those outside running circles to see the person within the athlete: someone inspired by music, words and ideas, a dreamer, curious, hopeful.

Heading into my final high school track season, I was still growing, a late bloomer. Doug Whistance, our coach with the Brantford Track Club, had planted the seed in my mind that it was possible to run much faster. I had Nick's committed guide-running support. In his mid-thirties then, he put his body through so much to guide me in our workouts, to say nothing of the countless hours he dedicated to our running during my years in high school. But as the weeks progressed through the spring of 1997, it became clear that he could no longer push me as he had. I needed somebody who could guide me comfortably at a fast pace. Typically, a good differential between a guide and a blind runner might be 15 to 20 seconds in a 1500-metre race, meaning that a blind runner capable of running 4:52 needs a guide able to run 4:32 or faster.

On a night in May 1997, I competed in a 1500-metre race for blind runners at our regional high school championships. I was guided this time by another of Doug's middle-distance athletes, Jeff Summerhayes. As we came through 1200 metres, I heard Jeff say that if we could maintain our pace, we had a chance to run 4:30. It was exhilarating to be running faster than I ever had.

Ultimately, we finished in 4:34, a massive eighteen-second improvement for me.

That night, the stars had aligned. This race led me to believe I could train and compete with the University of Guelph's varsity team and the possibility of racing internationally. Most of all, I realized that running had given me a lens through which I could see and connect with the outside world, that there was freedom in movement, and that I had now forged dynamic roots and a foundation to build upon for the future.

4 Chasing Dreams

I arrived at the University of Guelph in September 1997. I had only been on the campus a couple of times for brief visits, so I didn't know my way around. Like other first-year students, I was curious, nervous, and excited to be striking out on my own. For many, this was their first time living away from home. Having attended a residential high school, that part wasn't a big change for me. My transition was more about stepping out of the comfort zone of attending a school of about 250 students, all of whom had a visual disability, and going to a university with 13,000 mostly fully sighted students.

My high school had provided Braille textbooks, an accessible library, and adapted equipment, such as a Perkins Brailler, with which we could take notes or complete assignments. When I arrived at Guelph, none of these accommodations was a certainty. I had known the layout of my high school like the back of my hand, but during my first weeks living in the Schooner wing of the South residence on the Guelph campus, tree-lined and vibrant beneath the warmth of the September sunshine, I wondered whether I might be out of my depth.

Someone I met early on assured me that I wasn't. Barry Wheeler was a student advisor at Guelph's Centre for Students with Disabilities. He had a degenerative neurological condition, Charcot-Marie-Tooth, which affected his speaking and walking, necessitating the use of a scooter. In his early forties at the time, Barry had recently graduated with a degree in sociology and was now in a position to support other students with a disability.

With his help, I was matched with students in a peer help program whom I could call on to guide me to and from classes and generally from point A to point B anywhere on campus. I soon began to memorize these routes and travel alone, using a cane to identify obstacles and differentiate sidewalks from grass, listening for the open spaces between buildings that might be a cue to turn, paying attention to slight up-hills, to tiles or carpet, to the smell of fallen apples, or the sound of a coffee machine – each was a key in the mental map I created. Eventually, I joined the peer help program and became a guide for other visually impaired students.

From the outset, Barry assured me that with the right accommodations, I could succeed academically. Part of his role was to liaise with professors to create conditions that would better equip students with disabilities to excel in their courses. Being granted additional time to complete exams and being permitted to tape-record lectures were among these accommodations.

He also worked closely with the library to coordinate adapted text material. At that time, before the ubiquity of audiobooks and e-text, visually impaired students relied on volunteer readers. Often, material only became available a few chapters at a time, so it was not uncommon to be without assigned readings when I most needed them. As I quickly learned, the twelve-week university semester moved fast, and it was everything I could do to keep up.

Initially, I taped lectures and then returned to my room to transcribe the recordings on my computer using JAWS, a screen-reading speech program. The JAWS acronym stands for Job Access With Speech. Relistening to an entire lecture took considerable time and energy, and while it helped me absorb the material, it was far from the most efficient method. Eventually, I got a laptop and started bringing it to lectures to take notes, saving me a lot of time.

The varsity running team at Guelph was renowned across Canada for its competitive success; I wanted to train with the team but wondered how, as a blind runner with a very modest 4:34 1500-metre time to my name, I

4 Chasing Dreams

could ever hope to integrate with this group of accomplished athletes, several of whom had already represented Canada in junior international competitions. Brian Rattray, who led the Outdoor Education program at my high school, drove to Guelph to help me break the ice. We met with the new cross-country and track coach, Dave Scott-Thomas, who, in future years, would develop the varsity program into a running powerhouse. Dave had never previously worked with blind athletes but was open to me coming out with the team and offered to support me in any way he could.

Many years later, Dave was dismissed and received a lifetime ban in track and field by Athletics Canada for exploiting a high school athlete through an inappropriate sexual relationship. After his dismissal, some former athletes spoke out about what they termed an unhealthy competitive environment. The challenge for a coach in any highly competitive program is to focus on his top performers without ignoring less accomplished athletes. The difficulty was that Dave tended to neglect the underperformers to the point that they no longer felt they belonged on the team.

That being said, I learned a great deal from Dave. He introduced me to training concepts that ultimately made me a better athlete. He taught me the benefit of slowly increasing running volume over time as a key to improvement and the value of doing regular tempo runs at the top end of my aerobic ability so that I became habituated to running fast while staying relaxed.

I'm grateful to Dave for these lessons, which greatly contributed to the team's success over many years, for the space he offered me in the program, and for helping me link with guides, particularly in the beginning. Although it wasn't easy connecting with him, it was the connections I developed over time with teammates that came to flavour my experience and shaped so many of my positive memories.

Initially, training with the varsity athletes was intimidating, largely due to my anxiety about being a blind runner. Could it work practically when it came to training and racing?

These fears evaporated quickly, however. Although my 1500-metre personal best of 4:34 was not fast compared to most of the other athletes, I found I could keep up on the training runs as long as we stayed on smooth roads or trails that had relatively good footing, something the other members of the team thankfully came to understand.

Although I never raced at or near the front in either cross country or indoor track during my five seasons in the Canadian Intercollegiate Sport system, I felt fortunate to be part of a committed, driven group of athletes and to be connected with what would grow into a tradition of running excellence, predicated on humble principles of hard work and community, set in motion with only modest facilities at our disposal. Guelph did not have a 400-metre rubberized track to train on until long after I graduated in 2003. What we did have was a critical mass of young athletes who were committed to succeeding.

In my first season of training with the team during cross country, Dave initially connected me with one of the volunteer assistant coaches, Pat Gordon, who would guide me in workouts. Soon after, other runners stepped up, particularly on easy run days that separated tempo or interval sessions or on our Sunday morning long runs. Perhaps people realized that guiding was not especially difficult and that it came down to paying attention and being a little more careful than normal.

During the cross-country season, the team routinely worked on terrain that closely resembled the conditions they might expect to encounter in their upcoming races. While I participated in some of these sessions, the undulating ground was mostly too unsafe for me. On those days, I headed to the gym and replicated the workout on a spin bike, sometimes for up to 90 minutes. On other days, the team trained on the road or the cinder track, and I joined them during these sessions. Distance runners operate solo, but they derive tremendous benefits from the synergy of training with others. We worked out in a pack, and over time, athletes began to take turns guiding me through our intervals. On a workout such as 12 times 400-metre repetitions, for example, I sometimes ran with as many as twelve athletes, each guiding me in a single interval throughout the session. This enabled everybody to run at their own pace within the pack without forcing anybody to slow down or speed up for more than one interval at a time.

As I got to know other members of the team – such as Shaun

Kingerlee, who came to Guelph from British Columbia and who had run an outstanding 1:52 for 800 metres in high school; Peter Sullivan, a 1500-metre runner who became one of my closest friends on the team; and Phil Wiebe, who also played bass guitar and with whom I shared a passion for music – I came to realize that in hoping for acceptance, it was up to me to introduce people to my world. In doing so, I could dispel any reticence or uncertainty they might have felt about blindness. Being open, approachable and present at training sessions, team dinners, and parties helped put people at ease. It broke the ice. Like everybody else, I was there to train hard, with hopes to improve and ultimately contribute to our team in the best way I could. Running was the common denominator we shared, but as I learned, it was far from the only connection.

This isn't to say that it was easy. Many blind people live with debilitating shyness that manifests as social anxiety. I haven't been immune to this myself over the years. I've spent nights in a quiet corner, questioning if I should have come out in the first place. But over time, I realized the importance of reaching out to others who might never have met a blind person before and, in so doing, encouraged them to interact with me.

This is why I don't get upset when a server in a restaurant asks people I'm with what I'd like to eat. When I answer myself, the server usually understands and will address me directly for the rest of the meal, and for me, that's enough.

A few years ago, I wrote a poem about the stereotypes and perceived limitations that can pigeonhole blind people – if we let them.

> BLIND
>
> I see it in the spaces in between,
> The glances, stares like lances, under sound,
> Sixth sense activated through a dark screen
> To register a smile or catch a frown.
> I feel it in the questions people ask
> With courage even through the feared unknown.
> I wonder how to penetrate the mask
> And permeate allusions etched in stone.

VISIONS OF HOPE

So many of us walk a narrow line,
Impoverished, alone, misunderstood
Though writers or musicians by design,
Or astronauts or doctors if we could,
Or lawyers. Politicians if we dare,
Or grand piano tuners as we should,
Or teachers or translators, though it's rare,
Or artisans who fashion rock or wood.
There is so much that others just don't see
Beyond the image of a man and dog,
Or a girl reading with fingers carefully,
Or a grandmother squinting through a fog.
And yet, it's up to us to lift the cloak,
To look at skepticism in the eye,
To open our own doors, to go for broke
And not to let this lifetime pass us by.
I met a stranger riding on the bus
Who spoke to me with a sympathetic look.
He told me that his friend is just like us
And how he listens now to every book,
And how he's extra sensitive to sound.
And I smile despite myself. For the man's refrain
Was nothing if not a search for common ground
In rendering insanity more sane.
Our vision manifests within the heart,
Beyond the narrow lens of open eyes
Which register a fragment, but a part
Of a deeper shade of truth that underlies,
With this vision, we make sense in our own way
Of the world. And setting out on our own course,
We choose a route and make our furtive way
With the coins and currency of our life force.
We can cut against the grain of history,
For the leaders, the visionaries in our crowd

> Have eclipsed tradition. There's no mystery,
> They're simply not afraid to live out loud.
> So if I fail to meet your eye, don't blink,
> But extend your hand. Let's let go of our fear
> And chart a seed change sketched in braille and ink
> Towards a better world, on the other side of here.

During the indoor track season in my first year, Dave set up a 1500-metre time trial for me at Toronto's York University facility, where our team ran intervals one night a week. Nowadays, in addition to a rubberized 400-metre outdoor track, Guelph has a 200-metre indoor facility, built the year before I graduated.

Our goal in the time trial – my teammate Jay Henricksen was one of my two guides, and unfortunately, my memory is shaky as to the other – was to run the 1500 metres faster than 4:25. This was a significant jump from my 4:34 personal best, but necessary for me to be eligible for selection to the national Para Athletics team heading to the International Blind Sports Association World Championships taking place in Madrid that summer.

In a hand-timed run observed by Dave, who afterwards had to provide a signed affidavit affirming its validity to the Canadian Blind Sports Association, which oversaw team selection, we ran the 1500 metres in 4:24. I was over the moon. Training alongside runners who were better than I, the bar had been set high. I was on the upswing. There was still so much room for me to improve, but the intervals and mileage, the nights of peddling on a spin bike on my own – all of it was worth it, every second.

Consideration for performances run under those circumstances, without electronic timing, would be out of the question today. Governance of track and field in Canada for blind athletes, as with most sports contested by athletes with a disability, rests today with mainstream national sport organizations. In the case of track and field, Athletics Canada has, since 2003, been the governing body. Under its watch and in response to stricter competition-sanctioning regulations imposed by the International Paralympic Committee and World Para Athletics, athletes are today required to chase selection standards at specific designated competitions. A meet director can apply to have their event sanctioned by the International Paralympic Committee, although the process takes some time and administrative work.

There's a perennial debate within the Para sports community about the merits of integration of sports for athletes with a disability in Canada versus the old system where disability-specific sports organizations, such as the Canadian Blind Sports Association, among others, oversaw sport development and national team programs. Although this integration was intended to streamline sport delivery and technical services for high-performing para-athletes, the flip side is that fewer athletes with disabilities may be entering and remaining within the sports system.

In high school, I had wonderful opportunities to train for and compete at disability-specific competitions, such as the Windsor Indoor Games held each March and regional, provincial, and national disability sport championships. Without many of the disability-specific developmental opportunities available to me during my early years in Para athletics, today's aspiring young athletes with a disability who may not yet be at the national level may sadly give up.

National sport organizations such as Athletics Canada and provincial disability-specific sport organizations such as the Ontario Blind Sports Association continue to reach out to schools, clubs, and individual families of young people with disabilities to encourage their participation. Hopefully, these efforts will reach many more young people who might benefit from sport, as I was fortunate to.

With a national team qualifying mark heading into the spring of 1998, I next needed a guide runner who could train consistently with me in the weeks leading up to the competition in mid-July. While I had wonderful support from the athletes I trained with, much of it was cobbled around their training and schedules. I needed to find someone I could count on to train with me more regularly.

Greg Dailey was a twenty-five-year-old runner who had formerly been coached by Doug Whistance, who had overseen my training with Nick in high school. Having recently completed his undergraduate degree, Greg contemplated applying to a teacher's college. He had a personal best of 3:48

for 1500 metres, meaning he could easily guide me, even at my fastest.

Doug connected us in the early summer after my first year at Guelph. For our first run together, Greg picked me up from the house I was sharing in Brantford with my brothers and the Swerdfiger twins, Rich and Ron.

We set out, with Greg running beside me on my left. He was a natural when it came to guide running. The technique I used most often on the roads – occasionally bumping shoulders and being manoeuvered in or out by a touch of the elbow – seemed to work almost instinctively between us. We were both six feet tall, with identical stride lengths and similar body types, muscular for middle-distance runners. In subsequent years, many people thought we were brothers, such was the uncanny resemblance in our physical appearance.

Greg and I trained and competed together until 2011. If there had been a competition that ranked guide runners, he would have been among the best for his composure and judgment in placing us where we needed to be amid the free-for-all of blind track running in which we often found ourselves. Yet, in our first run, even Greg had a momentary lapse in hand-eye coordination. As he explained later, he watched as we approached a curb but hadn't foreseen how quickly the curb would arrive.

I went down but got back up quickly, and we continued our run. Other than tripping when we were cut off in a track race at York University a few years later, I can't think of another fall when Greg and I ran together.

After that initial run, Doug had Greg and I do two tough track workouts, including one memorable session where he had us run a 400-, then an 800-, and finally a 1200-metre interval, with lots of rest in between. We ran times of 1:04, 2:09, and 3:24. I had never done a workout like that before, and it gave me the confidence to believe I was ready to take another big leap in our racing.

Greg and I flew to Madrid in mid-July 1998, where we met up with other team members. There was Lilo Ljubisic, a blind discus thrower and world record holder from Vancouver, whose coach, Norma Jordan Suarez, was our team head coach; France Gagné, a male discus thrower from Quebec who had partial vision; and Stuart McGregor from Ottawa, an 800- and

1500-metre runner, also with partial vision, who at nineteen, a year younger than I, would later become a close friend.

Before the competition, I underwent a process known as classification. Athletes are examined by a doctor and differentiated into functional categories based on their type of disability and its severity. There are five overarching disability groups, each with several degrees of impairment; these include categories for athletes who are blind or with low vision, athletes with intellectual disabilities, athletes with cerebral palsy, athletes with an amputation, and athletes who use a wheelchair.

Within the blind and visually impaired disability group, there were three categories: B1 for athletes with no vision, B2 for those with up to 5% of their vision, and B3 for athletes with a visual acuity of up to 10%. In later years, the international classification system was updated, and these categories were redesignated to T11, T12 and T13.

After performing a basic eye examination that involved shining a light in my eyes and determining whether I could discern printed letters, the panel of eye doctors confirmed that I should be classified into the B1 category.

The hot temperatures in Madrid, in the mid-thirties, thankfully came with low humidity so that you could find some measure of relief in the shade. We were entered in the 800-metre and the 1500-metre events in our category. We would compete in the 800 first, an event that, in Madrid, had a first-round, semi-final, and final.

We qualified easily from the heats of the 800, but in the semi-final, we were cut off by a Portuguese guide runner who stepped in front of us, nearly tripping me. Ultimately, we did qualify for the final, running a new personal best of 2:08, but it had been a close call.

After the race, Greg, who had worked on a chicken farm with Portuguese workers during high school, confronted the Portuguese guide runner who had cut us off. People described the look of utter shock and surprise on the guide runner's face at hearing the angry obscenities Greg hurled at him, the only few words of Portuguese he knew.

Once the dust settled, we had a final to prepare for on the biggest stage to date of my athletic career. We would be racing against seasoned runners, blind athletes and guides at or near their prime. Greg and I weren't supposed to have competed in the 800-metre event, and because nobody expected anything of us, we felt less pressure than we normally would.

We thought that if the race were to be tactical, with the surges and moves that so often characterize championship races, and given our relative inexperience, we wouldn't stand a chance. At that time, the B1 800-metre world record was 1:59.99, set in the late 1980s by an Englishman named Bob Matthews. As ridiculous as it seems in hindsight, we felt that our best bet in the final was to go out hard, at a sub-two-minute pace, putting us in world record contention. Doug, ever ambitious, was convinced that our training had me ready to attempt to run in under two minutes with Greg's support, and with nothing to lose, we felt it was worth a try.

Running at the front would also help us avoid the trouble that had nearly derailed our semi-final. The stadium was sparsely populated with few spectators under the late morning sun as we lined up, four teams of two on the track, with two laps ahead of us. The magnitude of the moment wasn't lost on me. Here I was, together with Greg, at the culmination of years of work, hoping, trying, and imagining what could be; of dreaming and coming to believe; of finding traction and sure footing in the shifting sands of immigration; and of setting down tenuous roots in an adopted country whose singlet I was now wearing and about to represent.

The starter prompted us in Spanish: *"A sus puestos"* (are you ready) … Bang! The crack of the gun propelled us forward, and we were sprinting out around the curve, within our lanes for the first 100-metre stagger, at which point we could cut to the inside lane. Greg and I wanted the early lead, and our aggressive start ensured that we got it, meaning that we could run unimpeded with a clear track ahead, in control of the race, as the other teams fought for position behind us. We built a sizable lead as we flew down the backstretch, rounded the curve at the 200-metre mark, and prepared to enter the home straight for the first time. I was running flat out. We were flying full throttle. We were floating, two runners, blind athlete and guide gliding as one, covering metres of track with each unified stride, effortless, excruciating.

I didn't hear our 400-metre split time as we hit the bell, though I found out later we had gone through in 57 seconds. I hadn't ever run a 400-metre interval that fast in my life, let alone come through at that pace in the first lap of an 800.

Though it might seem counterintuitive, the first lap is almost always run faster than the second in an 800-metre race. This is because most athletes start fast to capitalize on the free energy available early in the race before dipping into their anaerobic energy system, at which point they settle, and the pace stabilizes. As the race progresses and athletes run low on aerobic energy, it becomes a race of attrition; in the 800, it's said the person who slows down the least wins.

Still, Greg and I maintained our lead, and as we rounded the curve into the backstretch, 300 metres lay between us and a most unlikely win in our first international final. Then we had only 200 metres left to go, which we reached in 1:28. I was a long way into new territory, past the point of no return, and there was only one road ahead.

The field of runners behind us was too good to let us get away. If it had been a 600-metre race, or even a 700, Greg and I would have had a great chance. But in an 800, the finish line can seem like an unattainable mirage where even a few metres feel interminable.

As we came off the last curve and into the final straightaway, I was swimming in lactic acid. There was nowhere to go but forward with everything I had. Greg yelled at me, "Go, go, go!" Runners approached us as we seemingly inched along the final straight, my legs shaking beneath me. First, one pair passed on the outside to my right, then a second, and there wasn't a thing I could do. And then my legs gave way, and I found myself face down on the rubberized track, and Greg was yelling at me, "Get up! Get up"! In a blur, I got back to my feet, and Greg and I jogged across the line; I had fallen just a few metres short, but it might as well have been a marathon away, such had been my utter exhaustion. We finished fourth.

Despite losing so dramatically, I knew I couldn't have tried any harder. Greg and I had raced unconstrained. We were naïve, new to this level of competition, yet unencumbered by pressure or expectation. Sometimes, you must make a move that common wisdom might call irrational.

Greg and I still had the 1500 metres ahead of us. We qualified for the final by winning our semi-final heat comfortably in under five minutes. It was strange to think that just over a year ago, during my final weeks of high school, my 1500-metre personal best had been around the same time.

I was nervous warming up for the final the following evening around a grass field close to the main stadium. The 800 metres had been pure experimentation for us, and perhaps because we had been able to assert ourselves and come so close to winning, I felt a sense of expectation going into the 1500-metre final, which was, after all, our better event. We had decided to be more cautious than the front running approach we had taken in the 800. We planned to run near the front without leading and to let somebody else do the work.

We found ourselves running behind Carlos Ferreira, a Portuguese runner who was strongest in the marathon, who, along with his guide, Ricardo Mestre, took the race out in 66 seconds for the first 400 metres and about 2:15 through the 800-metre split. I felt comfortable, poised and anxious; the other teams were right there with us. The race could have been anybody's at that point.

The pace slowed in the third lap as everybody readied themselves for the inevitable last-lap sprint behind Carlos and his guide. I heard 3:27 called as we passed 1200 metres. Then, Greg and I started to accelerate as Doug had taught us. Moving a little to the outside, we were right on the shoulder of the Portuguese athletes, and then we went past them, into the final curve and around the corner, with a clear track ahead.

There are moments in running when you feel intuitively that you have an extra gear that the other person doesn't have, and you use it to your advantage without regret. I felt strong, with the exhilaration of a small crowd urging us on. We never looked back. We hit the line in a new personal best of 4:17 – no collapse this time, running through it, two runners, one team, on top of the world!

5 Paralympians

Over the next two years, I continued training with the team at the University of Guelph, returning to Brantford in the summer to rejoin our club, still coached by Doug. He challenged me to believe in my potential and to approach our training and racing with assuredness, which is not to say that being coached by him was easy. In his late fifties then, a retired teacher from England, eccentric and experimental, he believed in hard training, challenging us to dig deep, and inspiring us to have confidence in possibilities.

For Doug, the training was about quality over quantity. I did workouts I never imagined being able to do, such as his classic series of eight 400-metre repeats, which I worked down to do in an average of 67 seconds for each interval, taking just a minute's rest in between.

Doug drove regularly to Guelph to coach me through unguided training sessions around the Turfgrass Institute, a grass farm adjacent to the campus. He wanted me to develop a feel for running freely and to get used to swinging my left arm. Typically, I was guided on my left side, so I tended to keep that arm more rigid. Doug wanted me to open up my stride, not to hold back, to feel a sense of freedom and autonomy, moving through space in an uninhibited way. He used a whistle to tell me to veer to the left or right: one whistle signified left, and two meant I should turn right. He also helped me work on my form, having me sprint uphill toward the sound of his whistle.

5 Paralympians

It was simple and ingenious.

Doug saw no reason why Greg and I couldn't run much faster than we had. His training was direct, intense, and uncompromising, inspired by the coaching philosophy of Frank Horwill, the iconic coach who famously founded the British Milers' Club and who also developed a five-pace training theory that many middle-distance coaches around the world have adopted as a foundation of their training.

Doug's 800-metre work often involved two or three fast 500-metre repeats with long rests, or he would prescribe 1500-metre training involving 800-metre repeats at a 1500-metre pace or faster, again with a long rest. And then there were the eight 400-metre workouts at our goal 1500-metre pace, taking just a 60-second rest between each interval and striving to run these progressively faster each week; it was a brutal workout, but it hardened us to cope with the specific demands of 1500-metre racing.

I've known talented national-level athletes who couldn't handle the intensity of Doug's training. Where other coaches might prescribe higher weekly mileage with moderate interval and tempo running, Doug's training went for the jugular. You knew what you were capable of when you trained that way. But it broke me sometimes; it broke all of us at some point. You couldn't train like that year-round.

In the summer of 2000, Greg and I set our sights on selection to the Canadian team headed to Sydney in October for the Paralympics. A few months earlier, we had dropped another four seconds off our 1500-metre time at an indoor race at the University of Western Ontario. This breakthrough came after a few weeks of Doug having me run on my own around the Turfgrass Institute. I felt strong after the sessions on the grass and the uphill sprints he had me run every two days. We did few conventional intervals or long runs, but my body felt good.

I wanted to immerse myself in the same environment that led several athletes coached by Dave to nice breakthroughs in the 1500 and 5000 metres. I knew it would be the key to a forward leap in our performance, propelling us onto the Paralympic team and potentially enabling us to contend for a medal.

I lived in a house near the university campus with four other runners:

Shaun Kingerlee, Peter Sullivan, Reid Coolsaet (who improved to 3:52 and 14:39 for 1500 and 5000 metres that summer and went on to become a two-time Olympian in the marathon), and Mark Volmer. Mark regularly guided me at Guelph on easy and tempo runs, which he excelled at.

We had fun that summer with a couple of memorable parties counterbalancing the hard training. Even without the top facilities that some runners had access to, we embraced training in an austere athletic environment. We made it work with what we had: a network of dirt trails, an old-school gravel track, good coaching, and uncompromising determination. We chipped away, each of us making quiet inroads into our potential, carried on the shoulders of others trying to do the same, moulded by the interval training and recovery runs that gave us a foundation and by the ethos of conviction, the dreams of summer, and the quiet understanding that lay at the root of our vision, which each of us guarded closely.

If you are healthy, motivated, working out consistently, running with people who are faster than you, raising your level of expectation and unlocking the best you have, you stand a good chance of breaking new ground. In June, that is what Greg and I achieved when we ran 4:10.8 in a 1500-metre race at York University, and a month later, having by then run a new 800-metre personal best of 2:01.8, we lowered our 1500-metre best to 4:08.2 at a Twilight competition held at McMaster University in Hamilton. These Twilight meets welcomed local athletes on Tuesday evenings during the summer months and, in 2000, enabled Greg and me to pursue and ultimately attain selection to the Paralympic team. We knew we were ready to take on the world on the biggest stage possible.

The Sydney Paralympics were held in October, in the Canadian fall, corresponding with spring in the southern hemisphere. Typically, in Canada, the outdoor track season ends in August. Greg and I continued running hard track workouts in September when most other middle-distance athletes had taken a break and were starting to train for cross country. The weather was cooler, and I was tired. It was difficult to maintain the intensity and momentum from the summer, and with no current racing opportunities on the track, we had to make our own.

We ran two time trials with the support of athletes from the team that ran slightly ahead of us at our target pace until halfway. Neither of them went very well. In the first, a 1500 metre, we ran a hand-timed 4:18 on a cool, rainy night, and in the second, a 2000 metre, we fell off the pace early; I didn't have it. Still, our foundation of training was solid. I knew it was important to take a breath and absorb the ebbs and flows that are inevitable when you are at or near your peak. I also knew I needed to stay positive and be ready to embrace the incredible opportunity that lay ahead.

Friends were thrilled that Greg and I had been selected for the team. My friend and future roommate, Carin Headrick, also blind and studying at Guelph, organized a surprise party for me at the university's Grad Lounge.

It was difficult not to get swept up in the excitement in the days and weeks leading up to our departure for Sydney. Deep down, I felt I'd lost a step from the summer. I was still in good shape but found myself feeling a bit flat. The strides or wind sprints we did as part of the warm-up for our workouts weren't as snappy as they'd been, and I found I wasn't looking forward to training in the same way; it had been a long season by then. But here we were, heading to Australia, where we would be welcomed with outstretched arms by a fan audience that had cheered their own Kathy Freeman to Olympic gold in the 400-metre hurdles only a few weeks before.

We landed in Sydney in the morning, descending across its coastline and touching down on land bathed in eternal spring. We drove to the Athlete Village where we would be staying, then were led through a seemingly endless check-in process before finally receiving our accreditations. We were then shepherded through the security checkpoint into what was referred to as the International Zone.

Thirty minutes later, we found ourselves in a vast tent cafeteria with an incredibly diverse array of food choices, round-the-clock access, and all the free McDonald's you could eat – they were one of the sponsors. Coke machines were scattered throughout the Village, where you could get free soft drinks using a token attached to your accreditation.

The Athlete Village was a beehive of activity: it was easy to feel like a tourist amid the music and the movement, with live bands near the cafeteria, an arcade, and an internet café where people surfed the web or checked emails. In the building assigned to Canada, a lounge had been set up for athletes to watch movies, view live action from the Games, or simply hang out. It was stimulating and sometimes draining to coexist with so many competitive personalities who, like you, were nervously and excitedly waiting their turn to represent their country.

Greg and I were running in the 800 metres in a combined category of B1 and B2 athletes. The latter group had some eyesight and could opt to run with or without a guide. We knew we would have a difficult time against B2 athletes, a few of whom had run well under two minutes, but our goal was to try to make it through to the final out of our semi-final heat. Our primary event was the 1500 metres, where we would run with a B1 field of athletes we had a good chance against.

One day during our first week in Sydney, Greg and I did a workout where we ran five 600-metre repeats on the track, finishing the last one in 1:34. I felt great; it was one of my best sessions in the weeks leading up to the Games, and it helped solidify my confidence.

Then, before we knew it, the day of the Opening Ceremony was upon us. Many of the athletes competing in the days immediately following the Opening Ceremony opted not to go, but as it was our first Games, Greg and I wanted to walk into the Olympic Stadium with the team.

In the hours leading up to the moment that athletes marched onto the track, teams were assembled in the stadium's bowels, arranged alphabetically by country. The atmosphere was exciting and emotionally charged. It was the first time I had ever been a part of anything so visceral and patriotic. The Mexican athletes, for instance, sang to the beat of drums they played rhythmically, like an ode to their nation's heartbeat. It resonated with me, contrasting, as it did, with the more sedate and conventional cheering of the Canadians and other contingents.

Finally, when it was our turn, we walked with Team Canada into the stadium, past the cheering Canadian fans seated next to the entryway, and out onto the track, where only a few weeks earlier, Haile Gebrselassi and Paul Turgat had contested an Olympic 10,000-metre final for the ages. Greg and I were swept along, past thousands of cheering fans with flags held out, in the vanguard of the biggest athletic celebration of our lives, bar none. After we reached our seats, we listened as Kylie Minogue sang Waltzing Matilda,

5 Paralympians

the unofficial Australian anthem. The Games were officially declared open as the Paralympic flame lit up the packed stadium, and nearly 5000 athletes from every corner of the world fell under its warmth, brought closer within a community of sameness, anointed as Paralympians under the stars of the heady Australian night.

Two days later, the Paralympic competition began for Greg and me, as we lined up for one of two 800-metre semifinals; we ran what for us was a solid race but missed going through to the final, finishing third in our heat in a time of 2:03.09. We were disappointed because we had run faster in the summer, but that first race let us wet our feet. Now, we were truly Paralympians, ready to compete in the 1500 metres against athletes in the B1 category only, where we knew we had our best chance.

We had nearly a week to get ready for the 1500-metre semi-final. Other than going for easy runs or doing a couple of small track workouts that week and occasionally watching our teammates compete in other track events, we ate, napped in the afternoons, and eventually ate again, but otherwise, there was little else to do.

It became important not to overthink things and to remain relaxed and composed while all around you, people were jumpy and on edge, nervous, and primed for their events. Some had already finished competing and were ready to let their hair down. Inwardly, I wished we could get on with it.

On a couple of those days, I headed into the city with Greg, Stu McGregor, and a few others to walk around the harbour, but we felt the shadow of the competition following us.

Finally, it was the morning of our 1500-metre semi-final. In Sydney, the Athlete Village was only a couple of kilometres away from the stadium, so Greg and I skipped the mass athlete transportation and jogged over to join our Canadian teammates on the warm-up track. We stretched, relaxed, completed our drills, and ran a few strides.

Then, fifty minutes ahead of our race, an announcer summoned us to the call room. Once inside, I remember the pressure cooker of pent-up energy: the physicality of nerves, sweat, and rapid heartbeats. I heard many languages spoken in staccato rapid fire. On that day, as on many other days in the years that followed, I asked myself, do I belong here? Do I have it? Am

I ready? And I hoped I was, for the people who I knew believed in me: my guide, my coach, my family, my team, my country, and myself.

Officials checked the length of our track spikes to ensure they complied with regulations, covered any logos on our track gear that promoted sponsors other than those that supported the Paralympics, and checked the darkened glasses or eye shades that B1 athletes were required to wear in races up to 1500 metres. The glasses were intended to completely obscure our field of vision so that those with even a tiny amount of light perception, as my brothers and I had, would have no visual advantage.

Although the process of medical classification was rigorous, we became quite sure over the years that some athletes we had run against had broken or attempted to break the rules. I had my first experience of this in our semi-final.

After the call room officials' inspection, just moments before the start of the race, Greg noticed that some of the blind athletes had readjusted their glasses to allow light in. He even saw one runner replace the proper darkened glasses with another pair. Greg told an official what he had seen, and thankfully, the official insisted that the runner wear the original glasses or face disqualification. Still, the system of classification and its implementation was and continues to be problematic despite greater rigour in the testing protocols put in place over the years by the International Paralympic Committee.

Finally, we were brought onto the track and led to the beginning of the backstretch to line up for the three and three-quarter laps of our 1500-metre semi-final. We lined up at the start, seemingly in slow motion, with a momentum calculated and inevitable. Then, the gun sounded, and there was no more talking or thinking, just racing.

Henry Wanyoike from Kenya and his guide initially took the lead. The pace was quick from the start, and it seemed that it wouldn't be an easy road to the final. Greg and I positioned ourselves just off the lead, in the slipstream of the leaders, and let them do the work. We might have split through our first 400 in 64 or 65 seconds and passed through 800 in about 2:11. The pace was fast but not suicidal. Then it slowed, and suddenly Greg and I found ourselves at the front. The leaders had fallen back, and we had a clear track ahead of us. We did enough to maintain our lead without expending undue energy and went on to win with a time of 4:16. Behind us, Henry and his guide also qualified, as did the Spanish runner Pedro Delgado and his guide, against whom we had competed in Madrid in 1998, and Portuguese runner Paulo de Almeida Coelho, the 1996 Paralympic 1500-metre champion and his guide.

Greg and I were thrilled to have made it to the final, which would take place two days later.

Being new to international competition, we were still riding the wave of a breakthrough summer track season despite the fatigue I had felt in the preceding weeks. We had a seasonal best time of 4:08.2, ranking us first in the field. Greg and I believed we were in shape to go after the then-world record of 4:05.11 by abandoning the usual slow and tactical approach to championship races in favour of setting and maintaining a fast pace, as we had tried to do in the 800 metres in Madrid two years earlier.

Two days later, as we lined up for the 1500-metre final and were introduced by the announcer under the morning sunshine, I tried to calm my nerves. I thought about what it had taken to reach this point: the years of hard work, the seasons of uncertainty, the inspired moments of possibility and action, and the ebbs and flows of my life. This moment represented a dream long in the making, and now here we were, living it for real.

The crack of the starter's gun penetrated through the hushed crowd, and we were away, fast off the line, intent on claiming the lead. Others had a similar idea because it seemed like everybody had started quickly, but nobody quicker than we, so intent we were we on getting to the front. We were leading and running fast – faster than I was used to. Ahead of us, the track was clear.

Coming around the bend and into the home straightaway in front of the main stand, I was struck by the increasing intensity of the crowd's cheering. It was hard to hear Greg or the other runners around us. It meant I had to trust Greg to position us where we needed to be. In Canada, our workouts and most of our racing had taken place in relative silence. Here, the element of hearing, so vital to how I conceptualized the space around me, was taken away.

At that moment, I needed to turn inwards and harness the mental coping mechanisms that helped me get there in the first place. The prism of my awareness narrowed. It felt strange, unsettling, and destabilizing, demanding tremendous emotional energy. The solution was to run on autopilot.

Even though I competed for years in such a way, I never got used to it. I've come to understand that being able to brace myself for these psychological challenges was integral to the reality of being a Paralympian with a visual disability. I had to accept that life is not about being perfect, it is about doing your best.

In retrospect, the race passed by in a flash. I heard 62 at our 400-metre split and 2:09 at 800. It seemed like we were running away with it. But you don't run away with a Paralympic final.

We hit the 1200-metre mark, splitting in 3:18, and still, we were leading, but we weren't running efficiently; I was slowing down. People said afterward that we had run with courage, but fear was motivating us to run hard in a Paralympic final where strategy was everything. As we hit the corner with 200 metres to go, my form was falling apart. And behind us, Paulo and his guide were suddenly right there. I knew it was them. Over the din of the crowd, I could discern the Portuguese guide runner yelling at Paulo. They were poised, and they were coming.

Around the corner and into the home stretch, my legs were wobbling. Now Greg was yelling, too, "Go, Jay. Come on, Jay, fucking go! Everything! Go!" To my right on our outside, the Portuguese guide was also yelling as the line approached. Everyone was yelling!

Paulo and his guide crossed the line four-hundredths of a second ahead of Greg and me – 4:10.13 to 4:10.17. It couldn't have been closer, yet it couldn't have been more definitive. In the aftermath, it felt like we had lost first place rather than winning second.

6 Stepping Back, Stepping Forward

There is a letdown following a major competition. You pour your heart and soul into training and getting into top shape in hopes of first qualifying, then trying to get into even better shape and then navigating the pressure cooker of tension, excitement, tactics, and expectations that are difficult to avoid at a global championship. The Paralympics are an experience unlike anything else. Your whole life becomes subsumed within the paradigm of Paralympian. When it's done, you climb out of the fishbowl and into everyday life again.

I was drained after the Games in 2000. I got a cold. This became a pattern for me at the end of almost every competitive season when my body realized it could finally rest. Back home, there were parties and get-togethers to celebrate our medal-winning run. Friends said we'd raced courageously. I was inducted into the Sports Hall of Fame in Brantford, where I had attended high school. I was grateful for the support of friends who wanted to celebrate with us, but inwardly, I felt deeply conflicted about our experience at the Games.

Greg and I came close to winning in Sydney – within a hair's breadth. It haunted me because the race had been within our grasp. Opportunities like that are fleeting, and I wondered if we'd ever have another.

Over time, though, I began to appreciate how we had raced; we took a calculated risk that felt like the right thing at the time, and I was grateful we honoured the integrity of that decision.

I'd stayed in school part-time during the semester the Paralympics had taken place, which made for some late nights catching up after we returned home. Many national team athletes who were also students had taken time off to concentrate on training before the Paralympics or to travel afterwards. I would be travelling again soon enough, though, joining a group of international development students from the Universities of Guelph and Saskatchewan who would be leaving in January 2001 for a semester abroad in Antigua, Guatemala.

I flew to Guatemala early in the new year with forty other international development students and a few professors from our home universities. Most of us were hosted by local families. We studied Spanish intensively at a language school for the first five weeks and then took courses in Guatemalan history, politics and literature.

Many times, in the late afternoon, we'd meet in the central square, sit and talk with locals, and then head to the Rainbow Café or Café Loca with fellow students.

On the weekends, we travelled around the country, often taking what were referred to as chicken buses, where humans and sometimes livestock rode together. We travelled in small groups to the beautiful beaches of Monterrico, enjoyed fresh fish and rum in coconut shells, or went on organized field trips. One of these trips took us to the Mayan ruins in Tikal in the north, known for its epic sunrises.

I did little running when I was in Guatemala. I tried training at first, but it wasn't the environment for it, and in the end, the break probably did me good. The few runs I went on were around a coffee *finca* with a fellow student named Ryan from the University of Saskatchewan.

Having brought a guitar with me, on many evenings, I played and sang with Janet McLaughlin, who I'd gotten to know through the international development program at Guelph. We wrote several songs and eventually recorded some of our music together. It was a creatively charged time for me as I sought to come to terms with the heartache of our Paralympic 1500-metre

6 Stepping Back, Stepping Forward

race and a romantic relationship in Canada that didn't work out.

Guatemala had recently emerged out of a long period of civil war dating back to the 1950s that saw the indigenous Mayan people repressed by land reforms and American foreign influence. It had become a proxy war, where forces on the left fought against the right in a battle of ideologies, and its victims were predominantly the Mayan people, martyrs of a genocide that decimated their population and threatened their very survival.

In that beautiful, tortured country, where time seemed to move more slowly, and there was less of a middle than anywhere I had ever been, the hope and generosity of so many of the people we met attested to the strength of its beating heart. I learned firsthand how privileged we were as Canadians to live as we do, secure within our high walls of hope, fear, and individuality.

I came to realize as well how fortunate I was, as a person who is blind, not to live in a country where people with a visual disability were referred to as *minus vàlido*. Any limitations I might have internalized were, I came to realize, fictions of my mind.

Back in Canada in the spring of 2001, I moved in with my university friend Carin Headrick and her boyfriend Steve Wettlaufer, whom I'd known from high school.

I also reconnected with Doug Whistance, my old coach, and got back into reasonable shape that summer. Greg and I competed at a Para Pan American Championships for blind and visually impaired runners in South Carolina. We won both the 800 and 1500 metres, each in a slow tactical race. I went on to run 2:06 for 800 metres and 4:17 for 1500 metres that summer. I wasn't in the same shape as the year before, but with consistent workouts, I knew I could get myself back to a higher level of training and racing.

Except when September came, life would change. I didn't go back to school. Over the summer, I applied for a job with the Royal Bank of Canada, a summer position in a call centre in Toronto, but they offered me a full-time job instead, and something compelled me to take it. I had a year of university to complete, but I was excited about a chance to earn real income.

I took a Greyhound bus to Toronto early each morning, answered inbound service calls for eight hours, and then took the bus home. It was exhausting and soul-destroying.

It's difficult for persons who are blind to find employment, and this was an underlying reason for my decision. The bank had accommodated me, and it felt like a vote of confidence at that time. My mother and Maurice were happy to see me working. They and others may have wondered whether I would return to finish my degree, but I always knew I would.

That fall and winter of working, and a three-hour daily commute meant my training was limited to weekends and some nights. The following spring, however, I set my sights on getting back into shape in preparation for the International Paralympic Committee (IPC) World Championships in Lille, France, in July 2002. I had left my job by then and planned to return to school in September.

After a layoff from running, starting back is physically painful and psychologically exhausting at first. When you're fit, even intense training can feel easy. When you're not, though, everything hurts. Returning to a training regime after a layoff is harder as the years pass, but it's still possible with time, patience, and determination. At a certain point, usually a few weeks in, there's a run or a workout where you begin to notice that everything feels a little better. It gives you hope and validates the weeks of discomfort you've put yourself through.

After three months of consistent workouts, Greg and I flew with the team to Lille, France, in July for the World Championships. I was not in my best shape, even though each workout had been a stepping stone to improved fitness. We only raced the 1500-metre B1 event, contested as a straight final.

The early pace was slow. Nerves, always strained in a slow-moving, tightly-knit pack where no one wants to commit, are especially palpable in a field of blind runners and guides. Blind runners are listening, and the guides are looking around, and you can cut the tension with a knife. You don't want to get caught on the inside and risk being unable to react to a move. I would have my elbow ready if anyone tried to box us in.

All 1500-metre runners, be they able-bodied or athletes with a disability, whether at the Olympics or elementary school track meets, believe they have the best kick in the field. In Lille, Greg and I felt confident that we did too.

The race continued to be slow and tactical, and Greg and I guarded our position near the front just to the outside.

With 300 metres to go, suddenly, the race began in earnest. Greg and I were well-placed, and we got on our toes and flew. For all the missed training that would have seen us buried in a faster, less tactical championship race, I knew Greg and I could kick hard for this one. I had the will to win and the belief we were going to. You have to believe without a shadow of a doubt. We hit the finish line in a slow 4:22, but it didn't matter because nobody cares about the winning time in a championship final.

7 Seasons of Change, Hope and Heartache

After returning home following our successful World Championships, I felt more motivated than ever to train to regain the level of fitness I had back in 2000. Before competing in Lille, I had been able to get into good shape relatively quickly with Greg's help. With more consistent training, I was sure we could return to top form.

Of course, more is not always better, and when I reflect on my running over the years, this has always been true. Doing specific training has always been the route to success; quality over quantity has always mattered the most.

In September 2002, I returned to the University of Guelph to complete the final year of my degree in international development, minoring in Spanish literature.

I trained with the Guelph Gryphons varsity team and ran two cross-country races, each on reasonably flat courses. Though I was never very competitive in cross country, it was still good for me to race and remain connected with the psychology of competition; for me, the outcome in these races mattered less than simply running hard.

That fall, I increased my training volume to 60 miles, or just under

100 kilometres a week. While this amount of weekly running is considered moderate for many competitive middle- and long-distance runners, it was a lot for me. Over the years, I worked up to as much as 80 miles, or 130 kilometres, during some weeks, and while higher volume training can work very well for some, I always seemed to do better with more intensity and less distance; this was true even with the marathon training I've done in more recent years.

There's a time for running more, a time for running faster, and perhaps a time in one's athletic career when it's possible to do both for a little while. Learning to be self-aware and read your internal signals is key to healthy running. I'm still learning this lesson. As runners, we're constantly learning, and it's not always a linear process. I look at how my African running friends train: intuitively, naturally. When it's raining, or if they're tired, they don't train; when they feel good, they're unbeatable. I hope to learn to be more like them.

Now, in my forties, I'm not the same type of runner I was in the fall of 2002 when I was twenty-five. Today, for example, I can do faster long runs than I could when I was younger, but the shorter, intense intervals leave me sore for days.

I'm not the same person I was back then, either. Life changes us; we mature, get hurt, and grow in new ways. Our journeys teach us about love, resiliency, the inevitability of change, and the healing force of gratitude. We learn that time takes away, but it also replaces as we evolve. Running has offered me a gateway to a deeper sense of myself.

In November 2002, I took a weekend trip to Ottawa to visit Krista, a high school friend. Like me, she had been a residential student, but each Friday afternoon, she flew back to Ottawa, returning to school in Brantford on Sunday night.

This was only my second time travelling up to see her. On Friday evening, Krista invited friends over, including a new one. Colleen, as I would learn, had lost her eyesight only three years earlier as a result of diabetic retinopathy, a condition where, over time, fluctuations in blood sugar can damage the blood vessels of the retina.

We talked through the night and into the early morning, long after everybody else had left and Krista had gone to bed. Colleen said she had started to experience blurred vision after completing her diploma in Early Childhood Education. As many young adults might have reacted, she was initially in denial but eventually let her parents take her to an eye doctor. Over the months that followed, she had a series of surgeries that attempted to salvage her diminishing eyesight, none of which was successful; eventually, she lost the rest of her vision.

I admired her stoicism and quiet acceptance as she shared the story of her vision loss. Being born blind, I never had to adapt to living without sight – it was the only way of being I'd ever known. For Colleen, losing her vision necessitated a complete transformation. The final realization occurred when she could no longer drive.

Her dad took her vision loss very hard. She disguised any vulnerability she might have felt, endeavouring to show her parents that she could adapt well. After a year of coming to terms with this change in her life, she returned to study psychology at Ottawa's Carleton University, accessing the support available to students with disabilities, as I had done at the University of Guelph. She learned to use a white cane and, with the help of an orientation and mobility instructor, navigated the walking and bus routes she would take regularly on her own.

Walking in her neighbourhood meant coming across people who knew her; she found herself having to explain what happened and relive the whole story of her vision loss. I'd always known that some people were less comfortable around those who were blind, but Colleen became painfully aware of it when some of her friends started calling less frequently after her vision loss.

We talked into the early morning about our families and my running. She said she wasn't athletic but had started going to the gym. We had very different life experiences, but there was a feeling of connection.

She seemed rooted and courageous; it made me want to keep listening and talking. Finally, I said goodnight and went upstairs. Colleen ended up on Krista's couch while, for some reason, I took the available bed, but she didn't hold it against me.

Following my return to Guelph after that weekend, we began messaging, at first occasionally, but as the weeks passed, with increasing regularity.

We each had end-of-term exams. And then it was Christmas. My brothers and I, who had also moved out by then, spent the holiday with our parents in Hamilton. Jon was attending Sheridan College in Brampton; by then, he had Luther, his first guide dog, and was taking a diploma program in animal care. Chris was doing studies in social work at Fanshawe College in London, Ontario, but had taken a semester off to focus on his new passion, bodybuilding. As teenagers, Jon and Chris had lifted weights – a key contributor to their success in wrestling. In addition to the strength this had given them, each had known intuitively how to maneuver around the fully-sighted wrestlers they came up against.

Chris had continued lifting weights and, at his bodybuilding peak, weighed 240 pounds; he was six feet, one inch of pure muscle. Like me, he was quiet and more introverted than his gregarious twin brother, but he was committed to being the best bodybuilder he could be. He placed fourth in the Mr. Brantford bodybuilding competition in September 2002, a notable feat in a sport where competitors tended to reach their prime in their late twenties. Chris was just twenty-two. Jon, our mother, Maurice, and I were in the audience, proud and cheering. I felt he had gone for it and put everything on the line.

But what is the cost when we give everything we have? We risk having nothing left to fall back on. How do we recognize the human vulnerability we are susceptible to and our need for safeguards to hold us up against the gravity of a downward spiral? How do we pull ourselves back up when the effort might feel too great? I heard former Canadian Lieutenant-General Romeo Dallaire say that what ultimately lifted him out of his own descent toward depression was love.

That fall, Chris was living in a house with one of the Swerdfiger twins, our old high school friends, and spent most of his time in his room. We knew he was a bit down after placing fourth in a competition he believed he could win. I visited a few times. We tried unsuccessfully to persuade him to come out with us. We never thought that Chris might have been struggling with mental illness.

I knew that Chris was in debt, although how much I learned only later.

Lack of money was one of the reasons he took a hiatus from school. He had borrowed from me over the previous months in the lead-up to the Mr. Brantford competition. At Christmas, I asked Chris if he could begin paying me back a little at a time, which he then started to do. He had registered for classes in January. It seemed as though he had broken out of the inertia of the previous months and that his life was moving forward once again.

As it often is with brothers, we were casual about regular communication. When we left my mother and Maurice's and headed in our respective directions following the Christmas break, I couldn't have known we would never see Chris again.

I returned home one Friday evening at the end of January 2003 to the apartment I shared about a ten-minute walk from the University of Guelph campus with Steve and Carin. They told me I needed to call home. Maurice answered, saying I should come right away. With no bus service at that time of night, I took a $75 taxi.

In my parents' apartment, there were floods of tears. My mother was inconsolable. Jon was there after being picked up by Maurice from his college dorm. The police had been there a couple of hours earlier to break the news that Chris had taken his own life.

Somehow, I knew deep down, before arriving, that Chris was gone, but the brutal confirmation of it hit home unlike any pain I had ever known before.

Each of us has crosses to bear. We carry the scars of our lived experience, some superficial and others that run deeper. Family, love, loss, buried feelings that ache sometimes and abate at others. Each of us carries a million scars. They can strangle us if we let them, or we can push against their rigidity, pull ourselves back up, and wear them as a symbol of healing, hope and experience.

It has been over twenty years since we lost Chris. There have been other losses since then, but what was so devastating about Chris's death was his youth. That night in my parent's apartment, Jon cried uncontrollably for a few intense, heart-wrenching minutes, grieving his twin, his littermate. In the years since, he has hardly ever talked about Chris's death. He would remain stoic, forward-thinking and outwardly strong. For me, the pain has ebbed and flowed. At times, I have felt profound guilt. If only I had known what was coming. I am haunted by the thought that I could have done more.

I miss Chris. I miss him when I'm reminded of the cricket or soccer games he, Jon, and I played for hours and endless afternoons when we were children, improvising in our own adapted way with a ball wrapped in a plastic bag. I miss him when recalling our wrestling, back when I could still win. I miss him when I remember the homesickness we felt together in the first months after our emigration to Canada. I miss him when I think about his fearlessness in taking on the best high school wrestlers. I miss his aggression. I miss his calm.

Brother

He makes his way to the secret place
That's hidden away, behind the human face.
He hits the bottom, reaches base
And he's gone without a trace.
Brother, you hold a special place
In our minds, one that time cannot erase,
for you fly the skies on wings of grace,
And one day we'll embrace.
You took it on your own to bear,
We didn't know. We weren't aware,
And it wasn't that we didn't care-
I wish I'd been there.
We make our way along the line
To pay our respects at your lonely shrine,
Through the cold. And snowflakes mark the sign
Of a moment in time.

You held the world up in your hands.
You sold your soul. Your dreams were grand
And you went back to school as you had planned,
But you were walking on quicksand.
So much denial, so much doubt.

VISIONS OF HOPE

I held you down when you were out,
And I was deaf to your silent shout,
So much we didn't know about
It wasn't fair, it wasn't right,
You were in too deep. You couldn't see the light.
You came to view the world as black or white,
No silver lining in sight.
So I reach out to you across space and time,
Through the screen of years, the scheme of rhyme,
And through the stream of tears that trail behind,
And I hold you in my mind.

8 New Direction

In the weeks following Chris's death, I returned to university and started training again with the team.

Colleen and I continued messaging each other until I finally gathered the courage to call her, something my roommates Steve and Carin teased me about.

I returned to Ottawa during reading week in late February and saw Colleen a lot over several days. At a time of intense grief, Colleen helped me envision a new way forward. In losing her eyesight, Colleen had come to terms with a tremendous loss of her own. She helped me to realize that I could do the same.

I was curious to explore the world and had been fortunate to do so as an athlete and student. I saw myself as transient, having no fixed place. In Colleen, I recognized stability. I knew I would always keep moving in my own way, but with her, I could also embrace a new sense of rootedness.

It took another weekend bus ride up to Ottawa and a night out at a karaoke bar with friends for us to become a couple. That was in March 2003. By September, with my degree completed, I said goodbye to my roommates – still good friends to this day – moved to Ottawa and rented a bachelor apartment, a fifteen-minute drive from the house where Colleen lived with her parents and brother.

The decision to move to Ottawa had begun to crystallize earlier that spring. I had been travelling to and from Ottawa every few weekends, staying with Krista at first and then, eventually, with Colleen and her parents. I was taking one final summer course that I needed to graduate.

I was also training and preparing, along with Greg, for the International Blind Sports Association (IBSA) World Championships in Quebec City that August.

Through my Ottawa friend and national teammate Stu McGregor, I connected with Ray Elrick, Stu's coach with the Ottawa Lions track and field club. I called Ray in April 2003 and asked to attend one of his workouts.

I felt welcomed when I came to his practice at the Terry Fox track two evenings later. Before heading out for the warm-up, Ray told the group: "Jay is here. Please take him with you on the warm-up, and he'll show you how to guide." That was all it took, but it set the tone.

A runner named Vladimir Radovich guided me on that initial warm-up. Also, there was Berry de Bruijn, Chad Pawson, Stéphane Gamache, Blair Walker, Michel Cormier, and André Okinge, an eclectic group from different parts of the world who had come to call Ottawa home as I soon would. They guided me in 400-metre repeats on the track and many subsequent workouts over the months and years. They formed the cornerstone of my new running community and became a seminal source of support as I made the exciting, disorienting transition to life in Canada's capital.

It was our coach, Ray, however, who opened the door for me to continue my running as a blind athlete and newcomer to Ottawa. A retired RCMP officer known for his directness, he created enabling conditions for me to train by simply asking his athletes to guide me. Too often, I hear about young people with visual impairments who don't participate in sports at school or within their communities because the coach doesn't know how to include them or is concerned about liability. Having coaches who can think creatively makes all the difference in the world.

Ray coached me for six years until 2009. Greg and I competed in two Paralympics and captured two World and two Para Pan American championships under his coaching.

My decision to move to Ottawa raised the question of how Greg, then living in Toronto, and I could continue training together. Toronto was only

8 New Direction

an hour's drive from Guelph, while the 450-kilometre commute to Ottawa took four hours or more, which was hardly practical for regular back-and-forth trips. We decided to give it a try. I planned to regularly visit family in southern Ontario, allowing Greg and me opportunities to meet for workouts. He was also willing to travel to Ottawa for occasional weekends or to guide me in local races. We would continue to train separately when not together. The support of Ray's athletes helped make this arrangement possible.

When I was in Guelph that summer, I trained with the varsity team, and Greg came up for workouts once or twice a week. I was getting into good shape and had run 2:02 for 800 metres and 4:13 for 1500 metres. We both felt positive heading into the Quebec City World Championships, where we would compete in both events in the T11 category for runners who were blind. My brother Jon would also compete in Quebec City in judo, finishing fifth in his weight division.

Greg and I had no problem qualifying for the final in our 800-metre heat in Quebec City, winning it comfortably in 2:04. I felt relaxed and strong. Our approach for the final was to sit in the main pack and then, with 200 metres remaining, kick and go for the win.

Two days later, in the final, I itched to go for it, as we ran in the main group. Finally, with 200 metres to go, we kicked hard and pulled away to win easily, again running 2:04.

At that time, the T11 800-metre world record was 1:59.90. It had been set seventeen years earlier, in 1986, by Bob Matthews, an English runner who also held the 1500-metre world record. Sir Robert (he was later awarded a knighthood) passed away in 2018, but in 2003, then in his early forties, he was still competing and had moved up to contest longer events on the track and roads.

I was twenty-five in 2003, and it was Bob Matthews' records that Greg and I had our sights firmly set on. We had introduced ourselves to him three years earlier at the Sydney Paralympics, where he and his guide had captured gold in the T11 10,000 metres. We ran into him again in Quebec City, and our encounter went something like this:

Bob: "So, how has the running been going this year? What have you boys run?"

Me: "We've run 2:02 so far."

Bob: "Oh, okay, so you're still jogging then!"

Me: Socially appropriate laughter and inward angst.

Bob: "Do you boys know where we can find a place around here to have a pint?"

Bob Matthews represented Great Britain at six Paralympic Games between 1984 and 2004, winning eight gold medals with support from several guides. His eyesight had gradually diminished as a young person due to Retinitis Pigmentosa, a condition involving a gradual loss of cells in the retina, and one which his father also had. Bob became completely blind by the time he was twenty. As he later wrote in his autobiography, Running Blind, running enabled him to face his fear of vision loss. He went on to a prolific international athletic career and became a pioneer in the sport. He was my role model.

Greg and I chased his records for years, and while we came close to his 800 and 1500-metre marks, we never eclipsed either. Being at different ends of our running careers, we never ran against each other in the same race. I looked up to him for what he did as a blind runner, but even more than that, for who he was – a down-to-earth, funny, resilient, and authentic person. He enjoyed beer and laughter. He embraced life. He was a trailblazer in our Paralympic movement who set the bar very high for runners like me.

Greg and I felt positive heading into our 1500-metre semi-final on the heels of our 800-metre win. In our semi-final heat, we deliberately pushed the pace over the first two laps, coming through 800 metres in 2:11 before slowing down the pace and winning comfortably. We had done this to test our competitors and ourselves. Heading into the final, we felt ready for any race – almost any race, that is – though not the one we got.

When the gun sounded, Greg and I found ourselves at the front of a group bunched behind us as we headed down the backstretch. As is usual in races with blind athletes, there was some jostling and bumping, but we seemed to be away from the worst of it. About 70 metres in, though, somebody clipped my left heel from behind. Suddenly, my running spike was half

8 New Direction

off. I knew I couldn't stop to fix it, and there was no way I could continue running like that. I did the only thing that came to mind and kicked it off to the side, so I was running barefoot, still wearing a running spike on my right foot. The race had changed for Greg and me in a split second, and rather than place ourselves at the front, we sat back and let other teams do the work.

Pedro Delgado, our old competitor from Spain, and his guide were in the race. The pace slowed dramatically, and Greg and I ran at the back of the group, a little outside our preferred spot to avoid congestion. I wasn't thinking about my bare foot. I was focused on the rhythm of the race, the footsteps around us, waiting for the moment somebody made a move.

The pace remained slow through 800 metres, and then there was a subtle increase, and suddenly we pressed. It wasn't a dramatic increase, just enough to string the field apart. We were still on the outside, alongside Pedro and his guide, and working hard. We completed the third lap in 66 seconds, and with 300 metres to go, we were together with the Spanish runners. I could tell where they were by the almost constant chatter between them. We had lost to them only once before, in the 800-metre final in Madrid in 1998.

Heading down the backstretch for the final time and into the curve, Greg and I were going for it. This was not the decisive move we pulled off in the 800-metre final a few days previously. I was running on fear; we were running on desperation.

We had the lead coming into the home stretch. I gutted it out, putting every ounce of energy into those final metres, and hit the line utterly spent but simultaneously elated. We had won.

As we celebrated in the moments following the race, I became aware of my throbbing left foot and the sticky blood between my toes. Our team physician patched it up and sent me to the hospital, where a doctor examined me and made sure the wound was clean. I was on crutches for several days as the abrasions healed. None of this stopped us from savouring our success in the pub across from where we were staying, the same place we had sent Bob Matthews a few days earlier.

My brother Jon and his teammates had also found le Pub, as we called it. I ran into him the night after our 1500-metre success on his way back to where we were all staying. He had competed that day and believed he had been eliminated from the judo competition, so he decided to hit the town, only to learn from another teammate at le Pub that he had qualified for a consolation round. Well-inebriated by then, he was in great spirits – deciding to lift me over his shoulders. Suspended in the air with only one useful leg, I only hoped he would return me to earth with care. Thankfully, he did.

The celebration couldn't fully suppress my feeling of slight disappointment. There might still have been a fast race in my legs if my season had not been brought to a forced end by my injured foot. But I also knew it was time to rest and appreciate what the season had given me – an opportunity to begin to heal and move in a new direction. I knew Chris's memory would follow and inspire me wherever I was. I had just completed the final course in my degree. Ahead of me lay a move to Ottawa, a deepening relationship, and a year to prepare for the Athens Paralympics.

9 Transition

My mother and Maurice drove me to Ottawa during the Labour Day long weekend. We spent a night with Colleen's parents before they moved me into my bachelor apartment in Ottawa's west end.

Her family was very good to me as I transitioned to life in a new city during those first weeks. They had me over often and fed me well. After some orientation and mobility lessons from an instructor working with the Canadian National Institute for the Blind, I learned how to get around my new neighbourhood, including the grocery store and Tunny's Pasture transit station.

I also began running again after the better part of a month away from training. By then, my foot had fully healed, though I felt slow and out of shape. Athletes work so hard to get fit over weeks and months, and then once we take our foot off the gas, fitness seems to disappear so quickly. My first workout after joining Ray's group at the Terry Fox track was a set of twelve 400-metre repeats on only thirty seconds of rest. This was a typical fall fitness-building session: the objective was to run each repetition in 80 seconds, but with such a short rest, I couldn't sustain it.

As a member of the national Para Athletics team, I was receiving what is referred to as carding through Sport Canada's Athlete Assistance Program, which provided athletes with financial support for basic living and training expenses; it helped me survive those first weeks and months.

I didn't have a job when I first arrived in Ottawa. I'd applied for several and had a couple of interviews, but no offers initially.

As autumn temperatures cooled, I began to feel increasingly down. Meet-ups with our training group involved a long trek on foot and a crosstown bus ride. During the workouts, I felt like I had lead in my legs. I started to miss the occasional workout. My training became spotty. Getting to and from practices and the practices themselves began to feel like a grind.

Colleen continued to be supportive, and the closeness between us deepened. She was an intelligent and resilient person who had overcome serious health odds. She bore with humility the scars of her past and painted them over with a resolve that I respected and admired.

Jon, my mother, and Maurice drove up to spend Christmas with Colleen's family. Over the years, we celebrated many Christmases and other holidays together. Our families were markedly different, but somehow, we seemed to get along. That Christmas in 2003, the first one following the death of my brother, my family was looking to do something different. It was important for us to begin to nurture new traditions.

As winter set in, the biting wind hit hard as I walked along Scott Street from my apartment to the bus at Tunny's Pasture Transit Station. There was no indoor track in Ottawa and very little access to indoor training, which wouldn't come until the Dome, a 400-metre indoor track, was constructed at Louis Riel High School in 2005.

The training group Ray coached met at the Aberdeen Pavilion in Lansdowne Park, where we could leave our gear and run a few wind sprints on the short section of rubberized turf. Following this warm-up routine, we ran outside, as the pathway along the Rideau Canal was mostly cleared of snow. When it was too cold, Ray kept the workouts short; you couldn't run outside for long when it was below minus 20.

Finally, I received a job offer in March from MBNA Canada Bank to work in their call centre. It was similar to the job two years earlier with the Royal Bank, so I knew what I was in for. Even so, I was grateful for the job offer, my first out of university, which I readily accepted.

The shift work, which sometimes had me working late into the night, was not conducive to consistent training, as our group worked out mostly in

9 Transition

the evenings, but I did my best that spring to balance work with preparing for the 2004 Paralympics set to take place in Athens in September.

In June, Greg and I raced in the 1500 metres at the Paralympic Trials in Sherbrooke, Quebec.

It was my first, or perhaps second, race of the season, and my limited training showed. We won in our category, but in a slow 4:22, a performance that triggered a doubt that sometimes crept into my psyche when a race hadn't gone well: was my best running in the rear-view mirror? I would be twenty-seven that summer. Was I still hungry to keep going?

I was training, working full-time, and adapting to a new city. It had been a tumultuous eighteen months. I was still coming to terms with losing Chris. I felt overwhelmed. Wouldn't I rather do what seemed normal and go out on Friday nights and sleep late on Saturday mornings rather than get up early for our track workout? Did I still want it enough? Was my heart still in it?

Greg and I had already been to the Paralympics and were world champions. Nothing was forcing me to continue. Nobody would have faulted me for walking away. It had been a fantastic journey, and I felt deep gratitude for every step of it.

I recognized, however, that while I was feeling burned out, things could quickly change.

I needed to continue training, not worry about what the stopwatch said, and remain committed. Running has its ebbs and flows, and I needed to give myself a chance to ride the currents of uncertainty, which are inevitable from time to time in high-performance sports.

Greg and I were named to the Athens 2004 Paralympic team after our win at the Paralympic Trials and our World Championships success the previous summer. We ran several solid 800-metre races at the Ottawa Twilight meets in June and July 2004, getting down to a time of 2:04.

The Ottawa Twilight meets were low-key competitions held at the Terry Fox track in Ottawa each Wednesday evening between seven and nine PM throughout the summer. Hosted by the Ottawa Lions, these meets provided weekly opportunities for athletes looking for competitive opportunities.

I took a short leave from my job at MBNA to focus fully on our preparation ahead of the Paralympics. That summer, Greg and I travelled frequently between Ottawa and Toronto for races and spells of training. Greg stayed with Stu and his wife Becky when he visited Ottawa since I was then living in a small studio apartment.

When I travelled to Toronto to train with Greg, I stayed with him and his then-wife Diane. We ran along the boardwalk by Lake Ontario and in the cemetery immediately behind their house in The Beaches neighbourhood. We ran our track sessions at Centennial High School in Etobicoke.

In early August, Greg, Stu and I had an opportunity to spend several days training in Seattle. We planned to run 1500 metres at a local competition and then fly to Edmonton for another race, where we'd also be joined by most of the Paralympic team ahead of the Athens Games.

I had never visited Seattle before and appreciated the opportunity to walk its streets and take in its music and coffee culture. Unfortunately, I picked up a minor hamstring injury in a workout, putting me out of both the Seattle and Edmonton races as a precaution. Our training had been going well, though, and I was not overly worried. I knew my hamstring just needed a few days of rest.

While in Seattle, with Greg and Stu as accomplices, I took the step of buying an engagement ring, which I planned to bring with me to Greece.

Back in Ottawa after our trip and before heading to our pre-Games training camp in Grosseto, Italy, Colleen arranged a surprise send-off for us. The party coincided with my twenty-seventh birthday and caught me totally by surprise. It was great having my training partners, friends, and family together; my mother, Maurice, and Jon drove up for the send-off.

Grosseto, a city on the Italian Adriatic coast, was where our Paralympic team adjusted to the six-hour time difference and put the finishing touches on pre-Games training. We stayed in a small resort hotel and ate together in a dining room where waiters served multiple courses; they brought loaves of fresh bread and bowls of pasta, which we thought was the main meal, until it was followed by salad, meat, and vegetables, washed down with bottles of

9 Transition

San Pellegrino mineral water.

Between track workouts and recovery runs, Stu and I hung out at the hotel bar terrace– drinking espressos and cappuccinos. We drank so many that week. We also joined Greg for exploratory walks along the old cobblestoned streets.

When you're a couple of weeks away from peaking, you try to be optimal in your readiness for your main competition. You don't want to do too much training, but you also want to remain sharp. Usually, this means you run less but continue with some faster running, which is specific to the race you're preparing for.

Greg and I ran a 1200-metre time trial a few days before leaving Grosseto, where our objective was to run at our goal 1500-metre pace of 65 seconds for each lap. This would expose us to the specific feeling of running at our target race pace for 1200 metres.

We were on pace at 800 metres, which we split in 2:10, and at 1000 metres, which we passed in 2:42. Then, the lactic acid caught up to me, and we finished the 1200 in 3:18 for an average lap pace of 66 seconds. While it was still a good run, I'd slowed down a lot in the final 200, which triggered the inevitable question in my mind as we prepared to take the bus from Grosseto back to Rome for our flight to Athens: did I have the fitness I knew I'd need to contend with the best in the world?

The Olympic and Paralympic Athlete Village was a 40-minute drive from Athens, so we couldn't just walk out and take in the energy of the Greek capital. Colleen and Stu's wife, Becky, flew into Athens a couple of days before we competed, and while it was terrific to have the support of loved ones, we saw very little of them before our competitions. We were cloistered away, and this took a toll on Greg especially.

One afternoon, he and I did a workout on the track, running a series of six 300-metre repeats in 44 to 45 seconds, taking three minutes of recovery in between. As we worked our way through the intervals, the guide for an Australian runner had inadvertently left a shoe in the lane we were using. It was a forgivable mistake, but Greg lost his temper and angrily kicked the shoe across the track, triggering a heated exchange with the Australian guide runner; such was Greg's pent-up rage, precipitated by the pressure and the sense of responsibility he felt in that hyper-energized, emotional echo chamber.

As in my previous Paralympics, there was no T11 800-metre race, so we participated in the T12 category, which offered the option of running with or without a guide. The goal was to make it out of the heats and into the final. We fell short by running a solid but not spectacular time of 2:03. However, that race helped to disrupt the inertia I felt during the preceding days and weeks; for Greg and me, it diluted the pressure.

We cheered for Stu as he clinched bronze in his T13 800-metre final. And then it was our turn. There was only a straight final in our 1500-metre event. We knew relatively little about our competition aside from Mustapha El Aouzari and his guide, a Moroccan pair we had raced in the 1500 metres two years earlier at the World Championships in Lille, and our old Spanish rival, Pedro Delgado and his guide Carlos.

I knew I was in good shape – perhaps not the shape I'd been in at Sydney, but still fit. But on the afternoon of the final, I felt flat. You like to feel springy and light on the day of your competition, but my legs felt like lead as we boarded the bus that shuttled us to the warm-up track adjacent to the Olympic Stadium. I attributed it to nerves and tried to relax.

The Olympics and Paralympics are unique in that they challenge athletes to find the best within themselves at a pre-set moment. The Games occur just once every four years, and on the day of your competition, you owe it to yourself and those who supported you to show up with the best you have. I vowed to do this here in the birthplace of the Olympic movement, as countless athletes had done before.

Greg and I ran in the Sidney Paralympic 1500-metre final in 2000 purposefully and aggressively, and it was nearly good enough to win. In 2004, we approached the final more cautiously, deciding it would be better to let somebody else lead to conserve our energy and then try to move up late in the race. In retrospect, I took this too literally. You develop a race plan, but you have to remain open to changing your plan on the fly based on how the race plays out. I wasn't feeling at my best, so I was comfortable with the plan to run from behind and trust that we could make our move when required.

9 Transition

Even at the best of times, this is hard to do.

We split through 800 metres in about 2:14. I heard Greg say we were in third and that the others (the Spanish and Moroccan teams) were twenty metres ahead. I felt disembodied, disconnected from the urgency of chasing a race that was slipping away from us, but I also knew we couldn't afford to wait any longer.

Over the next lap, I put my head down and worked hard, and gradually, we began moving up. Mustapha and his guide had taken off and would go on to win impressively in 4:08, but Pedro and Carlos were coming back into range.

Finally, I heard the Spanish guide runner yell frantically at Pedro as Greg and I dug deep, moved even with them, and then passed them, heading into the final 200 metres. We had to keep our foot on the gas; we were going for it, putting everything into our kick.

We hit the line in 4:14 and clinched second – a very different second from our Paralympic final four years earlier. I'd nearly let this one slip away: I'd woken up just in time.

The night after our 1500-metre final, I proposed to Colleen in a restaurant beneath the Parthenon, the venerable marble temple built in the fifth century BC that overlooks the city named after the Greek goddess it was dedicated to. Greg and I had picked Colleen up from her hotel and walked the kilometre to the restaurant. Colleen wore the wrong shoes for walking uphill on the cobblestoned streets and strenuously complained. After we finally made it, Greg left us at a table, promising to return in two hours.

Before leaving Canada, I had called Colleen's dad to ask his permission. His initial, disconcerting reaction had been one of silence and then laughter. He told me that he never expected his daughter to marry a blind man, but I had his blessing and warm welcome into their family.

I procrastinated as we had dinner, with the ring weighing heavy in my pocket. Eventually, I got down on one knee, and finally, the question came out. She was shocked and emotional and did not immediately say yes. There were tears and fears, and then, the beginnings of plans. I said we could arrange a quick wedding, whereas Colleen had entirely different ideas.

10 Winning in the Rain

That December, Colleen and I moved into a sixteenth-floor apartment a short walk from her parents. Jon and his yellow Labrador guide dog Luther came to live with us briefly before leaving for a three-month internship in the Bahamas, where he would teach basic computer skills to children who were blind.

I was back training and ran more consistently that winter. We had a gym in our building with a good treadmill, which I used often. I was still working at MBNA, but when the opportunity came in the summer of 2005 to work part-time from home with Paralympics Ontario, encouraging physical activity providers to include persons with disabilities in their programs, I jumped at it.

Although I had been training consistently through that winter and spring, it typically takes me a few races to hit my stride. I ran times of 2:10 and 4:29, respectively, in 800- and 1500-metre races early in the season, wondering how in the world I could be running so slowly.

After running just 4:20 in a 1500-metre race at York University in June, Greg and I had a nice breakthrough 800-metre race in early July, running 2:03 at a Twilight meet in Ottawa. We followed it up with a couple of 800-metre races in 2:02 during the subsequent weeks.

Each race included my training partners, Vladimir Radovich and Berry de Bruijn, who also guided me regularly in our workouts. They would run beside me on my left, pushing my elbow out slightly to cue me to veer to the right or touching the inside of my elbow to bring me closer to the inside. Because of how much track running I had done, I came to know intuitively when a guide and I were reaching the end of a straightaway and it was time to lean into the corner.

Every athlete has particular strengths. Vlad was always strong on hills and the short, fast intervals we would typically run at the end of our practices; no matter how he felt, he always found that extra gear on hills or end-of-workout sprints.

Berry was steady and consistently strong no matter what we did in training. He could run a 53-second 400 metres and, at the other end of the spectrum, a 1:10 half marathon.

One of the workouts coach Ray liked to have us do once or twice during our summer track training involved a series of three 500-metre repeats at an 800-metre effort, taking long rests of eight to ten minutes in between. These sessions were not only physically excruciating but psychologically as well, with the long rests building up the anticipation of what was coming next. The workouts were specific and effective at getting you into race shape and engendered a kinship among us for having survived them.

Greg and I travelled to Regina, Saskatchewan, in early August to compete in the National Championships. Although we only managed to run 2:05 in the 800 metres, we broke 55 seconds in the 400 metres, a first for me, albeit in an event I rarely ran. Still, it gave me confidence as we prepared to fly to Helsinki, Finland, to compete in the European Paralympic Open Championships, to which athletes from Canada and several other non-European countries had been invited. These Championships were held following the 2005 International Association of Athletics Federations (IAAF) World Championships, which had been hosted in the same venue just weeks earlier.

I remember feeling good a few days before the competition, following our arrival in Espoo, the small town outside of Helsinki where the Championships would take place. Greg and I did a small workout involving a couple of 300-metre track repetitions that we ran in 44 seconds before finishing with 200 metres in 27 seconds, and I knew we were ready because of how relaxed and in control it had felt.

We raced the 800 metres once again against athletes who had the option of competing with a guide in the T12 sight classification. Our objective was to make it past the heats and into the final.

We ran our heat as well as I thought we could have, splitting through 400 in 60 seconds and finishing in a solid 2:02 against several runners who had broken two minutes, but it wasn't quite enough to qualify for the final. However, it had given us a dose of racing in preparation for the 1500 metres against athletes in the T11 class, who, like me, ran with a guide.

Greg, Stu, and I took the opportunity to explore Helsinki. It is a beautiful port city, and in its cool, clean August air, which felt not unlike home, we traversed its streets for hours. Taking the train the short distance into the city offered us a change of scenery and a welcome break from the cycle of training, eating, and sitting around, which, as we had learned the year before, could easily lead to negative ruminations in the lead-up to championship races. Our experience in Athens a year earlier taught us the importance of keeping things relaxed to alleviate pressure.

When travelling with the national team, the three of us very often spent our non-training time together. Our three-way relationship provided a healthy counterbalance for Greg and me. Stu and I had also become good friends away from the track; coffee was a passion we shared, often before or after practices.

Greg and I won our T11 1500-metre semi-final, running 4:24; it wasn't easy, and I had to work for it. It might have been only our third 1500 metres that season, as we had been focusing more on the 800, but even so, we believed we were ready to run much faster in the 1500 metres if we had to.

It was pouring when we arrived at the track for the final, and I was not feeling great. I was hungry and achy, which might have been nerves. Greg encouraged me to play it by ear and do what we could in the race. We were up against the Brazilians Carlos Barto Silva and his guide; we would compete against Carlos many times in subsequent years.

We planned to start at a moderate 68-second pace and gradually increase the pace with each lap, which is exactly what we did. We led from the start. The Brazilians were on our heels, but Greg and I were in control even as the

10 Winning in the Rain

rain pelted down. Gradually we turned the screws, and the Brazilians fell away, and we went on to win in 4:12, our fastest 1500 metres since the 2000 Paralympics.

11 Riding the Currents of Life

Back in Canada that fall, I was determined to build on the positive momentum of our success in Helsinki. The future seemed bright. Colleen and I were planning our wedding for June of the following year. I had also started a new part-time job with Paralympics Ontario, working from home and coordinating an outreach program called Ready, Willing & Able, which connected program ambassadors, many of whom were athletes with disabilities, with schools and community groups to deliver adapted sport demonstrations.

In early November, coach Ray had our group run a 5000-metre time trial at The Dome, Ottawa's new 400-metre indoor track. Utilizing this pressurized indoor dome would completely change our winter training, allowing us to run intervals a few times a week and escape the elements.

Berry de Bruijn guided me in the time trial, and we decided to target a 3:20-per-kilometre pace, which would have us running 16:40. We ended up running 16:41, almost exactly as we'd hoped. This was my first time running 5000 metres on the track, and while our time wasn't fast, it indicated good early-season fitness I was sure I could build on. Or at least I thought so because just four days later, Stu and I were involved in an accident that changed everything.

It was a rainy, chilly Sunday afternoon. Stu had invited me to an Ottawa

11 Riding the Currents of Life

67's junior hockey game. After it ended, we planned to jog the few kilometres from the Lansdowne arena to his house in Ottawa's south end. Stu had enough vision to guide me on an easy run, as we had done many times before.

At one point, we needed to cross the busy Colonel By Drive. It was raining, and as the late afternoon light diminished, visibility was poor. After waiting for a lull in traffic, we started to jog across, but then Stu spotted an oncoming car racing towards us from the right.

Everything seemed to happen in slow motion after that. There was no good decision to be made. There was no going forward and no going back. I heard Stu yelling, "Jay, we're going to get hit!"

I've often wondered why we didn't try to run for it, but I imagine Stu assumed we would never have made it. We stood there on the line in the middle of the road and braced ourselves as the car hurtled towards us at 70 kilometres an hour.

We had turned our backs to the oncoming vehicle, and this is how we took the crushing impact of the SUV. We were thrown into the air, and I had the sensation of hanging, suspended in a vortex of life and death, and not knowing where we would land.

I don't remember landing, but I do recall lying on the road. Instinctively, I tried to get up, but people told me to lie still. Stu was yelling, asking if I was okay, and I yelled back, "Yeah, I'm okay. Are you okay?"

Stu had landed on the grass by the side of the road. I'd landed in the path of an oncoming van that had seen me at the last moment and braked to a stop.

Drivers had pulled over. Someone placed a blanket over me, and then I heard sirens in the distance as I lay on the cold road. When the ambulance arrived, the medic asked me basic questions I struggled to answer. I couldn't remember the name of our Canadian Prime Minister or my date of birth. Somehow, I figured out that the date was November 6 by counting backwards from Colleen's birthday, which I remembered was November 9.

As they lifted me onto a stretcher and placed me into the ambulance, I asked the medic if I was going to make it. He said that I would. I wondered how often paramedics hear that question. How frequently do they give the right answer?

Stu and I spent six days in hospital. We were both in rough shape but lucky to have survived; Stu had sustained a compound tibia-fibula fracture that required surgery and unfortunately led to a post-operative infection and a painfully long series of follow-up surgeries.

I spent several days in the observation area of the intensive care unit, as I had hit my head during the accident and sustained a fractured skull. I also had a hairline fracture of my right fibula and, as I later found out, a partially torn meniscus, a section of cartilage in the knee.

My family rallied around me. Colleen and her parents visited daily, bringing coffee and food. My mother flew in a day after the accident and was stunned when she saw my swollen face. Jon, who by then was back from his internship in the Bahamas, visited regularly, devouring the food I couldn't eat. Friends, training partners, and our coach Ray trickled in.

Our accident now feels long in the past, but each November 6, either Stu or I will reach out – usually, the message goes something like, "Grateful to be alive!" It might be an overused cliché, but there is feeling and meaning behind it because of the close call we had.

I left the hospital for home with crutches, an air cast, and a prescription for anti-seizure medication. The accident caused some bleeding in my brain, and the doctors were concerned about the possibility of a seizure. Thankfully, I was able to discontinue the medication after taking it for about a month.

I needed to learn to get around using crutches. At first, I practiced in our apartment and then in the corridor. As I learned to step first with my good leg and then transfer my weight to the crutches and use them to propel me forward, I grew more confident. It was encouraging to move under my own steam.

During one of my night-time practice walks along the corridor, a neighbour came out of his apartment and yelled at me for making too much noise. That put an end to my late-night hallway walks.

I found hope in a gradually increased walking routine. Eventually, this led me outside to walk on Bank Street and to the Billings Bridge Shopping Centre, a short distance away, with its coffee shop, where Stu and later my

11 Riding the Currents of Life

brother and I would spend countless hours. I became adept at relying on one crutch and using my white cane with the other hand.

It was at this time that Colleen's mother, Janice, developed a persistent cough. A series of tests would ultimately lead to a devastating terminal cancer diagnosis. Nobody saw that coming.

Janice's brother Ian, with whom she had always been very close, flew to Ottawa from Saskatchewan to support her and Colleen's dad as the Christmas holidays approached. Ian returned several times during the following weeks as Janice became weaker.

Janice remained incredibly stoic throughout her illness. She struggled to make it to medical appointments and chemotherapy treatments, which left her exhausted for days. She wanted to remain at home for as long as possible. She wanted to die there. I learned so much about courage from her determined, dignified fight against a disease that ravaged her body but never broke her spirit.

Meanwhile, I continued along the path of recovery following our accident. I attended regular physiotherapy treatments throughout the winter, and early in the new year, my cast was removed, enabling me to use a stationary bike and begin jogging for short distances.

I rode the spin bike in our building's gym, beginning with short rides at first and working up to an hour and, eventually, two hours on some weekends. I used an old talking heart rate monitor to measure my effort. My heart rate reached 135 to 140 beats per minute on longer rides, which I alternated with shorter, easier rides, during which I maintained a heart rate of 130. This approach to getting back into shape wasn't sophisticated, but I enjoyed it and could feel it working. My resting heart rate dropped as the weeks passed, so I knew I was getting fitter.

I also started doing short jogs every second day. I would finish a bike ride and immediately step onto the treadmill, beginning with two minutes of running and slowly progressing throughout January to a fifteen-minute jog. Eventually, I rejoined our training group at the indoor track.

I had lingering doubts as I progressively began running more. Was the pain still there? Had I healed properly? Should I be training at all?

It can take time for our bodies and minds to realize that we're no longer broken. We need to pay attention to our internal signals, but at a certain point, when we've followed conventional medical advice and done all the right things, it's important to be able to take a leap of faith and trust in our own healing power.

The winter of 2006 brought with it a rollercoaster of conflicting emotions. I felt gratitude for simple movements and the growing knowledge that my body was rebuilding. Conversely, though, there was the feeling of helplessness as the illness Janice was battling took a deeper hold.

Being able to return to training provided me with a way to face the sadness, a sadness I saw etched in Colleen's stoic demeanour. Through training, I felt I could be stronger for her. No longer did I feel like I was recovering. I was an athlete again, still bruised but not broken – never broken.

Colleen and I married on February 18 in a small ceremony at her parents' house, with only our immediate families attending. It was a day tinged with sadness: what normally would have been the biggest celebration of our lives was juxtaposed against the poignancy of terminal illness, which was draining the life out of the woman who had set such a positive example for Colleen.

Following the brief ceremony, we had some champagne before our families headed for a celebratory dinner. Janice courageously joined us but became too exhausted during the meal; Colleen's brother Shawn took her home.

She succumbed in early April to the cancer diagnosed four months earlier. She had put up a brave fight in her typical, understated, and stoic way. She was just fifty-eight years old.

The months since her diagnosis seemed to pass interminably, but in another way, it felt like only a skip of the needle back to the time when she had brought sandwiches to the hospital to offer to the doctors and nurses in the hours following my accident.

How quickly things can change. Life, I was learning, had very few absolutes. Through the grief I shared with Colleen and her family in the aftermath of her mother's death, I felt grateful to have known her, to have shared laughter, and to have been welcomed into her inner circle. I knew that her presence in Colleen's life was irreplaceable.

In June, Colleen and I had our unofficial second wedding ceremony and a reception with about 120 of our family and friends.

12 Back on Track

As spring turned to summer, I was finally able to join our training group on some of their track workouts. All the cycling gave me a good fitness base, but it wasn't running fitness, and it took time for me to transition into fast running. Ray was careful not to have me do too much, too soon. At first, I only ran parts of the workouts, gradually increasing the length and intensity of the training as the weeks passed.

In July, Greg and I competed in our first race at the Para Athletics National Championships held in London, Ontario, running 4:33 for 1500 metres. It was hard accepting a time I could ordinarily have run in a workout, but it also represented our return to competition, and that in itself felt like a win.

Athletics Canada had required that Greg and I race there to show our fitness and to earn a spot in early September at the International Paralympic Committee World Athletics Championships in Assen, The Netherlands. Although our time was slow, it was good enough for us to be selected for Canada's team.

I had wonderful support from the members of our training group, particularly Berry de Bruijn, who extended his season beyond the end of July to help me train in the weeks leading up to our departure for the Netherlands, his home country.

Ray was careful in how he trained me, and it was a testament to his experience and coaching knowledge that he got me ready with minimal training. In the weeks before Greg and I flew to Amsterdam with the team, Ray had me do workouts that were relatively low in overall running volume but touched on a variety of training systems, and every one of them left me feeling stronger and more confident. Confidence and self-belief are essential keys to athletic success, and even though I was not in the same shape as in previous years, every workout represented an improvement and contributed to an internal sense of growing self-belief.

One particular session from this time involved three 1000-metre repeats around a ten-kilometre effort with 60 seconds rest between each, followed by three 400-metre repetitions with about six minutes of recovery. Each of these was to be run progressively faster.

I did this session with Berry de Bruijn and ran the 400s in 68, 65 and 61 seconds. That workout was a psychological game changer for me because it affirmed in my mind that I could run close to a 60-second lap at the end of a workout, and I knew that if I was capable of doing that in training, I could do it at the end of a race.

At the beginning of September, I flew with part of the team to Amsterdam on an overnight KLM flight from Montreal. Greg arrived a day later from Toronto. The Championships were taking place in Assen, about an hour by train from Amsterdam.

My memories of Assen are foggy, like the mist that blew in off the Atlantic coast each morning. I do remember the fresh air, the wind and rain, the strong coffee, and the Dutch bread.

Other than a night out in Assen following the competition and a day walking around in Amsterdam before flying home, we didn't venture far from the residence we lived in on that trip, which was fine with both Greg and me as we were content to focus on preparing for our races, without the expectations or pressure we might have otherwise internalized in the past.

We spent evenings watching television with Dustin Walsh, a blind 400-metre runner, Steve Walters, his guide, and Blair Miller, who had previously guided Dustin before himself being classified as an athlete with cerebral palsy and competing for several years in the T38 category. We ate in a cafeteria. Apart from going to the track and doing our daily runs in an adjacent wooded area, we stayed close to home.

Greg and I were entered in the T11 800 metres, which had not been contested internationally for a few years as most of the recent major championships had offered only a combined T11 and T12 800 metres. We were to compete first in the T11 1500 metres, though, as a straight final with no qualification rounds. This was good for me, as less running favoured the low-volume training and minimal preparation I had been able to do.

Greg and I had raced so little that summer, which made the reality of lining up against the best in the world alternately disorienting and liberating, as we didn't carry the burden of expectation. Our simple strategy going into the 1500-metre final was to try to react to whatever happened around us, and this is where Greg's experience and ability to read the race were so key. I fully trusted that Greg would position us where we needed to be, on the outside and near the front of the pack but without leading, and that our communication and intuition would enable us to respond to the conditions of the race and to run to our potential.

As we hoped, the final was slow and tactical. Our main challenge as the pack jogged the first two laps was to stay out of trouble and avoid getting boxed in. The edginess and tension of the close-knit pack rose as we entered the third lap; so did the pulsating physicality of other bodies nearby as we approached the critical moment when the race would break open.

I'm not sure exactly who initiated the break for home. It came with under a lap to go. Suddenly, we were moving, and I was up on my toes with Greg beside me, sprinting together in lockstep, flying down the backstretch for the final time, rounding the corner and hitting the home straight, digging deep, and leaning into the finish line ahead. We won in a time of 4:22. We had run our final 400 metres in 61 seconds, as we had practiced in training.

If the race had been fast, as in the Athens Paralympics two years before, Greg and I never could have won; I just didn't have the accumulated fitness from a proper build-up. However, every race has its own unique story, and if you can make it to the start line, you have a chance to compete, and sometimes you can run out of your head. A part of me could barely believe we had pulled it off. A few months before, I'd barely been able to run at all. Going into the final, there had been no caveats or compromises in our approach.

12 Back on Track

We were there to win.

We had no time to rest on our laurels; we still had the 800 metres to prepare for. We needed to advance out of one of two tough semi-finals, where only the top three runners in each heat would make it through. My training had been more focused on the 1500 metres, so we welcomed the 800 as another chance to race without any pressure.

Our semi-final went out relatively quickly, with a 61-second opening lap that felt fast. Greg and I were in second and held our position, but I had to work hard as the lactic acid set in. We held on to second place, running 2:06, fast enough to advance us to the final two days later. I'd needed to dig deep, but Greg said afterwards as we cooled down, "Jay, that race will have done you a lot of good!"

Two days later, we lined up for the final with three other blind runner and guide teams, including our Brazilian rivals, Carlos Barto Silva and his guide. In 800-metre races contested in the T11 category, there are generally only four teams of two. For Greg and me, this meant we had a 75 percent chance of a medal. It was a Saturday afternoon, and the conditions were warm and calm. I felt springy and light as I hopped from foot to foot moments before we were called to the line.

The pace was fairly quick, and after the cut-in at 100 metres, where athletes break from their lanes, Greg and I settled into third place, behind the Brazilians and a Russian team. It can feel disconcerting to be in that position in a field of four teams, but things can change so quickly in an 800-metre race. It was important for Greg and me to be confident but equally cautious, as this was only our second 800-metre race of the year in an event where lactic acid can eat you alive.

We reached the bell again in 61 seconds, and I felt relaxed this time; I was getting used to that pace. As we entered the backstretch, the Russians switched their guide runner, which is permitted in T11 middle distance races; however, in shorter races particularly, it can be a major disadvantage as it forces the runners to move to the outside of the track and break their rhythm as the new guide takes over.

From then on, it was just Greg and I chasing the Brazilians. We locked onto their shoulder, and I was still relaxed and running easily. We waited and waited, and then at the top of the curve with 150 metres to go, we moved outside and drew level and then gradually moved past. At that point, I knew we were going to win.

We crossed the line and hugged one another, and uncharacteristically, I lifted Greg into the air, such was the spontaneous release of pent-up tension that flowed out of me in that heady moment. We had run 2:02, within a second of our personal best six years before. How had we done that after the accident and the months of compromised training? I'll never know.

None of it would have been possible without the support of many people during that time, not least Colleen, my coach Ray, the help of my Ottawa training partners, and, of course, Greg.

I accepted our success with profound gratitude and savoured the moment standing on the podium, listening to "Oh Canada" ring out across the stadium.

13 Getting Back to Prime

Following our improbable success at the IPC World Athletics Championships in September 2006, I felt like the gift of running had been given back to me. Less than a year earlier, Stu and I had been hit by an SUV and seriously injured. The road back to training and racing had been circuitous and often uncertain for me, but for Stu, it had been even less certain and significantly more painful. He was still dealing with complications related to the tibia-fibula fracture he had sustained and an infection following the surgery. Slowly, though, he was beginning to run again, although he continued to have residual pain, and his stride was never quite the same.

When we're young, everything seems possible. Over time, the compromises, the missteps, and the hurts we experience throughout life's unpredictable journey remake us as we age and, I think, better enable us to bear the brunt of whatever bumps lie ahead.

In 2007, Stu showed incredible resolve and determination by working his way back to the national team. He competed at the Para Pan American Games in Rio de Janeiro that summer, barely a month after the birth of his son, Will. Putting on the Canadian uniform again was surely vindication for him and for all that it had taken him to reach that transcendent moment. His recovery included several surgeries that continued beyond 2007. He had demonstrated to the Athletics Canada selection committee, the running community, the world, and himself that he had the will to overcome.

Heading into the winter of 2007, I was motivated by the knowledge that I was truly back. No longer was I in a recovery or rehabilitation mindset. Our success at Worlds hadn't been a fluke; Greg and I had worked with the tools we had there, and we'd been able to come out ahead.

Yet, I knew I hadn't been at full strength in Assen. There had been a confluence of circumstances that had worked in our favour, though, and we'd been able to capitalize. I knew I'd need improved fitness from consistent, progressive training to be ready to handle a 4:08 1500-metre race. My renewed confidence after the World Championships provided the impetus to launch forward into what, in retrospect, was one of the best years of my competitive running career.

In the fall of 2006, Colleen finished her BA in psychology and started working part-time with a company that transcribed textbooks and other documents into Braille for blind and low-vision readers; it eventually evolved into a full-time position. That fall, I also started a one-year contract position with the RBC Olympians Program.

The program enabled athletes to gain corporate work experience and function as athletic ambassadors by speaking at schools and to employee groups while working a flexible part-time schedule built around their training. I worked for several hours most days in a downtown Ottawa office alongside financial planners, although my work mostly involved writing content for the RBC corporate newsletter.

Though I lived in Ottawa, I worked with a boss and team based in Toronto. This was long before the ubiquity of remote work, and while it felt a bit unconventional, I enjoyed speaking to students and groups of RBC employees through the program – a great arrangement overall, enabling me to prioritize training.

Colleen and I had also started looking for a house to purchase, and in June 2007, we found the perfect spot, a two-bedroom, semi-detached townhome on a small cull de sac a stone's throw from where her dad lived and just a few blocks from the apartment we had shared for two and a half years.

13 Getting Back to Prime

Throughout that winter, which was mild by Ottawa standards, I stayed healthy, running 60 to 65 miles weekly. Our group met for workouts at the indoor track on Monday and Wednesday evenings and on Saturday mornings. We ran mostly on the track, with certain workouts taking us outside on milder days.

As usual, Ray had us run sessions that touched on assorted intensities but additionally focused on longer intervals. These had never been my strong point, as I'd always preferred shorter, faster repetitions, such as 200s and 400s. I struggled in November and December to make it through a session of four one-mile repeats on 60 seconds recovery at a 5:40 pace. By March, however, I could run this same workout, averaging 5:22.

Away from our practices, I ran outside for 60 to 80 minutes on most Sundays with Vlad, Jamie Stevenson, or Steven Drew from our training group. On the other recovery days between workouts, I ran for up to an hour on the treadmill, with double runs on some days and a day off from running most weeks.

In February 2007, I competed in a low-key 800-metre indoor race guided by my training partner, Berry de Bruijn, at The Dome, finishing fifth in a time of 2:07. I thought we could run faster because, compared to the World Championships, just a few months earlier, I was aerobically much fitter; however, we were in a training phase, not a racing one.

Later that month, Colleen and I took a five-day trip to Victoria, British Columbia, as a belated honeymoon. I did not want to miss any running, and although Ray's efforts to connect me with athletes at the University of Victoria fell through, there was fortunately a treadmill in our hotel, and I didn't miss a day. I wanted to be ready for the 5000-metre time trial our group would run at The Dome three days after returning home.

Rick Hellard, a top local masters triathlete who sometimes ran with our training group, agreed to guide me in the time trial, and as before, I was aiming to run a time of 16:40, or 3:20 per kilometre. Several athletes in our group ran it together on a Wednesday night in early March. I felt relaxed as the laps passed by.

Rick, who was in his early forties at that time, was breathing hard, and I was very grateful to him for digging deep, as so many other guides have done when helping me over the years. Guide running is a selfless act of enabling another person to experience the gift of movement. Guides allow people who are blind to participate in different sports. There are guide cyclists, or pilots, as they are referred to in competitive tandem cycling, where a sighted athlete rides on the front of a bicycle made for two. There are guide skiers who ski ahead of a blind participant, often wearing headsets to communicate. In swimming, tappers stand at the end of the pool and hold a long piece of foam to tap the swimmers on the head, so they know not to crash into the pool wall.

Rick and I finished the time trial at 16:39. The difference this time was that it had seemed so easy, like a tempo run. I couldn't believe how good I'd felt. Heading into the outdoor track season, I knew the consistent winter training had given me a foundation to build on, which I'd never had before.

In the spring of 2007, I felt life was expanding for Colleen and me. It was a period of broadening horizons for the two of us – I remember a sense of freedom and possibility juxtaposed against the rigour and routine of training. That spring, I was rarely in one place for long. Oddly, instead of feeling transient, I felt rooted and fulfilled.

In the days following our 5000-metre time trial in March, I took the train from Ottawa to Guelph to take part in a panel discussion on diversity and inclusion, an event Barry Wheeler, my former student advisor at Guelph's Centre for Students with Disabilities, had invited me to participate in. By this time, Barry had reconnected with Patti, his former long-term partner, following a fourteen-year separation. They had remarried a year before. Life takes a poetic turn sometimes. It was wonderful to see Barry again and return to a place where I had so many fond memories.

I then headed to Toronto and joined Greg on a flight to Flagstaff, Arizona, where we met up with Stu to spend two weeks training at an altitude of 2100 metres. This was the first time any of us had trained at that elevation. Flagstaff is an iconic destination for runners and endurance athletes of all types who hope to take advantage of the thinner air to adapt to living and training with less oxygen. The idea is that once back at sea level, our bodies become saturated with oxygen, which stimulates red blood cell

13 Getting Back to Prime

production and, in turn, the capacity for athletes to utilize oxygen and to train and race faster.

We stayed at a Holiday Inn, a short jog away from a gravel road where thousands of endurance athletes, including top Americans and world-class marathoners, have run countless miles over the years.

We did easy runs the first two days in Flagstaff, allowing our bodies to adapt to the unfamiliar stress of altitude. Greg and I ran eight to ten miles on most days, and Stu, who was training more specifically for the 800 metres, ran a little less, but mostly, the three of us trained together. Unfortunately, Greg picked up a chest cold several days into our time in Flagstaff. After resting for two days, he was able to run with me again, but only for easy volume, as fast running triggered his cough. Still, I came home from that training camp feeling light and strong, ready to put my full energy into our training as April approached.

As our group began training on the outdoor track that spring, workouts continued to go well as we started to do sessions that felt closer to actual racing. One workout Ray liked to have us do in the spring included two or sometimes three sets of a 400, plus an 800 and a 300, with about two minutes between intervals and a six-to-eight-minute break between the sets. We tried to run the intervals at what we believed to be our current 1500-metre pace. There were different variations of this workout, but the idea was to acclimate to the rhythm of 1500-metre running.

As in the past, Berry and Vlad guided me through many of these sessions, as did Kyle Desormeaux, a 1500-metre runner who had recently moved to Ottawa and who I knew from the University of Guelph.

Greg and I started our outdoor season at a track meet at York University in Toronto in early June, running 4:13 for 1500 metres and following it with a 2:04 in the 800. It was a good start; I felt sure I could go faster.

In the following weeks, Greg and I frequently travelled between Ottawa and Toronto to compete in races. I was still working with the RBC Olympians Program, which allowed me the flexibility to work around our training and racing schedule, and Greg, being a teacher, had much of the summer free.

When one or the other of us travelled, we typically spent two or three days together, during which time we raced, and, if time permitted, we would follow our race with a hard workout on the track. Sometimes, we'd even fit in a short, intense workout the day immediately after a race; this was unconventional as, most often, middle-distance athletes do an easy recovery run following a competition. Greg and I felt we needed to make the most of our limited time together; we didn't think much about the potential for injury or burnout because we were focused on getting into the best shape possible.

One workout we did several times that summer, on days following races, involved running one 500-metre interval. The idea was to run it like a 400-metre race but then continue the extra 100 metres and try to accelerate, even as your legs were tying up from the fatigue. The real training effect came from trying to run through the lactic acid over the final part of the single 500-metre interval.

I always felt nervous going into these workouts because of their intensity. In one, we reached 300 metres in 41 seconds and finished the 500-metre interval in 1:09. That was new territory for me, and I knew I was in the best shape of my life.

In an 800-metre race in July, once again at York University, Greg and I lowered our personal best to 2:01.4. Four days later, in Ottawa, we ran 4:08.8 for 1500 metres, just 0.6 seconds outside our personal best from seven years before.

We had not run that fast since 2000, yet I walked off the track feeling we could have run faster. I was ecstatic to be back racing at a level I knew we were capable of, but I hesitated for a moment with about 500 metres to go.

When you're in a fast race, sometimes there's an impulse to hold back because you're not sure what you're capable of. You're in an unfamiliar world. Your mind gets in the way. This had been my mistake.

For several days after that race, I was haunted by the thought of what ifs. How much faster could we have gone?

The best antidote for rumination is a good training session or race. Over the years, this has been the most successful strategy to clear my mind.

13 Getting Back to Prime

Within two weeks, Greg and I dropped our 1500-metre personal best to 4:07.05, once again in Ottawa, and the following day, we left for the Para Pan American Games in Rio de Janeiro.

On our overnight flight from Toronto to Rio via La Guardia International Airport in New York, we had to run to catch the second leg of our flight, and although we made it, our bags, which contained my running spikes, did not. When the bags finally arrived two days later, Greg and I went to the training track to run a 1000-metre time trial as a last hard effort before our 1500-metre semi-final in two days. We might have been pushing the envelope by running a time trial only two days before the semi-final, but it was important to be razor sharp, and there was no better way to do that than by practicing in race-like conditions. In the time trial, we reached 800 metres in 2:03 and finished in 2:35 – this was the fastest I'd ever run for that distance, my previous best being 2:39. I knew we were ready.

What made my time in Rio all the more special was the presence of my brother, who was there with his guide runner, Sean Young. A few months earlier, Jon had moved permanently to Ottawa to be closer to his then-girlfriend and to get more serious about sprinting. Jon was an all-around athlete who represented Canada internationally in wrestling while still in high school and later in judo, track and triathlon. He was a far more well-rounded athlete than I ever was.

Shortly after moving to Ottawa, Jon was introduced to Sean Young, a varsity middle-distance runner who had trained and competed with the University of Ottawa team. They were a great match: gregarious, extroverted, outgoing and fun to be around. In Rio, they competed in the T11 400 metres and the 4 x 100-metre relay.

Greg and I believed we were in world-record shape. Bob Matthews' long-standing records of 1:59.9 and 4:05.11 for 800 and 1500 metres, respectively, seemed not out of reach. We set our intentions on chasing these records in each race, with no real strategy other than to run aggressively and go after it.

Our first attempt was in the 1500-metre semi-final. The plan was to try to reach 800 metres in 2:08 or, at the most, 2:10, work hard on the critical third lap, and finish fast. Greg's focus would be on getting me to 1100 metres, and then, with a lap to go, it would be up to me.

After 100 metres of our semi-final, we were leading with runner-guide teams from Chile and Brazil breathing down our necks, but our lead slowly increased, and after a while, I could no longer hear them. August is mid-winter in Brazil, and conditions were perfect for fast running, with temperatures in the mid-twenties and no humidity. Usually, in a semi-final championship race, we would be concerned only with trying to make it into the final without focusing on time, but in Rio, Greg and I had our attention on the clock.

We reached 1100 metres in 3:03, which was a little slower than we needed, although the record of 4:05.11 was still possible if we could run a fast final lap. Now, it was up to me to get up on my toes and sprint. I went for it, but we came up short of the record, finishing with a time of 4:07.95. I was happy we'd run fast and set a new Para Pan American 1500-metre record in the process.

Our approach in the final the next day was much the same. This time, we got to 1100 metres in three minutes flat and finished in 4:08.00, winning over the Brazilians Carlos Barto Silva and his guide by seven seconds. The world record had eluded us, but we had run within three seconds of it twice over twenty-four hours and had captured a decisive Para Pan American championship.

The next day, Greg and I ran easy, and the day after that, we ran a single 500-metre interval where we split through 400 metres in 53 seconds. The following day, we ran a single 300-metre interval in 39.

I've often reflected on how potent and effective those short workouts were and what a difference they made for me. I wouldn't have recovered quickly enough from them without the long stretch of aerobic training, which had given me such a deep foundation throughout the previous winter and spring.

Two days later, Greg and I lined up in the 800-metre final against most of the same athletes from the 1500-metre final. The Chileans were there, and so were Carlos Barto Silva and his guide. I felt quietly confident. Our plan again was to run our race our way and aim for sub-two minutes.

Greg and I shot off the line when the gun sounded, sprinting out and

13 Getting Back to Prime

around the corner in our lane, hoping to lead at the cut-in after 100 metres. Cutting towards the inside of the track would minimize the distance which needed to be covered. Leading at that point would enable us to run unimpeded. While potentially leaving us vulnerable to being challenged later in the race, we were focused on running against the clock.

We got the lead we hoped for, which meant we could control our destiny. Now, it was really up to us.

We reached 400 metres in 57 seconds. The Brazilians were behind us, but I could tell there was a gap, and I knew I needed to stay focused and work hard as we headed into the backstretch. We were moving well, and I tried to run loose and stay relaxed.

We passed through 600 metres in 1:28, and as we came around the final curve, I knew we would win and that we still had a chance at the record. Lactic acid is unforgiving, though, and it caught up to me on the home straight. We crossed the line in 2:00.39, a personal best by a second and enough to win decisively, but just outside the world record, although it was another Para Pan American record. I was proud of how we asserted ourselves and came away with another title. It was time to celebrate.

We drank caipirinhas, Brazil's national cocktail made with cachaca liquor, lime, cane sugar, and crushed ice. I have a distinct memory of my brother, who had injured his hamstring early in the competition, doing push-ups, shirtless in a shopping plaza. We swam in the warm waves off Copacabana Beach, the perfect antidote for a hangover.

A day and a half after our 800-metre final, we boarded a plane bound for Miami, then onto Toronto, and finally back to Ottawa. It was August 21 when we touched down on Canadian soil. It was my thirtieth birthday.

14 Paralympic Preparation

Our summer of racing in 2007 had been the culmination of a consistent build-up and a series of races and hard workouts over the summer weeks, which got me into the best shape of my life. Heading into the 2008 Paralympic year, Greg and I felt we were more ready than ever to compete and win in Beijing.

I needed to force myself not to run for two weeks after returning from Brazil. You feel like you're losing ground when you take a planned break from training, but of course, rest is key within the cycle of training and recovery; taking a step back to take two steps forward.

We knew the Paralympic competition would be fierce as it's the event where everybody brings their very best, and I wanted to do the same. That fall, as I returned to training, I worked on my endurance. Outside of our group practices, I ran less frequently but harder. I routinely pushed the pace on the treadmill down to a six-minute-mile pace for a few miles. This built up my strength, enabling me to do workouts I'd never accomplished before, such as running a mile in 4:44 at the beginning of one practice.

In December, my friend and training partner Kyle Desormeaux guided me in a low-key indoor 3000-metre race where we ran 9:08, which was a big personal best for me; we ran our final kilometre in 2:54.

I was reaching a new level of training. I felt fit and strong and that I could handle any workout. It seemed like there were limitless possibilities.

14 Paralympic Preparation

In January 2008, Kyle guided me in an indoor 1500-metre race at The Dome in which we ran 4:12. I'd never run that fast in January before. Training had been going very well, but in the back of my mind, there was the lingering question: how long will I be able to keep this up?

A few weeks later, Kyle and I competed in a 3000-metre race once again at the Dome, which we entered intending to try to run under nine minutes. Although we kept to the 71-second lap pace we needed during the early part of the race, I faded, and we finished in 9:14.

I knew I was tired. Following that race, I headed to Toronto to join Greg for a few days of hard training. I got sick upon returning to Ottawa, however, and missed ten days of training as a result, bringing an end to my winter build-up. It was time to regroup and recharge for the outdoor season; the Beijing Paralympics were in early September.

After my contract with the RBC Olympians program had ended in the fall of 2007, I started working part-time as a braille proofreader with T-Base Communications, where Colleen also worked. It only amounted to a few hours of work a week, allowing me plenty of time to focus on training, which might have been a double-edged sword because one can focus only so much on training.

Achieving a healthy balance – making training a priority, yet not the only priority – means something different to everyone. This balance inevitably changes throughout our lives. There is so much more to someone than splits on a stopwatch, or one's finishing position.

Balance has to do with how we feel when we first wake up and how we relate to the family we inherit or the one we create. It's the fulfillment we derive from working or studying, with our unique sensibilities and the gifts we share with the world, with our quest to find inner peace and meaning, and with the totality of who we are. Without these different parts of us, what would we have to turn to when a workout goes badly, as it sometimes does? Or when we become injured, as we inevitably will?

I'm reminded of something Trent Stellingwerff, a former University of Guelph teammate and now a world-renowned exercise physiologist, said: It's those athletes who are healthy and happy who are most successful. He is so right. My health and happiness have been closely tied to training and competitive outcomes. Life is not perfect, and health and happiness operate on a spectrum, but in general, I've found that having a positive outlook goes a long way, even on days when it's hard to convince yourself to put on running shoes and get out the door.

I was restless in the spring of 2008. The Beijing Paralympics were only a few months away. The previous year had been a banner year for Greg and me, but what would we be capable of in Beijing? My winter training had had its highs and lows, and being employed only a few hours a week left me uncertain about the future. Colleen and I were managing financially between her job in marketing at T-Base and the Athlete Assistance Program support I received through the national team. We had enough to survive, but I was looking for more steady work and the security this would give us.

That March, as winter was in its last gasp, Greg, Stu and I flew to San Diego for a week of warm-weather training. We made a mini vacation out of it. Colleen, Greg's wife Diane, and their two-year-old daughter Olivia also came. Stu was there, too. We trained hard during our week there but also enjoyed the southern California sunshine. It came as a welcome break, and once back home, I found that things seemed to turn around.

Through a friend, I applied for a position with the Active Living Alliance for Canadians with a Disability, a national grassroots organization promoting active living among persons with disabilities and educating physical activity providers on inclusivity.

Following an interview in early April, they offered me the position of program coordinator. Jane Arkell, who had been their executive director since the Alliance was founded in 1989, was a supportive boss. I appreciated her allowances for my frequent travel to running events and allowing me to have a flexible work schedule. Throughout her career, Jane emphasized the value of a person's first experience with physical activity and how crucial this was in shaping their future relationship with an active lifestyle.

Another staff member at the Alliance was Chris Bourne, an avid triathlete who became paraplegic as a result of a car accident years previously. Chris and I knew each other through the Ready, Willing and Able

14 Paralympic Preparation

campaign, where he had been a program ambassador two years earlier.

I owe a debt of gratitude to Chris, who often picked me up on his way into our office in Ottawa's east end or dropped me off at the end of the day during the winter of 2008-2009 when Ottawa experienced a transit strike.

Over the years, with increasing work and family responsibilities after adopting two young boys, Chris still found creative ways of squeezing in a hand cycle workout before or after most workdays. I saw him as the embodiment of active living and a consummate role model, not only for those who acquire new disabilities but for anyone who values the freedom of the open road, the magic in movement, and the currency of courage. Chris still to this day offers support and mentorship to persons undergoing rehabilitation treatment following traumatic injury.

My work with the Alliance had me coordinate a national outreach campaign, All Abilities Welcome, to promote the creation of welcoming environments for persons with disabilities within recreation programs and facilities. It did so by connecting recreation and physical activity providers with a national network of speakers, most of whom either had a disability or an interest in promoting inclusion in recreation programming.

The campaign also encouraged individuals with disabilities to adopt an active lifestyle. In general, most people living in Canada fall well short of the 150 minutes a week of moderate to vigorous aerobic activity recommended by current physical activity guidelines, but this is even more so for the eight million Canadians who identify as having a disability. A lack of accessible transportation, dated facilities, and sometimes the attitudes of program leaders, teachers, coaches, peers, and even family members can all stand in the way.

In some cases, simple adaptations are all that's needed to attain true inclusion. It just requires an open mind and a bit of creative problem-solving. Here are a few examples. In 2003, when I joined the training group under Ray's coaching, he asked athletes to guide me on my first workout. A community centre arranged for an employee to meet a child with a disability and parent at the front of the building to walk them to a more accessible back entrance. Physical educators put a bell inside a soccer ball so a visually impaired player could follow the sound.

Persons with disabilities need to believe accommodation is an option. An active lifestyle comes down to having the necessary support to engage in health-promoting activities that enhance well-being.

According to the 2022 Canadian Survey on Disability, twenty-seven percent of Canada's population aged 15 and older had some form of disability that limited their daily activities. What are the future social and health implications for a society where sedentary living is the widely accepted norm for many persons with a disability? Without access, our world compresses. Each of us needs to move around, utilize community services, and perhaps most of all, benefit from the human connection that lies beyond our doorstep.

I've had moments when accessing community services and programs felt like an uphill battle, even as an athlete who has been incredibly privileged to enjoy a long, competitive career. Running has been my north star in so many ways, and I owe so much to those who have given me the encouragement and agency to turn to running as an outlet and an intervention in my life journey. Running has given me purpose, meaning, and freedom, and I owe it to those who have enabled and supported me to manifest the best within me as a runner, but at a deeper level, as an empowered human being. Much of my most lucid thinking has come to me while running, bringing clarity out of confusion. Sport has opened so many doors in my life, but perhaps most importantly, it has taught me about who I am. Working with the Active Living Alliance gave me a platform to promote meaningful inclusion and to encourage persons with disabilities to turn to an active lifestyle as a way to claim their place in the world.

It often takes a while for an Ottawa spring to unravel the coils of its warmth, so occasionally, our group would train inside The Dome until mid or late April; by then, any residual snow on the Terry Fox outdoor track had usually melted. The first few outdoor workouts were often windy and on the cool side. Typically, by June and July, the wind eases in Ottawa, and it becomes possible to run fast on summer evenings as the hot sun begins to set.

Greg and I opened our outdoor competitive season at York University in June by running 4:12 in the 1500 metres. It was a solid start. We had

14 Paralympic Preparation

run well under the Paralympic qualifying time, knowing then we would be heading to Beijing, so our focus was to get as prepared as we could to deal with a variety of race scenarios and, in particular, to be able to close fast in the critical final lap.

Our national championships were held in July in the humidity of Windsor, in southwestern Ontario. Greg and I were entered in both the 800 and 400 metres. The 400 metres was not an event we competed in often, but doing so in Windsor would enable us to work on our speed in a competitive race.

We ran 2:03 in the 800 metres, chasing Stu, who ran two minutes flat. We then turned our attention to the 400 metres two days later. We'd be running against my brother Jon and his guide Sean and Dustin Walsh and his guide Steve Walters, 400-metre specialists who lived and trained in Vancouver. With so few blind or visually impaired athletes competing in track in Canada, this would be a rare opportunity to race head-to-head with others in a domestic Para competition.

There was pride on the line between my brother and me. It was all good-natured, but I was determined not to lose because I knew he'd never let me live it down. Jon had only been training seriously for about a year, improving significantly over that time, having run 53.38 seconds over 400 metres to secure his and Sean's spot in Beijing about a month earlier. Previously, Greg and I had run 54.5 seconds, so we knew we had our work cut out. Dustin and Steve had run close to 53 seconds flat, and we knew they would be hard to beat.

Dustin and Steve were placed on the inside lane, with Greg and I in the middle and Jon and Sean on the outside. With the stagger start lines used in track, Dustin and Steve would be slightly behind us initially, with Jon and Sean slightly ahead to account for the differential created by circular tracks.

When the gun sounded, Greg and I sprinted out around the corner, our goal being to run flat out for 60 to 80 metres before taking our foot slightly off the gas. We wanted to let the momentum of a fast start carry us down the backstretch without accumulating too much lactic acid. Despite our quick start, I heard Dustin and Steve fly past us. By the end of the backstretch, we had caught up with Jon and Sean on our outside. Entering the curve with under 200 metres to go, I knew I needed to get up on my toes and go for it to keep the momentum going. You're not speeding up at that point in a 400, but you try to anyway, hoping the lactic acid won't hit too hard.

Coming into the home stretch, Dustin and Steve had a decisive lead. Jon and Sean were just behind us. It would be down to the wire, and I knew I needed to give it everything I had. Sean was yelling at Jon, so I knew exactly where they were. The fourteen seconds felt like an eternity as we battled back and forth, with Jon and Sean edging ahead sometimes and then dropping back.

In the end, Greg and I finished with a new personal best of 53.77 seconds, just behind Dustin and Steve and only 0.2 seconds ahead of Jon and Sean. All three teams had run under 54 seconds. It had to be one of the most exciting competitive races ever contested among blind athletes on Canadian soil.

The flight between Toronto and Hong Kong took fifteen hours, followed by another three-and-a-half-hour flight to Singapore, where Greg and I spent seven days training, acclimatizing to the heat and adjusting to the time difference before the start of the Beijing Paralympics. We were there with Dustin and Steve, Mikhail Gorbounov, a massage therapist and friend, and his wife, Olga.

I first met Mikhail and Olga, who were also visually impaired, at a track meet in 2000, where Mikhail competed in the masters category for athletes over 40. He had specialized in the 800 metres in the former Soviet Union before emigrating to Canada with Olga and their daughter Margarita in the late 1990s and, eventually, studying to become a massage therapist. Mikhail, a few others, and I would later launch the Achilles Ottawa running club for blind and visually impaired athletes in 2010.

I saw Mikhail for regular massage treatments – he always seemed to keep me healthy – so we asked Athletics Canada if he could be the official massage therapist at our pre-Paralympics training camp, which they supported.

Singapore has intense heat and high humidity, which left us little option but to run our track sessions early in the morning. Ray had developed a workout schedule for Greg and me involving short track intervals, given the

14 Paralympic Preparation

hot conditions, and easy running on the days in between.

The four of us – Steve, Dustin, Greg, and I – trained in the mornings, and then, most days, Mikhail gave us each a massage. In the afternoons, we explored the city, visiting its renowned botanical gardens and going to the beach to swim in the Indian Ocean, which felt like a warm bath. We also ate very well, as Singaporean food is inspired by the country's Indian, Indonesian, Malay, and Chinese diasporas.

Greg and I arrived in Singapore after running 2:00.60 for 800 metres in Ottawa a month earlier, finishing just outside our personal best from the year before. However, we only managed a 4:13 1500 metres in our final tune-up race before leaving for Asia. I'd picked up a chest cold and had missed several days of training.

When the stakes are high, doubts can inevitably creep in. You wonder whether you've done too little or too much. Are you as ready as you hope you are? Are you as ready as you need to be? Do you still belong in this game?

All the what-ifs swirl around in your mind. The Paralympics, held every four years, are the singular event where athletes hope to manifest their potential.

The past four years had brought with it injury and a very close call after being struck by an SUV. And yet, I'd been fortunate to have recovered fully, was coming off my best year of running, and was about to compete in my third Paralympics. Stu, who was still dealing with complications from his initial surgery following our accident, narrowly missed out on making the team. It was my first Games without him.

The previous four years had also given rise to heartache with the loss of Colleen's mother. It had also been a time of growth and renewal. Colleen and I had married and purchased a house, and we both had jobs we enjoyed.

Although there had been a few bumps on the road in the weeks leading up to Beijing, I knew anything was possible. We'd done some good workouts and had years of experience behind us. As our six-hour flight north from Singapore descended towards the Beijing airport, I rooted this perspective deep in my mind. I knew we could count on the work we'd done and that we would give nothing short of our very best. I knew we deserved to be there.

Jason and guide Greg Dailey running in the 2007 Parapan American Games in Rio de Janeiro, winning Gold in both the 800 and 1500 metres.

15 Paralympics

The mood as we marched into the 2008 Paralympic opening ceremony at the Birds Nest national stadium, the iconic centrepiece of the Beijing Games, was celebratory and festive. Beside us, Jon's guide, Sean, was snapping pictures, which he sent home instantaneously on his new iPhone.

The Birds Nest, which derived its nickname from the web of twisted steel sections that framed its roof, had been created as a unique venue embodying modernity set against Chinese artistic tradition. On the same track a few weeks earlier, a previously little-known Jamaican sprinter named Usain Bolt had electrified 90,000 fans and, in the process, signalled the arrival of a star who would change the face of sprinting.

The construction of the Birds Nest, for all its architectural ingenuity and brilliance, came at a financial and human cost: it had been built mostly by migrant workers for 500 million USD but also led to a mass displacement of migrant labourers as well as residents of Beijing, many of whom were forcibly relocated to make room for its construction. In all, as many as 2.5 million people were estimated to have been relocated.

The Olympics and Paralympics provide a venue for athletes to compete at the pinnacle of our sport. Athletes are not politicians, but an underlying question for me has been to what extent we might be complicit simply by association. Are we condoning the behaviour of a host nation where inequities run deep through our participation? As athletes, are we elevating our privilege at the expense of those whose host governments seem to have little empathy for their plight?

Athletes have a special opportunity to lift and inspire others, manifesting their unique talents and presenting them as a gift to the world. Through sport, hearts and minds can become more receptive to what is possible. Sport challenges the improbable as its records are broken and its protagonists elevated to an inspired level of human achievement.

This is part of what makes the Paralympics so meaningful, through the acknowledgment that persons with disabilities can transcend as athletes. Choosing to forego a competition because of the human rights record of its host nation wouldn't magically compel a government to change its policies because, as we see time and time again, the games go on anyway.

Athletes can have a profound impact on society by bringing their skill, courage, and integrity to the world stage when we receive the rare invitation to do so. By setting a positive example through the sport we practice, we can still care deeply about the plight of others and channel it into our performances through our attitudes and our empathy both on and off the field of play. It's a hopeful vision of athlete activism that, as protagonists, I feel we have the chance to uphold – the truth and goodness in sports.

In Beijing, Greg and I again focused on the T11 1500 and the 800 metres, where we would be running against both T11 and T12 athletes. As had been the scenario at our two previous Paralympics, the 800 metres would be run first.

Colleen took the long flight to Beijing to join us at the games and cheer us on with her friend Beverley, whom she had known since high school. They arrived two days after the opening ceremony on the Sunday afternoon leading into the main week of competition. I tried reaching Colleen unsuccessfully from the Athlete Village shortly after her flight touched down. Finally, she picked up. They were driving in a taxi from the airport to the hotel. Her voice sounded distant, and her speech was slurred. She had been sick on the long flight; her blood sugar had become very elevated. She assured me she would be okay, but I was shaken just listening to her.

Her friend Bev got on the phone, and she sounded panicked, not

15 Paralympics

knowing whether they should go to their hotel or directly to a hospital. I struggled through mental paralysis and tried to think clearly. While the prospect of dealing with the Chinese medical system felt alarming, Colleen was in bad shape.

We had a team physician in Beijing. While Bev went with Colleen to the hotel to drop off their bags, I spoke with him. Could he examine her before we start seeking outside medical attention through the Chinese healthcare system? He was sympathetic, but because of his jurisdiction, he was only permitted to treat Canadian athletes. He assured me that the Chinese medical system was first-rate, and ultimately, he was right.

As it turned out, there was a hospital steps away from their hotel. After dropping off their bags, they went directly there, and I took a taxi from the Athlete Village to join them.

Colleen spent two days in the intake section of the hospital before her insurance took effect, and she was finally admitted. Tests pointed to blood sugar levels that had become dangerously elevated, which explained her disorientation and slurred speech.

As a type 1 diabetic, it wasn't unusual for Colleen's blood sugar to fluctuate; often, it would rise when she ate something sweet or was under stress, but it could be brought back into the safe range by injecting insulin. Conversely, it would drop, particularly at night, if she had overestimated the amount of insulin needed to keep her blood sugar in balance.

The degree to which Colleen's blood sugar had risen was concerning, however, because of the risks of heart attack, stroke, and nerve or kidney damage. Although the doctors were able to administer insulin to slowly reduce her blood sugar, the bigger question was why it had risen to such a dangerous level in the first place.

I stayed with Colleen and Bev until midnight in the intake section of the hospital. Her condition had stabilized, and I headed back to the Athlete Village. Bev spent the night with her. I stayed the next night as we alternated nights in the hospital over the next week.

With Colleen receiving medical care, I tried to focus on the competition. The scare had been emotionally draining, but I realized I wasn't the person lying in a foreign hospital bed. I needed to harness this experience as best as possible to motivate and inspire me in our upcoming races.

In our T12 800-metre semi-final heat, Greg and I ran 2:03, which wasn't enough to advance us to the final; however, the race had served its purpose. It shook the cobwebs and steeled us for the 1500-metre semi-final happening in three days.

Colleen was admitted into a private room in a wing of the hospital reserved for international patients. It felt like the "Hilton" of hospital wings, superior to Western public health care standards. There were flowers on the table, a television, tasty food, and excellent medical care. The double standard of care for those with insurance versus those without was very apparent. While many patients in the intake area of the hospital suffered in miserable and unsanitary conditions, she received excellent treatment. While we were incredibly grateful for this, the visceral pain and discomfort of the other patients were impossible to forget. The potential for the Chinese medical system to offer advanced care was obvious, but it came down to economics. What privileges the plight of one human being over another? Weren't we each created the same?

One of the doctors who treated Colleen had completed her medical studies in Ottawa, spoke English fluently, and recounted fond memories of walking along the canal, the nature surrounding the city, and its fresh air.

Although her condition had stabilized, the doctor said that elevated creatinine levels in Colleen's bloodwork pointed to renal insufficiency, which, if left untreated, could result in kidney failure. She would need to receive follow-up treatment on our return to Canada. This was alarming, as previously, there had been no signs that her renal health was in jeopardy. She would need rest and recovery to be strong enough to take the long flight home.

Colleen's prognosis weighed heavy on me as I tried to come to terms with the implications. We knew dialysis was a treatment option and that kidney transplantation was another. Would Colleen be a potential candidate? Were there other possibilities?

The answers would become clearer in the weeks following our return to Canada. In the meantime, the Chinese doctors monitored Colleen's bloodwork closely. Bev or I stayed in the room with her so that she was rarely alone. When it was just the two of us, Colleen and I shared some hours of

15 Paralympics

quiet serenity, even under the duress of the situation; it helped me to understand that there are moments of peace to be found at every turn.

Bev remained composed and wonderfully supportive throughout. Without her presence, lightness, patience, and practicality, I'm not sure how we would have made it through those days when it felt like life was spinning out of control.

I would go back to the Athlete Village to rest or train with Greg and would later return so that Bev could go out for a while or rest. We formed a cloak of solidarity around Colleen and maintained this vigil for the week leading up to the T11 1500-metre final, the day she was released from hospital. She and Bev were in the stands at the Birds Nest, cheering us on.

To qualify for the final, Greg and I had advanced out of a tough semi-final to win our heat in a time of 4:15, running 48 seconds over the final 300 metres to clinch our spot. A few years earlier, we would have considered it a foregone conclusion that we would qualify, but athletes were running faster now. In 2000, when I competed with Greg at my first Paralympics, Canada had been one of the preeminent nations in Paralympic sport. Since then, many countries have started investing in athletes with disabilities, and the level of training and competition has greatly improved.

The Paralympics had evolved far beyond the post-World War II vision of Sir Ludwig Guttman. A German-British neurologist, Guttman, had fled Germany before the start of the war and was asked by the British government to establish the National Spinal Injuries Centre at the Stoke Mandeville Hospital to enable the treatment and rehabilitation of pilots with spinal injuries. Guttman believed physical activity therapy could help wounded military personnel build up their physical resiliency and self-respect.

On July 29, 1948, Guttman organized the first Stoke Mandeville Games for disabled war veterans, held on the same day as the opening of the London Olympics. The Stoke Mandeville Games would grow far beyond their modest beginnings; by 1960, just twelve years after the first competition, 400 athletes competed at what would become the first Paralympics, held in parallel with the 1960 Rome Olympic Games.

More than 4,000 athletes with disabilities gathered in Beijing in 2008

VISIONS OF HOPE

to push against the limits of what others might not have believed possible. Sir Ludwig Guttman's vision had broadened into a truly global movement.

While Greg and I had often competed against athletes from Spain, Portugal, and Brazil, nations recognized as traditional powerhouses in blind sport, when we walked out onto the track at the Birds Nest moments before the T11 1500-metre final, we found ourselves lining up beside a new generation of athletes from Australia, Brazil, Denmark, Kenya, and the host nation. The race, we knew, would be fierce. A few days earlier, the young Chinese athlete Zhen Zhang and his guide had raced to a 15:27 win in the 5000 metres against Samuel Mushai Kimani and James Boit, his Kenyan guide. My 5000-metre personal best at the time was a minute slower, which gave me pause, but I knew this was a 1500-metre race with its own rigours and unique demands.

My preparation in the days leading up to the final on September 15 had been anything but ideal. I hadn't been thinking a lot about the race. I'd slept every second night at the hospital. We'd learned there were treatment options for Colleen once we returned to Canada. We knew she would be okay. With this knowledge, I focused on the task at hand. It was time to do my job. As Nelson Mandela wrote, life demands that we be ready for whatever is in store for us, no matter how we feel.

In the moments before our group of six blind runners and six guides stepped to the starting line, a medal ceremony was held for another gold medal-winning performance from the host nation. We stood as the national anthem of the People's Republic of China rang out across the vast stadium, thousands of patriotic fans singing in unison. Somewhere among them were Colleen and Bev. It was a spine-tingling moment.

As the anthem concluded and we moved to the line, I turned inward and faced the existential question that had surfaced seconds before each of my two previous Paralympic finals. Was I ready? The answer was an unequivocal yes. The past year had not been a smooth path, but then life never is. I knew it had brought growth and learning with it. I knew I was stronger as a result.

The gun finally sounded, and there was no more time for thinking. We were jogging. Nobody was eager to push the pace. We ran together in a tight group. It was tactical.

15 Paralympics

Each time we circled to the home straight, the crowd was thunderous as the Chinese spectators attempted to exhort Zhen Zhang and his guide to bring home another gold. Greg and I were determined not to let that happen without a fight; as the race developed, we remained composed and content to run slightly to the outside of the pack as the 69- and 70-second laps ticked by. There would be a decisive moment, a moment of reckoning, and when it came, we knew we would be ready.

It came with 300 metres to go in the form of an aggressive injection of pace by Zhen Zhang and his guide. The field of runners reacted immediately, and the mood of the race suddenly changed. Greg and I got up on our toes and accelerated, practicing what we'd done so often in training. I couldn't hear anything through the din of the crowd. Down the backstretch and around the corner, we flew. I had no idea whether we were first or last.

I put everything into our sprint down the homestretch as we approached the last few metres and hit the line. In the seconds immediately following the race, Greg yelled that we had finished third behind Zhen Zhang and his guide, who had won, and the Kenyans Samuel Mushai Kimani and James Boit. We had run 4:12 to Zhen Zhang's 4:10.

We ran 44 seconds for our final 300 metres. It was our 800-metre training that made that possible, Greg later said. We hugged one another and shook hands with Zhen Zhang and the others. It had been a circuitous route to this post-race celebration, but it had culminated in another medal-winning race, and I couldn't have been happier.

16 Coming to Terms

Over the next year, we learned that Colleen had declining kidney function, which was irreversible. It could be slowed with a renal-friendly diet, which involved cutting out complex grains, bananas, potatoes, and carbonated drinks and eating moderate amounts of protein. Eventually, she would need to undergo dialysis to clean her blood and potentially become a candidate for a kidney transplant, but this would come further down the road.

She started on the renal diet and began to regularly attend the Progressive Renal Insufficiency clinic at the Riverside Hospital, a short bus ride from our home. She was treated by an interdisciplinary medical team consisting of a dietitian, a doctor and a social worker.

Young and otherwise in good health, they told her she was an excellent candidate to receive a transplanted kidney when the time came and that she could live a full life even as her kidney function declined.

A transplanted kidney could come either from a person who was recently deceased or a living donor who could function with only one kidney. Whether it came from a deceased person or a live donor, the donated kidney needed to be healthy and the right match, based on blood markers and other criteria to optimize the likelihood that Colleen's body would accept it.

Potential living donors undergo an extensive medical screening to assess their eligibility. I knew I would be tested to determine whether I could be a donor when the time came.

16 Coming to Terms

The next two years did not have a major international Para Athletics competition. On July 1st, 2009, Canada Day, Greg and I ran 4:10 in a 1500-metre race at the Aileen Meagher track meet in Halifax. Shortly after that, we joined a few of the other visually impaired national team athletes, including my brother, Sean, and Stu, at an International Blind Sports Association Pan-American championship in Colorado Springs. We ran 4:32 for 1500 metres at an altitude of 5,000 feet, winning the T11 category but finishing second overall against other visually impaired competitors.

Back at home, our training group was changing. Several athletes, including Kyle Desormeaux, my former University of Guelph varsity teammate, had begun to drift away to train with other coaches, and Berry de Bruijn wasn't running as much by that time; the energy wasn't the same. The guides I normally worked out with were no longer there. I was beginning to feel it might be time for me also to make a change.

I wanted to try to coach myself. Ray had been my coach for six years; he'd overseen my return from injury, guided my training in capturing two World Championship titles the next year, and coached me to two Paralympic medals. I appreciated everything he'd done for me, including integrating me within the group that first night I'd come out to the track six years ago, setting the tone for years to come. I told him so over coffee one Saturday morning in September 2009; I was grateful for everything he had done to help me.

In the following months, I connected with guides to help me with workouts, or I would join sessions they were doing. I also ran on my treadmill at home, focusing on long-tempo runs, feeling there was room to develop my stamina.

Late in the fall, I drove with Matt Stacey, another runner who had previously been in our training group, to the Canadian Cross Country Championships in Guelph. He had agreed to guide me in the 10-kilometre open men's race on the rolling terrain around the Guelph Lakes. Cross country had never been my strength, but I wanted to compete, given that the event was taking place in Guelph, a place which had been instrumental to my running during my years as a student-athlete there. Although Matt and

I finished well back, it felt good to be back in a place I knew so well while simultaneously stepping out of my comfort zone.

One of the perks of my work with the Active Living Alliance for Canadians with a Disability was the opportunity to travel and visit much of Canada. In February 2010, I spent several days in Yellowknife, Northwest Territories, leading an orientation training for All Abilities Welcome speakers.

A poignant memory in Yellowknife was dogsledding on Great Slave Lake. With a coastline spanning 3,057 kilometres and a depth of up to 614 metres, it's the deepest lake in North America and remains frozen from November through mid-June. I can still remember vividly the powerful pull of the huskies gliding us out across the ice, smooth as silk as we swished along, and the sound of their breath hung in the silence of that awesome stillness.

It was the year of the Vancouver Winter Olympics and Paralympics. I'd been accepted as a volunteer member of the Canadian Paralympic team mission based in Whistler, the satellite location hosting the Nordic and alpine skiing events.

I was able to bring Stu McGregor with me as a guide and to work with me as an athlete services officer, which involved setting up the Canadian Athlete Lounge and offering support and encouragement to athletes ahead of their competitions. It was a great experience and a chance to learn about another side of the Paralympics and the work behind the scenes as part of the mission staff.

The Games were opened on March 12 at Vancouver's BC Place by Michaëlle Jean, Canada's Governor-General. In all, 506 athletes representing 44 nations participated in the tenth Paralympic Winter Games, Canada's first as the host nation. Canada had previously hosted the 1976 Summer Paralympics in Toronto, which began two days after the conclusion of the Montreal Olympics.

Fifty-five athletes represented Canada across the five sports contested at the 2010 Winter Games, including cross-country skiing, downhill skiing and biathlon, which took place in Whistler, and wheelchair curling and sledge hockey, held in Vancouver.

16 Coming to Terms

The Whistler-based team mission staff met most evenings, usually over a beer. We connected by video conference with the mission staff based 125 kilometres away in Vancouver, where my friend Marie Dannhaeuser, who had been with me on the 2000 Paralympic team in Sydney competing in swimming, was the Athlete Services Officer.

These meetings involved the Integrated Support Team lead, who co-ordinated physio and other preventative treatments; the medical lead; the media attaché; the chef de mission or the assistant chef; and the team staff. Discussions centred on the day's results; any athlete or team issues, such as illness or other logistics; and the event schedule for the day ahead.

The Canadian team ultimately finished third in the overall medal count at what was then popularly labelled in Canada as the best-ever Winter Paralympics. They would be remembered as the Games of Lauren Woolstencroft, the amputee alpine skier who earned five of Canada's ten gold medals, and of Brian McKeever, the legally blind cross-country skier who earned the unique distinction of being named to both the Paralympic and Olympic teams that year. Ultimately, he wouldn't compete at the Olympics because of a last-minute coaching decision to have another athlete compete in his place.

After returning home from the Games in late March, I continued training throughout the spring of 2010 using my home treadmill and with the support of running friends and former training partners. When summer came, Greg and I once again tried to eclipse the two-minute barrier for 800 metres. We ran 2:00 and 2:01 several times but fell short of the elusive 1:59 we'd been chasing for years.

We began to set our sights on the upcoming International Paralympic Committee World Athletics Championships, scheduled in January 2011 in Christchurch, New Zealand. The timing was unusual as major outdoor championships are not often contested during winter in the northern hemisphere. We would be racing during the New Zealand summer. This meant we would need to train more intensely than usual throughout the fall to be ready.

Before starting our training build-up, I took my usual ten-day end-of-season break at the end of August. Colleen and I went on a five-day

Caribbean cruise, something she had always wanted to do and a trip we could take on our own, given how easy it was to meet people and learn our way around the ship.

Colleen's kidney function continued its slow decline, but she remained relatively healthy. We had a great time on the cruise; the time away allowed us to temporarily escape the uncertainty and future unknowns brought on by Colleen's health prognosis.

In the fall, when I started to train again, I did too much, too soon, resulting in an Achilles injury, which limited my running for several weeks. This pattern of early-season Achilles injuries would plague me over the next several years until I finally learned not to rush into hard training too soon.

I run on my toes, my calves absorbing the impact of each step, making them more like a sprinter's. Calves shorten during periods of inactivity, so if I don't take the time to slowly increase the duration and intensity of my running at the beginning of each season, my Achilles becomes susceptible to injury.

I was 33 years old in the fall of 2010. Injury aside, I felt good and was still running near my best. I remained motivated to train and to get the most out of my body in hopes of running faster, but I also knew the clock was ticking.

While some runners have been known to extend their prime running years well into their thirties and even into their forties, our physiology changes in degrees that become more apparent over time. Not the least of these changes is a decline in muscle mass, which can begin in our early thirties, and a drop in VO_2 max, a measure of the maximum rate of oxygen a person can use during exercise. Training cannot prevent these inevitable declines, but it can slow them down, which requires committed action and the right mindset.

One of the keys to athletic longevity is consistent training, balanced with plenty of rest and recovery; another is adaptability. Physiology is relentless; time will eventually age us, but there's so much we can do to maintain good health and push back against the gravity of the years; we don't have to grow old before our time. I learned this in my training and saw it in Colleen's ability to manage her declining kidney function through diet and a positive

16 Coming to Terms

mindset.

I knew I wasn't the same athlete I had been in my twenties. To get the most out of my training, I needed more recovery between hard workouts and an emphasis on endurance, as Ray had stressed in our build-up to the 2008 Beijing Paralympics. I couldn't give up on speedwork, but improving my endurance would be key if I hoped to remain competitive.

Greg, who was four years older than I, had also been dealing with plantar fasciitis, an inflammation under the soul of his foot that manifests as heel pain. It hampered his training for weeks. Our build-up wasn't perfect; we knew we were getting a late start, but we didn't lose hope.

I was fortunate to be able to recover fully from my strained Achilles within a few weeks. In the workouts on the treadmill and with a few of my old training partners, I focused on long intervals and tempo runs and felt my strength returning quickly. Greg was also turning the corner. On a trip to Toronto in late November, we did a twenty-minute tempo run beginning at a six-minute-mile pace and worked down to 5:27, indicating that I was in good aerobic shape.

A few weeks later, my old training partner Kyle Desormeaux guided me in a workout at the indoor track in Ottawa, where we ran four 1000-metre repeats with long rests, all in under three minutes; this was a breakthrough.

Then, on New Year's Eve, we set up a 1000-metre time trial, essentially a race against the clock performed as part of a workout with help from Ray, my previous coach. My brother Jon and his guide Sean ran the first 800 metres of it with us. I was guided by Cody Boast, who sometimes guided Jon in his training, in addition to Noella Klawitter, a female visually impaired athlete who was part of the national team for several years.

In the time trial, Jon and Sean ran a 2:05 800 metres while Cody and I split through 800 in 2:03 before continuing and running a hand-timed 2:34.

It was a personal best for me over that distance, and it gave me a boost of confidence in the days before our departure. I felt ready to take on the world.

17 Towards Transition

The year 2011 gave rise to many changes: a new coach, a new primary guide runner, and a new vision of the runner I wanted to become. It also involved a lot of travel. I competed in Australia, New Zealand, Brazil, and Mexico. I attended an Athletics Canada training camp in Florida in April and travelled to London in October for a pre-Paralympic site visit.

Greg, Jon, Sean, and I travelled together to Sydney on January 10, joining the Canadian national team at a one-week pre-World Championships training camp. I had been in Sydney eleven years earlier for the 2000 Paralympics and was excited to return.

The January Australian summer heat was intense, especially coming from Canada, where winter was in its full grip. We ran or worked out on the track mid-morning and had the rest of the day to recover and relax.

Two days after our arrival, Greg and I competed in a low-key track meet where we ran a 2:04 800 metres. I was somewhat disappointed at the slow time. We were also still dealing with jetlag and recovering from the long flight.

As we adjusted to the time difference and the heat, Greg and I also found time to relive aspects of our previous visit to Sydney, retracing our steps and wandering around the harbour with its iconic opera house, bars, and coffee shops. We also went to Manly Beach with Jon, Sean, Dustin, and Steve to swim in the warm Pacific waves.

17 Towards Transition

Then, in what seemed like a flash, we were leaving Sydney and embarking on the next leg of our journey, a three-and-a-half-hour flight to Christchurch, where the World Championships were taking place. We landed in the late evening, greeted by sniffer dogs looking for fruit and other items forbidden to bring into New Zealand and much cooler temperatures in the low teens.

Greg and I had several days before lining up in the T11 1500 metres, in which we would once again face Zhen Zhang, who, along with his guide, had raced to gold in the 2008 Beijing Paralympics in front of a home crowd.

With a population of 370,000, Christchurch, the most populous city on New Zealand's South Island, seemed more like a large town, parochial in its peacefulness. But this first impression was deceptive. We came to appreciate how warm and well-informed New Zealanders we met were. Being so geographically isolated, they were intensely curious about life in other parts of the globe; many travelled overseas on work permits or for education, giving them a wide lens through which to envision the world.

New Zealand was and continues to be very progressive in its environmental and social policies. In recent years, its government banned new offshore oil and gas exploration and initiated plans to generate one hundred percent of its energy from renewables to become carbon-neutral by 2050.

In 2011, it was New Zealand's integration of the Māori people within mainstream life that I couldn't help but notice. Although New Zealand had its share of inequities and divisions, the government's push for the Māori language to be taught in all schools reflected a commitment to preserve an essential element of Māori life within mainstream education.

In Christchurch, we met and spoke with Māori people as they went about their daily lives. We also saw Māori history and traditions reflected in the symbolism that defines New Zealand, perhaps most poignantly in the rendition of the Haka at the opening of the championships.

The Haka is a sacred ceremonial Māori dance that conveys strength, unity, and pride, complete with foot-stamping, body-slapping and rhythmic chanting. It's also now performed before matches by the New Zealand national rugby team known as the All-Blacks, and its synchronicity, controlled aggression, and singular conviction have resonated with me ever since.

Greg and I placed second in our 1500-metre semi-final and advanced to the final. It took place on a cool Christchurch morning with just a few fans watching. The semi-finals indicated that the final would be fiercely competitive, and this proved to be the case. The race was fast from the start.

Even though we had trained well leading into the competition, it felt like I had been left standing still in the first lap. Ahead of us, Zhen Zhang, Samuel Mushai Kimani and Odair Santos from Brazil and their guides ran away with the race. Santos won in a new T11 World Record time of 4:04.70, followed by Kimani and Zhang. Greg and I finished a distant fourth in 4:12.

Santos was new to competing in the T11 category after his vision had deteriorated following the 2008 Paralympics, where he had captured bronze in the 800-metre T12 event for athletes with a visual acuity of less than five degrees. The fact that he and his guide, Antonio dos Santos, broke Bob Matthews' longstanding 1500-metre world record was simultaneously exciting and personally jarring because of how hard Greg and I had worked chasing that elusive record.

After the race, the deeper question was why Greg and I had finished so far behind the leaders. Santos, Kimani and Zhang had raced at another level. This was the first time in our years of competing together that we had finished outside the medals in a major T11 competition, and it hit especially hard. Both of us had been injured, impacting the early part of our build-up, but things had turned a corner in recent weeks, making our fourth-place finish more difficult to swallow.

We had a few days to collect ourselves before the 800 metres, in which we would compete against athletes in the T11 category only. We used the time to go to the track and run a set of three 200-metre repeats very fast, slowly walking back to the start in between each repetition; we ran under 26 seconds on our final interval, which greatly lifted my confidence.

A few of us took a bus trip one afternoon to visit several wineries. New Zealand's hot days, cool nights, and periods of rain have enabled it to cultivate Pinot Noir and Sauvignon Blanc, among the best in the world.

Those few hours away from the immediacy of the competition did a lot to help me reset. One other event, however, shook my inertia, quite literally

17 Towards Transition

– a tremor that awoke us in our hotel room at six in the morning. The room swayed as the windowpanes rattled. I had experienced a similar sensation ten years before in Guatemala when its neighbouring country, El Salvador, was struck by a devastating earthquake measuring 7.6 in magnitude.

In New Zealand, tremors are not uncommon. Many buildings are reinforced to withstand the seismic shifts along moving fault lines. However, this particular tremor was among a series that followed the September 2010 7.1 magnitude earthquake in Darfield to the northwest of the city and, ultimately, a 6.2 earthquake that struck almost directly beneath the Christchurch central business district on February 22, 2011, just three and a half weeks after we left New Zealand to return to Canada.

Tragically, this series of earthquakes caused 185 deaths, liquefaction of much of the surrounding land, and significant damage to infrastructure within Christchurch and the surrounding area, including the destruction of many buildings; among these was the iconic Christchurch Cathedral, which we had often walked past.

That we had been in New Zealand just weeks before this tragic event was something I would think a lot about in the months ahead.

Greg and I won our 800-metre semi-final, advancing to the final, with my brother and Sean coming through in another heat. Also, in the final were our old rivals the Brazilian Carlos Barto Silva – and a young Columbian named William Sosa.

The final occurred on a cool, windy Saturday night at the Queen Elizabeth II Stadium in Christchurch. The less-than-optimal conditions played a significant part in how the race ultimately unfolded. Greg and I had discussed it beforehand, surmising it would not be fast and that our best strategy would be to let others do the work and look to make a move as the leaders tired in the wind.

The race played out almost exactly as we thought it might. From the start, the Brazilians led, followed by the Columbians. Greg and I hung back, as did Jon and Sean. The tension was amplified in the rapid-fire rhythm of the Columbian guide runner's verbal commands to his athlete as we settled into the backstretch, breaking through against the silence of our concentration. Even now, many years later, when I listen to the race replay on YouTube – with the commentators discussing the sense of urgency Greg and I needed to close the gap as we sat in third place – the anxiety I feel is almost palpable. Didn't they know we were waiting to make our move?

We split through 400 metres in 63 seconds. The Brazilians, Carlos Barto Silva and his guide, were leading and trying to control the race, opening up a little gap between the Columbians and us. Unfortunately, Sean and my brother did not have the race they had hoped for and were unable to move up from fourth position.

Greg and I had honed our communication over many years of running together, so we were very much in sync. There was always an intuitive feeling between us that enabled us to adapt and react in different race situations. As we reached 600 metres, still in third place, and moved into the final turn approaching the last 150 metres, we each knew the moment was now.

We moved up on the Columbians; I sensed they had nothing left. We still had work to do to chase down the Brazilians, but I felt good. Any doubts I harboured about my ability to kick had vanished in that vortex of energy as we chased after the Brazilians. We had run a 25.9-second 200 in practice a few days earlier, and I thought, I can do this! I can do it!

We flew into the home stretch, and the crowd noise was tremendous. I ran the last 100 metres for Chris, my brother, whom we lost eight years earlier, almost to the day. I knew we'd passed the Columbians and had drawn level with the Brazilians, but beyond that, I couldn't hear a thing. Then, Greg said, "Lean," and screamed, "Yes!"

The win was especially sweet because we entered the race as underdogs. It had been five years since we'd won at a major international competition, and the depth and competitiveness among blind runners in our T11 category had improved markedly. We knew we were not in peak form in New Zealand – the 1500-metre final had shown us that – but winning the tactical 800-metre final was deeply validating, and though I knew I had work to do with the London Paralympics only a year and a half away, it told me I still belonged at that level.

18 Change

World Championships normally occur at the end of summer in the northern hemisphere and mark the end of a competitive season. Still, because the Games in Christchurch were held in January, our season back in Canada was only beginning. I came home eager to jump back into training and build on our race performances in New Zealand, but within a couple of weeks, I started to feel pain in my Achilles – it was the left Achilles this time. I was tired, and my body's susceptibilities were heightened with prolonged fatigue. Sooner or later, hard training and competing without proper rest catch up to you.

It's not easy to train through Achilles tendonitis. I tried running for a few days before the pain forced me to stop. Greg and I joined the team at a week-long training camp in Clermont, Florida, in March. I was able to do some running, but I was only delaying the inevitable process of rest and rehabilitation that my Achilles needed. Soon, I found myself sidelined from running and turned to the stationary bike and, eventually, pool running to maintain my general fitness.

As the days of not being able to run led into weeks, I started wondering whether it might be time for me to call it a career. I would be thirty-four in a few months. Greg and I were world champions and had covered a lot of ground, travelling the globe together in our thirteen years as a team, competing and medalling at three Paralympics, and establishing a friendship that felt rooted and secure.

And yet, something was gnawing at me, telling me this wasn't how it was supposed to end. Somewhere, deep down, I knew there was still plenty of good running in my legs. I needed to get healthy and rehabilitate my Achilles, but I also realized that if I hoped to be successful, I needed to be less alone.

As committed as Greg was to our running, the reality was that we lived several hundred kilometres apart, and this meant we could train together only periodically, making the most of occasional weekends to work out together either in Toronto or Ottawa.

In addition to treadmill running, I also had wonderful guide running support, improvised with the help of a few former training partners, each incredibly supportive and gracious, but around whom I had to adapt my workouts to align with their training and availability. While I felt very fortunate to have their help, it was a constant compromise and not ideal for training consistently and in a focused way. I needed to be able to train in a manner geared specifically for me.

I also knew I needed a coach. During the previous two years, I had planned out my training, but I now realized that I needed a person in my corner with an objective viewpoint, someone with a broader lens to support me in becoming more complete as a middle-distance runner, somebody who could challenge me to go beyond my perceived limits in training and do things I sometimes didn't want to do.

I met with Ian Clark in April for an evening coffee after reaching out to him a few days earlier. Ian had coached a group of top high school athletes with the Ottawa Lions for several years and, more recently, had worked with an elite group of local runners.

He had been a standout high school distance runner, finishing fifth in the World Junior Cross Country Championships and breaking 14 minutes for 5000 metres on the track during his senior year, before heading to Berkeley on a running scholarship. Unfortunately, a series of injuries forced a premature end to his competitive running. "Back then," he told me, "I ran as hard as I could every day."

It was this intensity that made him so good, but it also caused his body

18 Change

to break down. Years later, as a coach, he stressed the value of recovery between days of hard training, and this had been one of the keys to the success of several of his high school runners who, like him, had pursued athletic scholarships at U.S. universities.

Ian believed he could help me rehabilitate my Achilles and return to competitive running, and so we began to work together. Although other athletes would be coached by Ian in the months and years ahead, at that time, it was just me.

Ian showed me how to do eccentric heal drop exercises on stairs, which, over time, helped generate new tissue and eventually healed my Achilles tendon. He also encouraged me to do deep water running to maintain fitness since riding the stationary bike aggravated my Achilles. I didn't enjoy water running, but I did it as a way to maintain fitness. The early morning pool running sessions at the Carleton University pool gave me a way to push hard without the fear of injury, and that made it worth it.

Ian also believed that once I was back running, I would not be able to train effectively by trying to cobble together sessions with my former training partners. I would need somebody available to work with me consistently, two or three days a week; someone who would be fast enough but also reliable, motivated, and willing to put time and effort into our training and eventually racing together.

As the weeks of rehabilitation and pool running continued, my Achilles pain began to ease, and I resumed jogging, initially only for a couple of minutes every second day, and eventually for 30 minutes when there was no more pain.

One of Ian's former high school athletes, Pat Marion, or Paddy as we called him, was back in Ottawa working and still running a bit. Ian had asked him if he could help with my training. Paddy agreed, and we ran together for several weeks before he accepted a job as a chef in British Columbia, thus ending our brief period together. It was back to the drawing board in search of a more permanent running guide.

Another of Ian's former proteges, Josh Karanja, had also recently returned to Ottawa, and on Ian's urging, he came out to the track one night. He was in the final weeks of completing a Master of Public Administration program at Eastern Michigan University, where he had competed within the National Collegiate Athletic Association (NCAA) system, renowned as a breeding ground for future world-leading talent.

Josh had specialized in the 3000-metre steeplechase, a gruelling track event demanding a combination of endurance, strength, and agility to hurdle a series of barriers and a water jump on each of its seven-and-a-half laps. He'd been able to stay mostly healthy during his four years of eligibility, and the years of high-level training and racing had culminated in him finishing an outstanding sixth in the NCAA championships in his final year.

Guide running was new for Josh, but he learned the basics quickly. We ran our first couple of laps clockwise around the track, opposite to the usual direction. Ian was especially careful not to have me doing all my running on the track in the same direction, given my recent Achilles injury.

Josh seemed quieter and more reserved than others I had trained with, but over time, we came to know each other well; we became close friends. Born in Kenya, his mother, Susan, moved to Canada to work as a nanny when he was seven. Josh lived with his aunt in Nairobi for four years before joining his mother, arriving in Ottawa on December 31, 1995. He had never seen snow before.

Life was very different. He quickly learned that children in Canada weren't supposed to fight one another at school. Susan involved her energetic son in many different sports, including ice hockey, downhill skiing, basketball, and eventually running with the Ottawa Lions. She also registered him into the French immersion stream at school, although Josh didn't know a word of French then. This was tough love, and although he'd been effectively thrown in at the deep end, he adapted as young people do. It was this ability to adjust to new circumstances that may have given him the resiliency to survive and excel within the tough NCAA running system, earn a running scholarship, and ultimately come away with a graduate degree.

It was summer as we undertook our first training session together – two emigres from very different parts of the world with uniquely different life experiences, yet who now shared a common trajectory. As we trained together on that warm evening in June 2011, Josh was fully dressed in long pants and

18 Change

a sweatshirt. We used to tease him about this because it seemed to us he was dressed more for winter training, but Josh was unwaveringly true to himself; he knew what he needed. He later told me that in his first year at Eastern Michigan, his coach had encouraged him to increase his weekly training volume to 145 kilometres each week during cross country. Previously, the most he had run with Ian in high school had been 80 to 95 kilometres a week, and to Josh, it made no sense to increase his mileage so quickly and to risk injury, so he didn't. He did great workouts and long runs, though, even without the extra miles, and raced well, so his coach eventually left him alone. There's nothing like success to affirm the truth of our self-awareness and intuition.

I was healthy and training again. I knew my fitness would return in time. In late June, I ran my first race, the five-mile Achilles Hope and Possibility Road Race held in Central Park in New York City, running just under 29 minutes on the rolling course; though it wasn't fast, I was thrilled to be racing again.

I made the eight-hour trip to New York by van with a familiar group of friends, including Mikhail Gorbounov – the massage therapist who had joined our training camp in Singapore before the 2008 Beijing Paralympics – his wife Olga, their daughter Margarita, and her husband, Cliff.

It was my first time visiting New York, and I remember the energy and vibration of the early evening traffic as we parked close to the YMCA on West 63rd Street, where we were staying. Our small group was there representing Achilles Ottawa, a new running club formed a year earlier as an offshoot of Achilles International, an organization supporting athletes with disabilities, with chapters in 70 countries around the world. Years earlier in Russia, Mikhail had been the President of the Achilles St. Petersburg chapter. He had brought groups of blind and visually impaired athletes to participate several times in the New York City Marathon and had befriended Dick Traum, the founder of Achilles International.

Mikhail had always hoped to form an Achilles group in Ottawa, and now here we were, a year after launching our small club. Its board of directors had chosen me to be the first president. A handful of visually impaired members and volunteer guides who met every Thursday evening would run in our Achilles t-shirts and afterwards be invited for tea at Mikhail and Olga's home.

Although my first race in Central Park would be a modest beginning in my return to competing that summer, it was the experience of being guided by a convoy of four local runners that stands out in my memory; the Achilles organizers had recruited some local guides for those of us without one, and somehow I ended up with four. In the race, they encircled me and created space for us to manoeuver amid the sea of other runners, and as we ran together, I felt propelled by their positivity and encouragement.

We reached the first mile, seemingly slower than our six-minute goal pace, only to hear one of my guides call out that we had run 5:47. It had felt so easy, and I knew it was because of the energy harnessed in the human chain around me. I was deeply grateful for the support of this eclectic group of road runners, each of whom had risen early on a Sunday to help me complete my first race in that most iconic running venue.

One of the runners, Paul Thompson, had moved to New York City several years earlier. Originating from the UK and in his mid-forties, Paul could still run under 16 minutes for five kilometres and 1:10 in the half marathon. He had competed in cross country and on the roads for years, balancing his training and racing around his career as an accountant, eventually settling in New York City with his wife Shamala in 2004.

Paul was almost always at or near the front of local races against runners much younger than he. We have kept in touch over the years, and he has guided me in races in New York City a few other times. In October 2022, we took a six-day trip to Boulder, Colorado, for a stint of altitude training. It was a trip we'd been trying to plan for a few years, and we did some great training there, including a memorable fifteen-miler on Magnolia Road, an excruciatingly hilly route where we ran with a group of very fit masters-aged runners. They certainly set the bar for what I hope will be my future self.

Paul continues to teach me that running at a high level is entirely possible as we age. Now in his mid-fifties, he's still running times that place him among the best in the world within his age category and well ahead of most younger runners. The ingredients of his success, as he explained, have been a deep aerobic foundation built up over years of consistent training,

18 Change

which involved running about 110 kilometres a week year-round, including a weekly 32-kilometre-long run and a couple of moderate interval workouts. Training in this way added up and enabled him to stay healthy and not overdo it.

Back in Ottawa after returning from New York City, I continued to do Ian's workouts with Josh's guiding support, and over the weeks, my fitness started to return. Josh's fitness also improved with his solo training on top of our work together.

Ian's workouts were longer than I had been used to; he typically had us run a variation of intervals on the track, followed by uphill grass sprints and a long cooldown of up to 60 minutes on some days. Josh and I dreaded these long cooldown slogs along the Canal when we were already tired, but we understood the purpose of these runs: building our aerobic engine, which would be the foundation for our future training.

Over time, as we introduced twice-a-day running on some of the workout days, I covered 30 kilometres on some days. On the days in between, though, Ian sometimes told me to run for only 20 minutes or not at all if I was tired. This was very different from what I had done before – a 20-minute jog hardly felt like training. The idea was that workout days should be intense, with complete recovery in between.

In July, I ran my first track race, a low-key 1500 metres at an Ottawa Twilight meet, which Greg drove up from Toronto to guide me in. We ran 4:22 – not fast, but it was my first race on the track.

Greg and I hadn't seen much of one another in the preceding months during my rehabilitation. With my return to training, however, and the dawning realization I needed consistent guide running support to be able to undertake the necessary workouts, I knew a change was ahead.

I think Greg sensed this as well, but I don't remember us discussing it at the time; that would come in the days and weeks that followed. Through phone calls and emails, I explained I needed local training partners, that the runners in the old training group had long since dispersed, and I needed Josh to train consistently and specifically. The London Paralympics were a year away.

Greg suggested that I find local guide volunteers to train with me. Of course, this had been what I'd done for many years when our old training group had been together, but that had been a unique situation. That group had welcomed me openly, and Ray, our coach, had been the architect of our individual and shared success. In 2011, I still ran with people from our old group periodically, but by then, most of them were no longer training as seriously.

Finding guides who could keep up and who were ready to show up and train consistently would be hard. I needed fast guides I could count on to be there when I needed them and who were ready to focus on doing the specific training that I would need. They needed to be dependable; I needed to feel I could place my trust in them, and, of course, we needed to get along. Guiding requires a commitment that is difficult to find among fast runners in what is essentially an individual sport, with little incentive other than the intrinsic value they derive from enabling someone to pursue their competitive potential.

Success in middle-distance running comes from weeks, seasons, and, ultimately, years of consistent training. For years, Greg and I had white-knuckled the compromise of living and training several hundred kilometres apart, coming together when we could. This unconventional approach, as improbable and imperfect as it was, brought us to the pinnacle of success many times over thirteen years. That summer of 2011, I was nearly thirty-four, and six months previously, we had raced to an 800-metre world title.

As national team members, Greg and I were each receiving a monthly funding stipend through Sport Canada's Athlete Assistance Program, otherwise known as carding, not enough to live on, but it certainly helped support our training-related costs and living expenses. Although I had occasionally paid guides in Ottawa to help me with workouts, I now had an opportunity to train consistently with Josh, who would then be eligible for carding.

In addition to being my long-time guide, Greg, who was four years older than I, had been my best friend, a mentor, and a confidant. On the track, he had known how to get the best out of me. Off it, I trusted him implicitly. We had represented Canada around the globe in places as eclectic and far-flung as Madrid, Helsinki, Colorado, and Rio de Janeiro; however, my more

18 Change

poignant racing memories with him were from local competitions, such as the Hamilton Twilight Series, where we had broken through in 2000 ahead of making our first Paralympic team. He had been at my wedding, and years earlier, I had attended his and subsequently witnessed his marriage break down. He had been there at my brother's funeral in the snow and cold. We had covered a lot of ground together, literally and figuratively, in running and real life.

I made mistakes with how I handled the conversations that led to the end of our running together. It felt like the worst breakup, with no shouting and screaming, but so much was left unspoken between us.

I yearned for something our situation couldn't give me: the stability and commitment of a local guide runner to help me become a better athlete and keep me in the sport longer.

Greg had given so much to our running, training on his own to be ready when we got together and spending countless hours over the years driving between Toronto and Ottawa. I appreciated everything he had given to our running, but my words felt empty and hollow.

I wish I could have done a better job of communicating with him clearly and with greater empathy.

Before the 2012 Paralympics, guide runners weren't awarded championship medals. I wish I could have shared a podium with him. I wish we could have set the 800- or 1500-metre world record we came so close to eclipsing multiple times. I wish we could have captured Paralympic gold together, the one medal that had eluded us.

Triple Crown. "Don't say I didn't try to warn you, kid. Have a nice life."

19 Para Pan Am Preparation

In August, Josh and I ran our first track race, a low-key 5000 metres, at an Ontario para-athletics championship in Sarnia, Ontario. It was Josh's first time being around so many people with disabilities. Our time of 16:43 was close to what I had run on the few previous occasions I'd raced the twelve-and-a-half lap distance. It wasn't fast, but it gave us a starting point to build our training.

Ian encouraged me to think about training for the 5000 metres in addition to the 1500. He reasoned that as runners age into their thirties, it becomes more difficult to maintain speed; however, longer intervals and more distance made it possible to develop better endurance. Many 800- and 1500-metre runners hesitate to move up in distance because they're more comfortable focusing on the events they've always done. There's often a feeling of fear and hesitation with the 5000-metre competition. I've heard it described as similar to what it might feel like hanging over the edge of a tall building by your fingertips.

Ian's reasoning made sense. Josh, who had raced it often, was fully on board. I needed to get used to the long tempo runs and intervals that would prepare me to face the rigours of the longer event. Josh said that racing 5000s will make the 1500 feel short.

A few weeks later, at the end of August, I travelled to Sao Paulo, Brazil, to compete in the World Para Athletics Grand Prix, where I would race against

19 Para Pan Am Preparation

one of our main rivals, Odair Santos. It was my second visit to Brazil, having competed in Rio de Janeiro with Greg at the 2007 Para Pan American Games. Although I was still not in top shape, travelling to Brazil allowed me to race internationally again, a year out from the London Paralympics.

Josh was unable to make the trip, as he was defending his master's thesis when we were to be in Brazil, but my friend and long-time training partner Kyle Desormeaux had agreed to run with me. Ian was also able to travel with us. The three of us caught an evening flight from Ottawa to Washington before we were to board a United Airlines flight scheduled to arrive in Sao Paulo the next morning. Only we wouldn't make it that night.

About 40 minutes after taking off from Washington's Dulles International Airport, we heard a popping sound, and the plane immediately began to drop. We could smell smoke in the cabin, and people started screaming around us as we lost altitude. A flight attendant announced in a shaky voice, which did nothing to conceal his panic, that the pilot and crew had everything under control.

We were told that the plane had blown one of its four engines but would be able to fly back to Washington, where we would make an emergency landing. The people around me reacted in different ways, from panicked screaming to stoic silence. Ian was composed and matter-of-fact, while Kyle was anxious and upset. Inwardly, I was in turmoil, but outwardly, I stayed calm. Many of the Brazilians on the flight were praying.

Finally, we touched down without incident. Eventually, we disembarked and were taken by bus back to the main terminal, given hotel and meal vouchers, and rebooked on a flight the next morning.

The memory still brings up a visceral feeling in me. Our lives hang in the balance when it comes down to it; nothing is for sure.

We finally made it to Sao Paulo late the following evening. We spent the next two days walking around Brazil's financial capital, doing some short training sessions, visiting a historic cathedral, and sampling some Brazilian barbecue. Then, it was time to get down to business.

Kyle and I would be racing the 800 metres and the 1500 the following day. In the 800, Odair Santos and his guide took the pace out hard as they usually did and went on to run 1:58. Kyle and I finished a distant second, running 2:04. It felt disconcerting to finish so far behind them, but 2:04 was a time I knew I could improve on. The next day, we won the 1500 metres in 4:19 in a race that, for some reason, Santos and his guide did not run.

We had a few hours following our race to walk around and take in the city, bathed in the early September sunshine of Brazil's late winter, before heading to the airport and boarding our overnight flight home. Just like that, our short trip had come to an end.

Through the fall of 2011, my fitness improved as the weeks of training accumulated. Josh, Ian, and I met for workouts at the track on Tuesday and Thursday evenings and again on Saturday mornings. Then Josh and I did a long run of up to 90 minutes on Sunday mornings with easy recovery runs or rest days in between. We covered all the elements of middle-distance training in our sessions, but increasingly, Ian was having us do longer intervals: 800s, 1000s, 1200s, and eventually, mile repeats with varying rests, depending on the goal of the workout.

If the objective was to focus on aerobic development, he had us run four or five one-mile repeats with 60 seconds of rest at a controlled pace. If we were doing a race-specific 5000-metre workout, we ran the intervals faster and took longer rest periods. These workouts were always intense. A classic workout began to make its way into our training: four intervals of 1200 metres, taking 3:30 recovery in between. That fall, Josh and I were running these in four minutes. By the summer of 2012, we could do them averaging 3:42.

In late September, I ran the 5-kilometre road race in the Ottawa Army Run guided by Mike Woods, a runner who had trained with Josh under Ian's coaching back in high school and who, like Josh, went on to compete in the NCAA. He eventually transitioned into professional cycling and represented Canada at the 2016, 2020, and 2024 Olympics, finishing fifth in the Tokyo 2020 Games. In the Army Run 5K, we ran 16:27 together, just two seconds slower than my personal best up to that point and good enough for fourth overall. Josh raced on his own in the Army Run half marathon that day, winning by nearly four minutes in a time of 1:08.40.

19 Para Pan Am Preparation

During this time, I was serving as our national team Para Athlete representative, which meant I was a point of contact between our national sport organization and athletes, bringing forward concerns related to the Athletics Canada national team program. This role enabled me to participate in discussions about the program at a time of increasing opportunities for athletes with disabilities.

I was invited in October 2011 to join a delegation of coaches and staff from Athletics Canada for a pre-Paralympic site visit to London. These visits were fact-finding missions intended to gather information about the conditions athletes might expect to encounter when training and competing in the Paralympic host city.

Given my visual impairment, Athletics Canada allowed me to bring a guide who could help me get around throughout our six days in the UK capital. Josh was the obvious choice, and he jumped at the chance.

Between sitting in on many logistics meetings with members of the host organizing committee, visiting the Athlete Village where construction crews were adding the final touches, a trip to Brunel University where Athletics Canada planned to hold a pre-Games training camp, and visiting the new Olympic Stadium in east London, Josh and I took in as much of the city as we could. Running allowed us to cover more ground than we otherwise could have by walking. Unfortunately, Josh picked up a minor calf strain partway through our time in London, which limited our running, but we made the most of the chance to take it all in. We felt the palpable energy in the city as it readied itself to lift the veil on its 2012 Olympic and Paralympic Games.

The zeitgeist of the impending Games was captured most poignantly on the subway billboards Josh described for me. As well as drawing the public's attention to the images and icons of the impending Olympics, they also highlighted the unique skills and talents of athletes on a quest to achieve Paralympic ascendancy. At this Olympiad, it seemed apparent that the Paralympics wouldn't be an afterthought to the Olympics but an integral part of a major celebration of sport in all its universality.

Josh and I were training in hopes of representing Canada in London in the

1500- and 5000-metre events in the late summer of 2012, but more immediately, we were preparing to compete at the Para Pan American Games in Guadalajara, Mexico, in November 2011. The timing of this competition was unusual, given that in North America, runners normally ended the track season in August. However, having competed in our World Championships in January, then being forced to take a step back because of injury in the spring and early summer, and then returning to racing later in the summer and into the late fall, 2011 had been anything but normal.

Josh and I had been training well. On Sundays, we did long runs covering up to 24 kilometres at a time, frequently joined by Mike Woods, who had guided me in the Army Run. These long runs, which often got progressively faster, stretched me to the limit, but they gave me a base of aerobic fitness I had never had before.

In our track sessions, we kept working at tempo and long intervals, but Ian also ensured we never got too far away from the 200- and 400-metre repeats needed to stay in touch with our speed.

A few days before leaving for Guadalajara, Josh and I ran a 1500-metre time trial on the indoor track in 4:12, a big step forward from where I had been back in the summer, and which told us what we were doing was working. I knew I could still improve and felt excited about the possibilities.

Guadalajara is 1500 metres above sea level, so altitude was going to be a factor there. I sure felt it in our first days running there. Any type of running felt harder.

Josh, who had grown up in Nairobi, which is 1800 metres above sea level, seemed to have little difficulty adapting to the thin air. We did a workout of one-mile repeats on the track a couple of days after arriving. We intended to run the intervals in 5:28, but the wheels fell off for me early in the workout. A couple of days later, I stood by the side of the track as Josh did five one-mile repeats between 4:55 and five minutes.

Unfortunately, Josh once again picked up a recurring calf injury that flared up during a 150-metre acceleration run at the end of one of our workouts. He could still jog, but when racing, he would need to be firing on all cylinders. The team coaches and medical staff were concerned that if Josh's calf acted up during one of our races, it could lead to a more serious injury.

19 Para Pan Am Preparation

We needed to adapt on the fly. There were two other middle-distance guides with our team in Guadalajara. Cody Boast, also from Ottawa, had guided me in workouts and some races in my build-up for the World Championships the year before. He was there guiding Noella Klawitter, a 1500-metre female athlete who was also being coached by Ian at that time and competed in the T12 category for athletes with a small amount of vision. The other guide was Simon Hodge, a student-athlete who ran at the University of Western Ontario and trained with and guided Jacqueline Rennebohm, who had previously been a Paralympic swimmer before transitioning into a 100- and 200-metre sprinter.

Both Cody and Simon were gracious in their willingness to step in. For the 1500 metres, which would be a straight final, we decided that Cody would guide me, while both Cody and Simon would share the guiding in the 5000 as it was permitted to use two guides in events longer than 400 metres; each would guide me for 2500 metres.

Heading into the 1500-metre final, we knew Odair Santos was in a league of his own. Realistically, we accepted that it would very likely be a race for second place. It played out as we thought, with Santos and his guide storming to a big early lead and running away with it to win in a time of 4:12, which was outstanding at altitude.

I felt light and fast, confident in my ability but unable to match Santos's searing pace, which ran the legs off the field. Cody and I ended up running mostly on our own and finishing second in a time of 4:20, ahead of another old Brazilian rival, Carlos Barto Silva. We immediately celebrated with Josh, who stood by the side of the track, and Ian, who had just arrived in Guadalajara.

Making it back to a championship podium again after months of injury and self-doubt, beginning to work with a new coach, and transitioning to a new primary guide runner was a vindication and an assurance that I was doing what I was meant to do.

There was little time to rest on our laurels because the 5000 metres was set to take place at ten the following morning. We soon headed back by bus to the Athlete Village, had a quick dinner and went to bed to be ready to wake up at 6 a.m.

The next morning, I felt a bit flat as we lined up in the moments before the gun sounded to start us on the first of the 12.5 laps of our 5000 metres. It might have been a rebound from the adrenaline of the previous night or a restless sleep, but I didn't have the usual snappy feeling in my legs.

Initially, Simon and I took the lead, but as we passed through the first 200 in what seemed like a reasonable pace of 38 seconds, Odair Santos and his guide felt the pace wasn't fast enough and moved past aggressively. At this altitude, and feeling the way I did, I was content to let them have the lead. In racing, there's a razor-thin line between contentment and complacency, and I knew in my heart that I was in a defensive racing mindset.

Simon and I tried to stay in contact with the front-running Brazilians, but they were strong. A Mexican athlete named Zapien Rosas Luis and his guide passed us, and now we found ourselves in third and losing ground.

On the back stretch of the seventh lap, just before 2800 metres, Simon and Cody switched, and Cody's renewed energy and fresh legs galvanized me a little bit, but I was struggling, and at that point, it was really about survival. We were able to maintain our third-place position, finishing in 16:47, far behind Santos and his guide, who won comfortably in 16:05, and the Mexicans, who seemed to run the race of their lives to claim second on their home soil.

Ian and Josh's disappointment in my performance hit hard. The burritos we ate for lunch at a place near the stadium far surpassed the cafeteria fare Josh and I had been eating, but I couldn't enjoy the meal. Ian and Josh weren't unkind, and it wasn't so much about having finished third but rather that I'd let the race get away without putting up a fight against the Mexicans, who had never beaten me before and never would again. Ian and Josh saw that I'd given up, and I'm sure for Josh, who had trained alongside me throughout that fall, it must have been difficult to watch. He thought I might not have what it takes to be competitive over the longer distance. I ruminated in bed later that night as I tossed and turned, determined to prove him wrong.

20 Winter Training and Racing Forward

Back in Canada in the days and weeks following the Para Pan American Games in Guadalajara, it seemed like something had changed. I felt supremely good and was flying on my runs and in workouts. I finished treadmill runs often under a six-minute mile pace, and it felt easy. Days after returning home, I floated through five 1000-metre intervals with Josh in 3:20, taking just 45 seconds in between, and a few days after that, I ran five 800-metre repeats with 2:30 rest, averaging 2:19. Never before had I been able to run workouts like that and feel so good doing them.

It might have been the aftereffect from returning to sea level after our ten days spent at high altitude, accumulated fitness from our training throughout the fall, or motivation to up the ante following my disappointing 5000-metre race in Guadalajara, but for a while, after returning home, I felt stronger than ever.

December in Ottawa came with its sub-zero-degree temperatures and first snow. We were doing our quality sessions mostly on the indoor track by then and continuing to run outside, though the conditions sometimes compelled us to slow down. It felt like we were pushing hard, but I never questioned it as I knew we were on a new path. I'd been to three previous

Paralympics but had never before trained for the 5000 metres in addition to what had always been my main event, the 1500.

I just needed to work hard and place my faith in the week-in, week-out training. We did workouts on the indoor track involving 400-metre intervals in 65 seconds and kilometre repetitions, which sometimes dipped under three minutes.

One memorable workout Josh and I did on Christmas Eve was around Revelstoke Drive, a 1700-metre road loop in a quiet residential area. It was usually well-plowed and included a long uphill section. Our warm-up was from my house to Revelstoke before running five 1500-metre repeats, then several 200-metre hill sprints with a jog back down in between, and finally our cooldown back to my place. In that workout, Josh and I covered 23 kilometres in the bitter cold. Ian came out to watch and time our intervals as he almost always did. When it's that cold, it's far better to be running than standing around. I appreciated Ian's dedication when he easily could have been keeping warm indoors and enjoying the start of the Christmas holiday.

In January, Josh and I ran 4:11 in an indoor 1500 metres at the Dome, and we repeated it two weeks later.

The following week, Ian had us run an 800-metre time trial at our practice. We ran 2:05 and then, after about 15 minutes, followed it with four 1200-metre repeats, taking 3:30 recovery between each. I think we ran 3:50 on the first of these, and there was still so much lactic acid in my legs from the 800-metre time trial that it was difficult to imagine how we were going to complete four of them; however, I found I was able to run faster on each interval, finishing our final one in 3:42. It was a big workout, and I knew it was a good sign.

Nine days later, we ran 4:08 for 1500 metres in a race at the Dome. It was the breakthrough we had been waiting for.

This period of training taught me about the value of consistency in workouts. For weeks in a row, Josh and I were executing good workouts one after another. We were dialed in, and I believe this was key to our success that indoor season. The sessions we did were tough, and they stretched me just enough, but not so far that I burned out.

20 Winter Training and Racing Forward

Having Ian and Josh there, committed as they were, kept me accountable and compelled me to dig deep. I trained harder than I thought possible even a few months earlier, and this opened new horizons in my mind.

In mid-February, Josh and I travelled to Miramar in southern Florida to join a week-long national team warm-weather training camp. Jon and Sean, who were training for the 400 metres as well as the 4 x 100-metre relay, also made the trip, as did Stu, who was attempting to make the team in the 800 and 1500 metres in the T13 category.

In previous years, when Stu, Greg, and I travelled, we spent plenty of time together. Without Greg being with us, the dynamic felt different during the training camp, but I appreciated Stu's familiar presence and was glad he was back training in hopes of making another Paralympic team.

Josh and I trained very hard that week. On our second to last day in Florida, we did a track session of three 2400-metre repeats, each run as a progression where we completed 1600 metres at around my half marathon effort, then accelerated into 400 metres at our estimated 3000-metre pace, then immediately into 400 metres at 1500-metre pace. We took six or seven minutes between the intervals. It was a brutal workout, but we mostly hit our goal paces. I was completely spent afterwards.

When you're fit, though, recovery comes more quickly, and that afternoon, Josh and I ran again for 40 minutes in the park near our hotel, cruising at a 6:30 per-mile pace with what felt like minimal effort.

The next morning, we did a long run along the beach. I hung on as Josh pushed the pace down to six minutes per mile or faster. Afterwards, we went out to have a quick burrito before heading to the airport to fly home, but my body rejected it completely. I couldn't keep it down.

The hard training paid off a week later, though, as we ran what was, for me, a huge personal best by 17 seconds in a 3000-metre indoor race back in Ottawa at the Dome. We finished third in 8:51.69, behind Alex Berhe, who would become our training partner in the following years. He was in his final year of high school at that time. Eventually, Alex would become my primary guide runner.

March in Ottawa can still bring harsh weather, but this particular March was milder than usual, and I remember Josh and I doing a workout on the outdoor track in shorts one sunny afternoon. If you can make it through a winter having trained hard and remained healthy, you've essentially given yourself a great foundation to set you up for a good summer of racing. As my old coach Ray used to say, it's winter that makes all the difference. We were very fortunate to have the indoor track to shield us from the worst of the elements. It enabled us to train in a way we never could have managed outside.

We were still mostly meeting at the indoor track for our sessions. As the evening daylight extended and when the outdoor footing was good enough, we began or ended many of our workouts on road inclines. The hills weren't overly steep, and Ian encouraged us to go up fast. We did 45- or 80-second hill repetitions, depending on the day, with a jog back down for recovery.

I always found these challenging but crucial to building functional leg strength, enabling you to sprint late in races when you were tired.

Our 3000-metre race in the Dome had been a stepping stone towards getting me ready to run a competitive 5000 metres in hopes of achieving the Paralympic qualification standard, and Josh and I had an opportunity to run one in mid-April in California.

The previous summer, when Josh and I started running together, he had mentioned his desire to qualify for the 2012 Olympics in his own right in the 3000-metre steeplechase. Together with Ian, we discussed how Josh might simultaneously guide me while also incorporating his training in hopes of qualifying for the Olympic team. In addition to the running Josh did on the days we weren't training together, Ian had Josh add additional intervals after many of our workouts to ensure he was getting the work he needed. One day in particular, Josh ran a three-mile tempo in under 15 minutes after a good session with me. This was the calibre of athlete he was.

That March, as we trained in preparation for travel to Arizona in early April for a 1500-metre race in Phoenix, followed by ten days of training before going to California, Josh started to incorporate jumping over indoor steeple barriers. The steeplechase is among the most demanding of endurance events on the track because of the anaerobic requirement to jump or hurdle over barriers, as well as negotiating a water jump on each of the

20 Winter Training and Racing Forward

race's seven and a half laps, all while sustaining a pace at the very top end of one's aerobic capacity. To be successful, one needs to have the speed of a 1500-metre runner combined with the endurance of a 5000-metre runner, complemented by determination, an extreme pain threshold, and nerves of steel.

Josh and I flew to Phoenix in early April 2012. The desert heat radiated from the pavement. The day after we arrived, we ran 4:08 in the 1500 metres at the Sun Angels Track Classic. I hadn't felt great warming up for the race, but our months of consistent training didn't let us down. The next evening, Josh ran his first 3000-metre steeple chase of the season by winning his section in just under nine minutes. Our trip was off to a good start.

We stayed in Scottsdale, a suburb of Phoenix. We rented a vehicle and would drive to the track or to pick up groceries, with Josh always scanning the neighbourhoods around us for good running paths.

We were there for several days before Ian, Stu, Noella, and Cody arrived from Ottawa. We had a lot of downtime between runs, and I used the time to catch up on work for the Active Living Alliance, read, or watch television.

Luckily, I had a very supportive boss in Jane Arkell. The All Abilities Welcome campaign to encourage recreation providers to include participants with disabilities was in its final year. Jane supported my ambitions to qualify for another Paralympics. I worked remotely from wherever I was. The campaign was winding down, and I was working on the final report and also applying for grants and other funding sources in hopes the program could continue.

A few days after we raced, Josh and I ran a session of 1200-metre repeats, hitting 3:38 for a couple of the intervals. I felt fit and fast. Around this same time, though, Josh started to feel persistent pain in his Achilles. At first, he tried to ignore it, never one to complain, but eventually, he needed to rest completely for a few days. This was hard for him because we were there to run, but injuries are part of the sport, and when they come, it's a signal to take a step back.

I ran on the treadmill in our hotel for the remainder of the week while Josh rested his Achilles. The others from our group arrived mid-week. It was good to have them there.

Then, before we knew it, we were heading to the airport to catch a short 55-minute flight across the Sonoran and Mojave Deserts into Los Angeles. Originally, everyone had hoped to compete at the Mount Sac Relays competition in Walnut, just east of L.A., but in the end, Josh was the only one to be accepted into the meet. The rest of us had been accepted into the Brian Clay Invitational meet in Azusa, close to Mount Sac.

Josh's Achilles had improved, but it still wasn't a hundred percent, and he missed several days of training by the time we all arrived in Los Angeles. He went for a test jog on our first night in LA as the rest of us ate dinner in a Mexican restaurant near our hotel. Twenty minutes later, he came in and said his Achilles felt okay. "Okay" would have been painful for many others. It took a lot for Josh to acknowledge he was hurting. Injuries work on a spectrum, and Josh was as tough as they came, but he also knew his own body and felt confident enough to be ready to race.

The next evening, he ran 8:55 in his section of the Mount Sac 3000-metre steeplechase. It wasn't reflective of his high level of fitness, as he fell early on in the water pit and spent much of the race working his way back up, but it was an improvement on his first steeple two weeks earlier at the Sun Angels meet.

The following evening, we prepared ourselves alongside the other 5000-metre competitors. I felt flat in our warm-up, which we did on grass. It felt as though I'd eaten too much in the hours before. There was no zip in my legs. With all that it had taken to get here, I felt I couldn't fall short in this race, which would be fast and set up perfectly for me. Stu had broken two minutes in his season-opening 800 metres a few hours earlier. Unfortunately, Noella had been feeling the effects of a lingering chest cold, and things hadn't gone as well in her 1500 metres with Cody. I wanted to seize the moment and take advantage of all the training and this opportunity to be in California in April with a perfect race scenario.

Josh and I reached 3000 metres in 9:22, sticking to our pre-race plan to run 75 seconds for each lap, and I thought, my god, there's still two kilometres to go! There were runners all around us. A number of them had

20 Winter Training and Racing Forward

gone out too fast, and we were able to pick off a few of them, even though we were slowing down.

It was early evening, and though the sun was still hot, most of the track was in shadows. This gave us a welcome break from the sun's intensity for most of the race. I was hurting but tried to concentrate and stay relaxed.

Between the third and fourth kilometre is the point in a 5000-metre event where you often hurt the most, and it's also when the real racing usually begins. Josh and I were not so concerned about our position, but we wanted to come away with a fast time. Our pace slipped a bit in the fourth kilometre, but I tried to dig deep over the last 1000 metres and give it my best.

We finished tenth in our heat with what was nearly a 40-second 5000-metre personal best for me of 15:46, well under the Paralympic qualifying standard of 16:15. The months of consistent distance training had made me into a different athlete from what I had been just eight months earlier. We'd had some minor setbacks but were consistent in our workouts, and while this race was a breakthrough for me, it didn't come as a surprise. Importantly, Josh's Achilles had held up well.

After cooling down, we headed back to our hotel, showered, joined Ian for dinner, and then headed back to the track, where we ran into the American marathon record holder Ryan Hall. He was there watching, and we chatted for several minutes. He was then nearing the end of his competitive career.

Then we stood by the track and watched another Canadian, Cam Levins, outrun a quality field in the elite men's 5000 metres with a speedy 55-second final lap. Cam, originally from Blackrock, British Columbia, had risen to prominence at the University of Southern Utah and was known for running up to 300 kilometres during many of his training weeks. He went on to represent Canada later that summer in the London Olympics, finishing ninth in the 5000 and tenth in the 10,000. After later transitioning to the marathon, he represented Canada in the 2020 and 2024 Olympic marathons and finished an outstanding fourth at the 2022 World Championships held in Eugene, Oregon.

The next afternoon, our group drove north up the Pacific coast to Santa Barbara, where we spent four days training. We stayed in cabins at a little bed and breakfast a block from the beach. In the days that followed, we trained hard and ate well, often driving further inland into the more arid hills to sample delicious local red wine.

Travelling with others can trigger tensions, and I remember a day of conflict between Noella and Cody that led to tears on both sides, though I forget the reason why.

I also got angry at Josh one day for pushing the pace on what was supposed to be an easy 60-minute recovery run. I couldn't understand why he wanted to run so fast when we had a hard workout the next day. Our argument didn't last very long, though. We were a team, after all, and we wanted the same thing.

On our last morning in Santa Barbara, we walked the block or so to the beach with Stu and Ian. We bought plates of pancakes at a little hut on the beach and sat there eating, listening to the sound of the waves lapping against the shore as the sun came up. I felt a sense of stillness and peace. Despite many layers of complexity, I was reminded that life in its truest manifestation has an elemental rhythm.

21 The Making of Medalists

Back in Ottawa, the weather warmed, and we transitioned back to training regularly on the outdoor track. Josh picked up his steeplechase training again in combination with the workouts Ian had us do together. His Achilles still wasn't perfect, though, and the demands of jumping over barriers and landing hard only further aggravated it.

Canada had multiple 3000-metre steeplers contesting the elusive Olympic spots, and to have a realistic chance, Josh needed to run in the 8:20s. He had a personal best of 8:37, and I don't doubt that if he had more time and trained solely for the steeple, he could have had a chance. He placed his dream on the back burner to run with me. I deeply appreciated his dedication to our training and racing, as he never harboured resentment for what might otherwise have been.

I felt tired in the workouts. It had been a tough couple of months. In one workout in May, I strained my left hamstring, not severely but enough for Ian to suggest I take a five-day break from training. It was a welcome pause, even if the timing, the beginning of the outdoor season, wasn't ideal.

When I started back again, I struggled to find my running rhythm in the weeks leading up to the Olympic and Paralympic Trials, which would take place in Calgary at the end of June. Everything seemed to feel harder.

I have seasonal allergies that typically flare up during the first few weeks of spring, so this might have been part of it. I was concerned because although Josh and I had raced well in our two early-season races in Arizona and California, our selection to the team wasn't guaranteed. We certainly wanted to run well at the trials, where we knew the selection committee would be watching closely.

Josh and I flew to the trials in Calgary at the end of June without having raced on the track together since our 5000 metres in California in mid-April. I had run a 35-minute 10K road race at the Ottawa Race Weekend a month earlier, guided by a runner named Mike Gill, who had briefly trained with our group in Guelph years earlier, but other than that, I wasn't race sharp, and it showed.

In our 1500, Josh and I ran a sluggish 4:28, and it felt like a struggle every step of the way. Stu won! Normally, he and I competed in different visual classifications, but we raced at the trials together with other athletes in different categories just to make it a competitive race since there simply wasn't the depth of athletes with disabilities to have multiple disability-specific events. After the race, I was randomly selected for drug testing. I was dehydrated and, as a result, had a long wait time, drinking endless bottles of water under the scrutiny of the testers before finally being able to provide a urine sample.

Two nights later, Josh and I lined up with mostly able-bodied competitors in the 5000 metres. In that particular event, the organizers allowed para-athletes to run together with the other athletes. We stood alongside soon-to-be Olympians, including Cam Levins, whom we had cheered for at the Mount Sack Relays in California a couple of months earlier.

Although I still wasn't feeling in top form, the race was an improvement over our 1500, and Josh and I went away with a slow but solid finishing time of 16:40. We were lapped by Cam Levins and others who were vying for Olympic qualification at the front end of the race, but we had done enough to prove our fitness and ensure our spot among the para-athletes who would represent Canada in London in a little more than two months.

Josh and I had every reason to celebrate, as did my brother and Sean,

21 The Making of Medalists

who had also qualified for what would be their second Paralympics. But it hadn't worked out for Noella, Cody, and Stu. They were despondent. Stu had sought out races, even travelling to Moncton, New Brunswick, to make a last-gasp effort to qualify in the 1500 metres in his T13 category, but narrowly missed the standard.

Back in Ottawa from the Olympic and Paralympic Trials, Ian had Josh and I run two good sessions the following week, including a workout involving four one-mile progressive intervals, each with three minutes and thirty seconds rest between. In each of the miles, we transitioned from a fast aerobic pace to a 3000-metre pace and then sprinted the final 200 metres as fast as we could. It was intense and effective in its specificity to 5000-metre racing.

A week later, the second week of July, Josh and I raced a 5000 at an evening Twilight meet in Ottawa, and I believe the mile repetitions from the previous week played a huge part in the outcome. Our plan in the race was to run the first 3000 metres in 9:30 or 3:10 per kilometre, and then, depending on how I was feeling, do what we could over the remaining five laps. We got to 3000 metres in 9:32, two seconds slower than our original plan, but I felt good. And then I remembered how it had felt starting into the final mile repetition in our workout from the week before. I felt better than I had then, and this gave me the confidence to attack the pace and not simply hang on, as I'd always done in the critical fourth kilometre.

We went on to finish second with a one-second personal best of 15:45, but most importantly, the race affirmed that I'd come through the rough patch in my training. Three days later, at the Athletics Ontario Provincial Championships, which our club hosted, Josh and I ran a 4:08 1500 metres and followed it up the next day by running 2:02 for 800. I was encouraged to finally turn the corner and be back training and racing at a level I knew I was capable of.

A few weeks later, Josh and I lowered our 5000-metre personal best to 15:37 at another Ottawa Twilight competition, getting to 3200 metres in 10:02 and hearing Ian's voice from the side of the track saying: "Chill out, Jason!" It was the perfect thing to say and a quintessential example of good coaching in real-time. Those brief words were enough to get me to relax and pick it up over the final laps.

It was another step forward in my metamorphosis as a distance runner. The work Josh and I had done under Ian's coaching meant that I was no longer limited to the 800 and 1500-metre events; I could compete over 5000 metres as well. Now, I had another option.

Having endurance also helped me recover more quickly between workouts so I could train harder and do more. Focusing on endurance training also helped me in the 1500 metres. Even if my speed wasn't what it had been, I could now sustain a fast pace longer and stay aerobic doing it.

Josh, Ian, and I requested to forego the pre-Games training camp at Brunel University in west London to maximize our training time at home in a familiar environment. First, Ian had us run a 1200-metre time trial to habituate us to the feeling of reaching that point in a fast 1500, finishing in 3:14, the fastest I'd ever run for that distance.

Then, a week later, we followed it up with a 3000-metre time trial where we ran 8:51, which equalled the personal best that Josh and I had set together indoors back in February. We started a little harder this time, reaching 1600 metres in 4:42 and then falling off a little, but still, it had gone well, considering we didn't have other athletes there to push us.

On a warm August Saturday night just before Ian, Josh, and I took a Monday morning flight to Gatwick, Colleen arranged a little party on the back deck. By then, my brother and Sean had already flown over. At the party, I gave a spontaneous speech thanking everyone for coming and letting them know how much it meant to have their support.

I deeply felt the vital energy, care and connection friends and loved ones extended to me. They would be there for me as I embarked on the next stage of my journey, providing support during moments of loneliness and uncertainty. Their support fueled my ambition to honour and appreciate those who stood by me. I had transformed into a new athlete, a new person. In London, I wanted to honour the new and former me, recognizing all the phases of my life with the highs, lows, and lessons that contributed to the totality of who I had become.

21 The Making of Medalists

We arrived in London on a Monday evening, four days before our 1500-metre semi-final. Josh and I were taken to the Athlete Village, and Ian to a nearby hotel. Josh and I spent the next couple of days familiarizing ourselves with the Athlete Village, doing a couple of light workouts, and adjusting to the five-hour time change. Our Friday 1500-metre semi-final would take place at 11 a.m. local time, which was six in the morning back home.

Josh and I watched the televised coverage of the Opening Ceremonies from the Village with others from our team who had also remained behind. Lying in bed, we could hear the crowd and the fireworks from the Olympic Stadium, only a mile away.

The London Games had an aura special among the Paralympics I'd competed in. Great Britain is the birthplace of the Paralympic movement, but much more than that, people seemed to connect with the humanity of athletes who had transcended the limits of their impairments to excel at what they did. People wanted to share that energy. Josh and I met taxi drivers and people on the street who told us they were more excited about the Paralympics than the Olympics, which had just taken place. To us, these sentiments felt genuine.

There were protests in London in the days leading to the Paralympics because of the involvement of Atos, one of the Games sponsors. Atos ran the technology behind the information system used by officials, athletes and the media. The British government also had hired the company to carry out controversial tests to determine whether claimants of incapacity benefits were fit to work. This led disability activists to protest against an insidious irony: Atos was the main Paralympic sponsor, but it would also be helping the UK government deny benefits to many people who had a legitimate disability.

I wrote earlier about the moral compromise of being an athlete at the Paralympics. This tension existed in London. Life places us in positions of constant compromise; it's almost unavoidable in society today. I don't think the answer is to detach ourselves from life but rather to be sensitive and aware, to be the best, open-hearted, and well-informed people we can be, even in situations that go against our conscience, and to look for ways to engender hope within our sphere of influence.

Before our semi-final, Ian obtained a guest pass into the Athlete Village to join Josh and me for dinner. These passes were difficult to get, and we would meet Ian only outside the Village from then on. The three of us sat over our plates in the athlete cafeteria and discussed the usual race strategy. In the semi-final, Josh and I hoped to do just enough to make it through to the final without expending any more energy than we had to.

Although Josh had represented Canada before in the 3000-metre steeplechase at the 2009 Jeux de la Francophonie held in Beirut, this was his first exposure to competition on this scale. He absorbed it with his typical cool head. Walking onto the track the next morning, he exchanged a few words of Swahili with a Kenyan guide runner who recognized him as one of their own.

I knew Colleen was somewhere out there in the stands. She had coordinated her flight to meet Maurice's sister Jacqueline, who had flown in from Northern Ireland. My mother and Maurice soon arrived from Toronto and stayed at a bed and breakfast in Pinner, a village just northwest of London.

We lined up, and finally, it was race time under the morning sun. The gun sounded, and we took off, and as is typical in most 1500-metre races, everybody immediately swung for the inside lane. Josh and I were a bit slow getting off the line, and I was tripped in the first few metres as other athletes cut us off.

It happened in a split second, and I instinctively slammed my hand down on the track to break my fall. Fortunately, I stayed on my feet and bounced up quickly.

We found ourselves at the back of the field, and it was clear it wouldn't be an easy path to the final. We were able to work our way into third and keep that position throughout the race, finishing in a time of 4:13. Ahead of us, the team from Morocco was disqualified because the guide had inadvertently crossed the line first, which brought Josh and me into second and an automatic qualification spot. We'd made it through, but it had been closer than we would have liked.

In the days leading to the final on the evening of Monday, September 3, Ian had Josh and I practice fast starts by sprinting off the line and running

21 The Making of Medalists

nearly flat out for about 80 metres. We knew we needed to be much more aggressive from the start to minimize the risk of being tripped as everybody went for the inside.

On Monday night, we lined up in the Olympic Stadium against a stacked field that included the Kenyan Samuel Kimani, Odair Santos from Brazil, and the Chilean Cristiano Valenzuela with their respective guides. The packed stadium pulsated with energy, and among the crowd were my mother, Maurice, Colleen and Jacqueline; Ian's mother and sister had flown over from Canada and were also there.

The race went by so fast. Josh and I got out quickly and avoided trouble, as we'd hoped. I could hear very little around us and was running on feel and instinct. I remember little else, other than the home straightaway and the sound of the Chileans approaching fast behind us, but not fast enough to take away our third-place finish. I later wrote about the race on my Winning Track blog:

> We hit 300 metres in 46 seconds and, as planned, backed off, splitting 400 metres in about 62 seconds compared to 60 for the leaders. Ahead of us, the Kenyans and Brazilians were in a two-horse race. Over the last 300 metres, the Brazilians did start to come back to us, but I was hitting the wall after splitting 1200 metres in about 3:16. On the last 100 metres, I just gave it everything I had, and thankfully it was enough to hang on for bronze. We ran 4:07.56, a half second off my personal best and 0.2 seconds ahead of the Chileans. Ahead of us, the Kenyan Samuel Muchai Kimani and his guide set a new world record, running 3:58, and Odair Santos and his Brazilian guide ran 4:03. All four of us broke the previous Paralympic record of 4:08.

We received overwhelming email and text messages of support from my sister, who was then living in the north of England with her two boys, and many of my relatives in Northern Ireland. We found ourselves on a natural high in the 24 hours following the race, but as Josh said, the high ends. We still had the 5000 to get ready for.

VISIONS OF HOPE

As we warmed up four nights later, Josh noticed that Odair Santos, seeded number one with a best 5000-metre time of 15:17, wasn't in the warm-up area. We heard later that he'd picked up a bug, which meant the race was wide open. There was a Kenyan team with a seasonal best of 15:42, and we anticipated they would make it a tough race.

Ian, Josh, and I had agreed on a plan to run 74 seconds per lap, which we knew would string out the field and put us in contention, no matter what others did. Our 15:37 5000 metres from a few weeks earlier had been at a 75-second pace, and we felt we were a second per lap fitter now.

In the call room, an official made sure each of the blind Kenyan runners switched from the regular sunglasses they had brought to the darkened eyeshades they were required to wear.

We lined up on the track in front of a sellout crowd of 80,000 people. There was a sea of noise as the gun sounded, and we were away. There was no more time for nerves or last-minute pep talks.

Within the first 200 metres, Josh and I moved easily to the front and established a relaxed but purposeful rhythm. Behind us were Cristiano Valenzuela from Chile and his guide Francisco Munoz, who had tried to reel us in during the final 100 metres of the 1500. Behind them, a gap started to open and would increase throughout the race.

Josh and I were locked into the 74-second lap pace we had often practiced in training. I told myself to relax. We rode the energy of the crowd as it waved around the stadium, letting it lift us. I remember Josh saying, "If we keep this up, we're going to win!" I tried to internalize the feeling of being back in Ottawa running at a Twilight meet, with no pressure or sense of expectation.

At one point, Josh told me that we were dropping the Chileans. The three Kenyans in the race, including the runner and guide who had previously run 15:42, had dropped out by then.

As the laps passed, the Chileans managed to reattach themselves to within a few metres, and by two miles, which we passed in 9:57, they were tracking us closely. In the two previous 5000s that Josh and I raced, our last mile had been the fastest, and I was determined that this one would be no different. But the Chileans were tough and hung on stubbornly. They had

21 The Making of Medalists

run just 16:01 for 5000, so we hadn't imagined they would be ready to contend, but here they were right with us. In a long race, front running becomes exhausting because there is no energy ahead of you to attach yourself to, and Josh and I had led the entire way.

With two laps to go, the Chileans surged past us. I remember thinking, just let them do some of the work for a bit. We tried to settle in behind them, but they accelerated, and I wasn't able to pick it up anymore. Over the final 600 metres, they pulled away and went on to win in 15:26; behind them, Josh and I finished second in a new personal best of 15:34.07.

I felt many emotions after crossing the line and hearing the Chileans scream with joy: respect for what they had accomplished, physical and emotional exhaustion, and disappointment for having come so close to winning. Yet, Josh and I had gone for it. We put everything into the race, and we nearly pulled it off. A year ago, I knew we would have been nowhere close.

Two hours later, Josh and I stood on the podium, looking out into the night as the stadium slowly emptied, alongside Cristiano Valenzuela and the Japanese athlete Shinya Wada, who had clinched bronze, with their respective guides. It was a proud moment to share with Josh because in 2012, for the first time, guides also received Paralympic medals. Josh now had a silver to add to his bronze from our 1500 metres. Later, Josh told me that standing on the podium together had meant more to him than if he had qualified for the Olympic team on his own. That has always stayed with me as a testament to who he was and what our running together meant to him.

The logistics were too complicated to meet my family immediately after the medal ceremony. So, Ian, Josh, and I found a Mexican spot to have a beer before Josh and I headed back to the Athlete Village for a midnight dinner with my brother and Sean. They had finished seventh in the T11 400 metres and had supported the 4 x 100-metre relay team to a sixth-place finish.

The following afternoon, Colleen and I flew to Northern Ireland with Jacqueline, Maurice's sister. It was Colleen's first visit and my first since visiting my ill grandmother in the fall of 1999.

We stayed with Jacqueline for five days in Lisburn, just southwest of

Belfast. We also got together with my mum's siblings Alan and Betty and cousins Susie and Mathew, who I'd spent so much time with as a child. Susie now had young children of her own.

I also talked with my sister Nikki. She couldn't make it to Northern Ireland when we were there, as her boys had just started school, but I was happy to hear her voice over the phone.

My uncle Alan took us to Jordanstown, the school Jon, Chris, and I had attended. Since it was rebuilt, I didn't know my way around anymore, but some parts were still familiar.

A few of the teachers I'd had were still there, though close to retirement. They were thrilled to meet Colleen and to hear of Jon's and my running success but saddened to learn about Chris. The school had played such a seminal part in our young lives. It was nice to feel welcomed and remembered.

One of the teachers brought my first-grade teacher, Mrs. Gibson, who had retired years earlier and was in the early stages of dementia. It had been over twenty years since my brothers and I had left, and even though her memory was shaky, I was happy to see the teacher who had taught me Braille and encouraged me at six years of age to learn to read.

The school arranged an assembly and asked me to say a few words to the students about my Paralympic experience. I encouraged them to follow their passions and to share them with others who could support them on their journeys. I shared the message my old high school principal, Mr. Bethune, had left with me so many years earlier: that our time as students would form the inner core of our life experience and that we should feel empowered in who we were and what we had to offer the world.

One night, when a few of my relatives and I were in a pub, my aunt mentioned that I had just won two medals at the London Paralympics. Before I knew it, people were descending on our table, drinks were offered on the house, and the bar was kept open longer than allowed. Our quiet drink had subsumed into a spontaneous party. Northern Irish people are passionate, generous, and hospitable, never missing an opportunity to celebrate and raise a glass in celebration of one of their own.

In the weeks after returning to Canada, Josh and I were invited to speak at several schools. We were named Ottawa's Para Athletics athletes of the

21 The Making of Medalists

year for 2012 and joined several other Canadian athletes as Queen's Jubilee medal recipients. We are both low-key people at the core, and the notoriety felt awkward. The only thing I could do was say thank you.

Jason and guide Josh Karanja win Silver in the T11 5000 metres at the 2012 Paralympic Games in London.

Jason and Josh win Gold in the Toronto 2015 Parapan American Games T11 5000 metres and Silver in 1500 metres.

Jason and guide Jérémie Venne win Silver in the T11 1500 metres at the 2017 World Para Athletics Championships in London.

22 Stepping Back to Step Forward

After the tumultuous weeks during and after the Paralympics, life slowed down. I slowed down, too. I was back working at the Active Living Alliance, running a bit, although with a sore Achilles, volunteering as a board member with the Ontario Blind Sports Association and the Achilles Ottawa running club, and spending Saturday mornings at home for the first time in years.

We knew that sooner or later, Colleen's kidney function would deteriorate to the point where she would require dialysis. For several years, she had been closely monitored by a medical team comprising nurses, a dietitian, a social worker, and a doctor. She was doing all the right things: eating a renal-friendly diet and taking care of herself; however, her kidney function continued to decline.

In late October, her doctor reported that the protein in her blood had become significantly elevated. This came as a shock because, physically, she felt good.

Although we had known that dialysis and potentially a kidney transplant might be options for Colleen to explore down the road, we didn't think she would be facing the possibility of either of these so soon. Yet, like everything, she accepted the news with pragmatic courage.

The next month, she began hemodialysis treatments three afternoons a

22 Stepping Back to Step Forward

week, each treatment taking almost four hours. She brought her laptop to the hospital so as not to fall behind at work and returned home exhausted and depleted, but her spirit remained intact. I drew strength from her resolve.

Over the previous spring and summer, I had undergone a series of blood tests to determine whether I might be eligible to be a kidney donor. As I learned, you can live and function fully with just one kidney; the remaining kidney expands to do the work previously carried out by both. Although the tests had revealed I wasn't a perfect match, I was compatible on two out of the three criteria. If Colleen took the right anti-rejection medication following the transplant, my kidney should work.

Through the fall, I underwent a battery of medical tests, including an electrocardiogram, chest X-ray, abdominal ultrasound, renal CAT scan, and a urine sample. I also had a consultation with a doctor and a surgeon, attended a presentation on kidney donation, and met with a social worker and a psychiatrist. Part of the assessment was to determine whether I was certain about going ahead with the procedure and clear about the risks.

In January 2013, I was given the go-ahead to become a donor. Our surgery was scheduled for March 7.

Josh and I started running again, but our nagging Achilles injuries hampered our progress. Water running and cross-training on the elliptical and stationary bike helped keep me in shape as I healed. Josh had shockwave treatment over several weeks, where a high-voltage current was used to promote blood flow to his Achilles to enable the tendon to mend.

Ian had mapped out a training plan for us leading toward the 2013 International Paralympic Committee Athletics World Championships in Lyon, France, that summer. Following the kidney surgery, however, I would miss six weeks of training and then need to ease carefully back into running over the next several weeks.

In conversation with one of the doctors, I asked whether I could cross-train on the stationary bike or elliptical in the weeks following the transplant. The answer had been a definitive no. Could I water run? No. Could I do any physical activity? Yes, I could go for slow, easy walks, but nothing more. He warned me that I'd be tired. It was important to be careful. I shouldn't lift anything that weighed more than 4.5 kilos.

Ian had encouraged me to get as fit as possible leading into the surgery so that we'd have good winter training in the bank.

There were some dark days during that fall and early winter when I wondered whether it was worth trying to train. After the year we'd had, I was tired.

A friend I knew through the Achilles Ottawa running group offered me a valuable perspective: "Running is forever, and it will always be there to enjoy, no matter at what level." He reminded me that I'd done a lot and could come back at any time, write a book or become a coach, and always derive inspiration from and remain connected with a sport that had been integral to my life for so many years.

Colleen was more nervous about everything that needed to be done before the surgery than the procedure itself. She had confidence in the medical team. I was both nervous and excited. I knew what a successful transplant would mean for her: improved energy, no more dialysis, and a normal life. She would need to be monitored closely after the surgery and take anti-rejection medication for the rest of her life, but these things hardly felt like compromises.

We met with two previous transplant recipients. The medical team prepared us well on what to expect but were also honest about the risks. We knew there was also a slim possibility that the transplant might not work if Colleen's body rejected it. There was about a 95 percent likelihood that the transplant would be successful, however.

At the end of February, Colleen and I found ourselves a week away from our renal transplant surgery date. We had spent so much time thinking and talking about it, and now it was nearly upon us. We had a house to clean, cooking to do, and paperwork to complete, including our Power of Attorney information and Colleen's employment insurance.

Colleen had two final dialysis treatments during the first week of March before being admitted to the hospital to begin the preparations for surgery on the afternoon of March 6. My mother arrived from Hamilton that

22 Stepping Back to Step Forward

evening. I was admitted into the hospital early the following morning, having been dropped off by Ian, who woke up extra early as he wanted to be the person to bring me in. At 8 o'clock, I was brought into surgery. My kidney was transplanted into Colleen in the hours that followed. As they wheeled me into the recovery area early that afternoon, I vaguely remember hearing the surgeon say that my kidney had started working for Colleen right away and that everything had gone exactly as they had hoped.

The surgeon had extracted my left kidney laparoscopically, performing a keyhole surgery that didn't require a major incision. Even so, I was very sore.

Two days later, I was released from the hospital with a prescription for an oral opioid, which, in the end, I never took. I knew the pain was natural and would pass in time.

Colleen remained for a few days of observation before coming home.

My mother spent three weeks with us, and Colleen's dad, who lived across from us, visited often. Jon and Lars, his new black Labrador guide dog, moved in temporarily. Jon laid claim to our couch, offering moral support and doing his part to ensure that no coffee or any of our mother's home cooking went to waste. I appreciated his humour and solid, reassuring presence.

A few weeks before the surgery, I had a call from a sports reporter named Martin Cleary, who for years had written about the Paralympics and local Paralympians in a weekly column in the Ottawa Citizen. He'd asked what was next after London, and I shared the news with him about our impending transplant surgery.

Before the article appeared in the Ottawa Citizen at the end of January, many people, including some of Colleen's friends from high school, were not aware that she required a kidney transplant. That made for a few interesting conversations, along with many offers of support following our surgery, from meals to promises of drives to medical appointments. We were even offered free teeth cleaning to minimize bacteria and the potential for post-surgery infection and free osteopathic treatment to help break up the scar tissue from the incisions. Such was the generous spirit of people in our extended circle.

Some people told me I was doing a heroic thing. To me, donating a kidney to Colleen was no different from what others would have done in my position. It was a privilege for me to be able to.

Colleen was a different person when she came home. She was sore as well, but she had a new brightness and vibrancy. In the beginning, she had more energy than I did. I was so happy to see her thriving in those early days and weeks.

The surgeon had been unequivocal – no running or strenuous physical activity for six weeks following our operation. I wouldn't have been able to anyway. I did start going for short, easy walks almost immediately, often joined by Colleen. My mother, ever a worrier, didn't let us go alone. She would put on her warm coat, and we'd walk in the frigid March air for just a few minutes at first, then extending the distance to a full block, and eventually, making it to the Billings Bridge shopping plaza nearby. It wasn't a lot, but it felt significant. I knew that forward movement of any kind was an antidote to pain. It was the currency of survival.

I also realized that for the first time in years, I was not thinking about running. And strangely, I was at peace with that. We continued to walk daily. Over the weeks, we became stronger. Colleen felt more energized than she had for a long time. Living for years with kidney disease had accustomed her to chronic exhaustion.

I knew I was stronger, too, not just physically, but at a deeper level of my being. I was less focused on myself. I knew I had grown as a person.

The weeks passed, and my mother returned home, Jon left the comfort of our couch, and we started to pick up the pieces of our previous lives. Colleen had regular follow-up appointments. Later that spring, she returned to work at the advertising agency where she had been working for the previous five years.

I also went back to work; however, the Active Living Alliance was struggling with its funding, and later that summer, I was laid off, though I continued to work there part-time while starting an MA in World Literatures and Cultures at the University of Ottawa.

Life returned to a familiar rhythm. If you were to ignore the bottles

22 Stepping Back to Step Forward

of medication on our table, it was almost as if little had changed. Colleen was feeling great. I was more tired than usual, but over time, my energy returned.

I started running again, slowly at first, gradually building up to small workouts on the track.

Even running a mile at a 5:40 pace felt almost impossible at first. Ian developed a training plan for Josh and me focusing on short interval runs to help me get used to fast running again.

Despite how difficult it was to get back into shape, I couldn't help but think about the IPC Athletics World Championships in Lyon, France, at the end of July. There would be a T11 800 metres event, and both Josh and Ian were fully on board with focusing on the 800 since I had missed so much training and didn't have the time to prepare for a longer event.

In May, my friend Vladimir Radovich guided me in the 10-kilometre Ottawa Race Weekend, and we managed to run 40 minutes. It felt great, and I was encouraged. Around this time, Josh and I ran a 2:10 800-metre time trial in windy conditions at Terry Fox track, and a couple of weeks later, we improved to 2:07 in a second time trial. Soon after, we ran 2:05 in a local race and followed it up a few days later with a 4:17 1500 metres.

Although these times weren't as fast as what we had achieved a year earlier, it was clear that I was getting back into shape. Athletics Canada also recognized this progress by selecting us for the Worlds team. I was determined to prove that their decision had been the right one.

Ultimately, competing in the T11 800 metres in Lyon didn't have a fairytale ending for Josh and me, as we narrowly missed out on advancing to the final from our semi-final heat, running a solid time of 2:06. We found ourselves needing to manoeuver around other athletes, unable to move up late in the race to secure a qualification spot. This was the only time I'd failed to advance out of a semi-final in an international competition against T11 athletes. While I felt some initial disappointment, I knew that, in reality, just making it to the Championships had been a win. Simply being healthy, running again, and returning to fitness was deeply gratifying.

23 The Years Between

In many ways, the contours of life as a Paralympic athlete are drawn in patterns of four-year increments. During the year the Paralympics took place, the activities around training and competing took on an even deeper shade of meaning. Life simultaneously contracted and intensified. Training and life were inextricably linked. Both required care and attention through their various seasons in the years between Paralympiads.

In September 2013, following our return from the IPC Athletics World Championships, I raced my first half marathon at the Ottawa Army Run, guided by Pat Marion, a good friend I had briefly trained with two years earlier. He hadn't been running a lot but graciously agreed to step in after Josh picked up a minor calf injury a few days before the race.

During the half marathon, Paddy wanted to push the pace, and we ran right at the edge of my maximum for ten miles, which we reached in 58 minutes, before the lack of training caught up to him, and we pulled back to finish in 1:19.35.

Over the months that followed, Josh and I trained well, but once again, I had a setback with my right Achilles around Christmas, forcing me to rehab for a month. It took time to get back to fitness. I later jumped at an opportunity to spend a week training in Phoenix in February 2014 with an Athletics Canada group, which allowed me to test my Achilles in workouts and to get some massage and athletic therapy.

Back in Ottawa in February 2014, Josh and I won an indoor 3000 metres in 9:17. It was not a fast time, but I was happy to be racing again and finally getting over the injury. By then, our training group was growing and included Stu and my brother Jon, who was training for the 400 and 800 metres with support from two guides, Brian Cummings and Andrew Heffernan.

In March 2014, Colleen and I celebrated the first anniversary of our transplant. She was continuing to thrive and seemed to have more energy than ever.

That summer, Josh and I had some good races, running 4:09.21 for 1500 metres, 9:02.33 for 3000 metres, and 15:52.23 for 5000 metres, all at local Ottawa Twilight competitions. The Achilles injury I'd had in the winter had held us back in our training and meant that I never quite reached the fitness I'd had in 2012, yet Josh and I still came away from that season ranked first in the world in both the 1500- and 5000-metre events in our T11 category.

I took a ten-day, end-of-season break from training in August, during which Colleen and I spent five days at a bed and breakfast in an old house in St Andrews, New Brunswick. We woke each morning to the sound of the ocean and descended the winding stairs to the kitchen, where the owners, Liz and Gary, prepared breakfast for the guests.

On warm days, we explored the town, feeling safe walking the streets, just the two of us. It was the kind of place where drivers stopped to allow people to cross the street. We encountered strangers offering help. The sunshine and sea air felt like a smile from nature. At night, we ate fresh seafood and fell asleep to the sounds of the ebbing tide.

I also completed my master's that summer. Not having been a student for ten years, it had taken me a while to readjust to student life, but I deeply valued the experience.

Studying novels in translation by such authors as Japanese writer Kenzaburo Oe and Turkish writer Orhan Pamuk exposed me to linguistic magicians and brilliant thinkers who painted portraits with their words. We had deep discussions in our courses, led by often multilingual professors who challenged us to interrogate the complex themes beneath the surface of the works we read.

Following eight months of coursework, my major research project

23 The Years Between

compared poetry by Ireland's Seamus Heaney with that of the Chilean Pablo Neruda. They were very different public personas, but each used the archetype of digging beneath the ground to reveal lessons from the past that were instructive in the time and place where their work was read. I was supported and advised by my patient supervisor, Professor Jorge Carlos Guerero, from the Department of Modern Languages and Literatures. Literature is a valuable echo chamber of human psychology and an avenue to reach for a deeper truth. Those who say that studying fiction is esoteric are missing the point. I think we can only benefit from approaching life's complexity through a gateway that opens us up to possibilities grounded in reality as well as imagination.

In the fall, I was able to pick up some extra hours of contract work at the Active Living Alliance. It was good to be back in that familiar work environment again. It was the best job I'd had, but it was becoming clear that our days as an organization were numbered.

When the Justin Trudeau Liberals later swept to a majority in the October 2015 federal election, there was a renewed emphasis on social programs that sought to advance health promotion at the grassroots. More federal funding was made available to support not-for-profit organizations, many of whom had closed down due to funding cuts while the Conservatives had been in power. The Liberals historically had also cut funding in the not-for-profit sector, but with Trudeau's pledge of "sunny ways," it seemed that a progressive new direction was possible. Carla Qualtrough, a visually impaired former Paralympic swimmer, took on a joint portfolio as Minister of Sport and Persons with Disabilities.

Late in 2016, the Active Living Alliance reopened, albeit on a smaller scale than before. Jane Arkell reassumed her position as executive director. She would later talk me into joining the Alliance board for a three-year term, later extended into a second term. Sadly, Jane passed away during Christmas 2023 after a period of deteriorating health. She had been the driving force behind the organization since its inception in 1989.

In the fall of 2014, I was invited to attend an annual student leadership conference organized by Physical and Health Education (PHE) Canada, which promotes equitable access to quality physical and health education and healthy learning environments. Educators and post-secondary students in health and physical education from across Canada met for several days of workshops, reflection and collaborative activities. I was asked to talk about inclusion in active living and physical activity for persons with disabilities. I welcomed the opportunity to encourage the students, many of whom would become educators, to create spaces of inclusion for students in the future.

At the conference, I met Professor Joannie Halas from the University of Manitoba during a team-building activity in which I climbed precariously across a high-ropes course, guided by the verbal cues of my teammates.

Joannie had spent her academic career writing and teaching about systemic racism and colonial structures that continued to disempower young Indigenous people in Canada. She delivered a talk in which she described the lack of inclusion within her field of physical education. As she pointed out, physical education in Canada tends to privilege white, heterosexual males, with very little representation among women, persons with disabilities, or visible minorities, and particularly, First Nations or Métis people. This led her to write a poem, "I Am Un-Canadian," penned as an indictment of her profession and the exclusion it perpetuated.

At the end of her talk, Joannie called on those in the room to help her write what she hoped would be a counterpoint to her poem from so many years before – a more hopeful message.

I was inspired by Joannie's honesty and her belief in the capacity of students to reimagine a more optimistic future through their words. I was also humbled by how she challenged us to look in the mirror and recognize our complicity as settlers who had been taught so very little about the legacy of violence and repression propagated against Indigenous people.

In the days that followed, I got to know Joannie a little more, and over meals and between workshops, the shell of what eventually became a trilogy of poetry crystalized, with involvement from Drs. LeAnne Petherick and Heather McRae, two other educators at the conference. Each student was asked to write one line summing up how they saw their place in the world as future physical and health education leaders. Each line was to begin with the words "I am" or "we are."

23 The Years Between

On our final evening together, each student drew a slip of paper out of a hat and read the I am/we are phrase of another participant. The individual lines became the sentiments of the entire group.

The emotional energy was palpable among the students, many from marginalized backgrounds and with intersecting identities, including a number with indigenous roots. It was a profoundly moving moment.

There was a feeling of deep connection and intention as we moved outside to sit around the fire. Later, I lay awake for hours. The memory of that shared experience still feels visceral and real. Life so often compels us to repress our emotions. That night, a space was cultivated to let go of them.

Over time, Joannie and I collaborated to integrate these phrases to form the middle poem of the trilogy: "Circle," "I Am, We Are," and "Frontrunners." *

CIRCLE

Tonight, we form a circle in time and space,
Young teachers, leaders, students on the sacred land
Of our first peoples. And in this venerated place,
We remember. Though we can never understand
What caused such denigration and disgrace
In schools which robbed young people of their youth
And scarred a generation's human face
With etches of illusionary truth,
Yet we pause. A history chapter seldom read,
A narrative uncloaked. And the repressed tears
Stream out. We cry for the victims, for the dead
For the survivors imprisoned in lost years.
Discrimination, prejudice, contempt
Metastasize within our culture still.
Nobody's innocent. No one's exempt.
But we can write a new prognosis with our will.
To begin, can we feel, hear, see and name
Our complicity and pain?
Through our silence we recreate
Echoes of sanctioned violence. Can we reclaim

Our shared humanity? Can we bear its weight?
Let's plant these seeds. Let's cultivate their fruit
To yield a new I am. And over time,
Allow this collective conscience to take root,
That we might harvest a new paradigm.

I Am, We Are

We are the future.
I am a leader.
I am passionate about inclusive PE.
I am a better person.
I am a leader. I am energized.
I am a part of this movement.
I am part of the change.
I am no longer sitting back.
I am inspired.
We are diverse and offer beauty, courage, and love to one another.
I am inspired.
I am a better person.
I am multicultural.
I am proud.
I am a believer, a dreamer, and will always have open arms.
I am an understanding person.
We are friends.
I am energized.
I am content.
I am changed.
I am ready to make a change.
I am re-energized.
We are transformative. We are not afraid to ask difficult questions that lead us to grow.
I am brave.

23 The Years Between

I am humbled.
I am courageous.
I am tired, but will keep moving along.
I am stronger.
I am empowered.
I am out of my shell.
I am worth it.
I am important. We are making a difference.
I am a hard worker.
I am committed.
I am inspired.
I am hopeful.
We are influential.
I am an outdoors woman, a leaf in the wind, a crest in the wave. A leader in my field, the changing of seasons.
I am wind.
I am the spark.
I am free.
I am in the midst of a transformation to a stronger, wiser and more courageous young leader.
We are the elements.
I am a visionary, striving to achieve balance in all aspects of my life.
I am aware.
I am enlightened.
We are collectively conscious.
I am myself.
I am you, you are me.
I am honoured to be able to change the world based on what I have learned from you.
I am, because we are.
I am beautiful, confident, intelligent, a student, a leader, spectacular, amazing, enthusiastic, young, compassionate, supportive, an athlete.

I am ... thrilled about the future.
I am more than can be summarized up by words.
I am the future.
I am a leader.
I am a stronger individual, both internally and externally because of this PHE conference.
I am a more creative, outgoing physical education teacher.
I am privileged, the opportunities and experiences we had this week are next to none, and I feel very fortunate to have been a part of it.
We are a team.
We are the future.

Frontrunners

I am and we are
Frontrunners
Laying a trail of transformation
I am and we are
Indigenous, proudly affirming our deep roots in this land now called Canada.
I am and we are
Settlers, recognizing our role
In truth ... and reconciliation
Together, the missing and murdered are our students
Our friends, our responsibility
I am and we are
A true north nation
Free to question the false narratives
that divide rather than unite
that destroy rather than build
I am and we are
Asian, African, Muslim and Jews.
We are white Canadians recognizing our racialized identities

23 The Years Between

And racialized minorities telling our own stories
I am and we are
The gay-straight alliance in our schools
The student with different abilities
The fat and unfit
The junkie the homeless the mentally ill
The disengaged and pushed out
Pulled back into the circle
We are passionate about inclusive PE
We create affirmative space
Re-centring the margins
of our playing fields
Because we can
Do better
We choose hope over fear
Frontrunners
Setting the path together
Laying the trail
Toward a new health and physical education
I am and we are ...
Hope.

---

* Dunkerley, J., Halas, J., Petherick, L., McRae, H., Gibson, B. & the 2014 PHE Canada Student Leadership Conference students and mentors. (2015). I am: A trilogy in reflection of the 2014 Student Leadership Conference. Physical and Health Education Journal, 80 (4), 35-37.

24 Continuing the Journey

Josh and I were back training again, continuing to build on the momentum from our summer of racing. There were now several new able-bodied athletes who had joined our training group. They were university and senior high school 1500-metre runners who had each run around four minutes in that event. Josh and I often pushed them at longer workouts, but they blew us away at faster intervals. Jérémie Venne, then in his first year at the University of Ottawa, was among these athletes. He later became one of my primary guides, and we shared memorable experiences training for and competing at the 2017 World Para Athletics Championships.

Athletics Canada, believing in our potential to contend for medals in international competitions, continued to offer financial support to Josh and me for travel to camps and races. While other athletes sometimes used the grants to train for months at a time in warm weather, this wasn't practical for Josh and me. We were both working, I was also married, and we liked the familiarity of our regular training routine at home. So, we used the funds to plan short, focussed periods of training intended to help propel us forward at specific times throughout the year.

That November, just before American Thanksgiving, we travelled with Ian to Carlsbad in southern California, close to San Diego, for a week-long training camp. With moderate weather almost year-round, a variety of great places to run – including the track at the University of California San Diego

24 Continuing the Journey

– the ocean just a short jog from where we were staying, and great Mexican food, I was in my element. We trained hard that week. One memorable session consisted of a twelve-minute hill run ending at the UC San Diego track, then going right into a three-mile tempo on the track, averaging a 5:32 per mile pace, then after a 90-second break, doing another three-mile tempo on grass. It was an exhausting but exhilarating workout. When training this way becomes commonplace within the running culture around you, you embrace the mindset that you can handle this type of intensity and more. You derive confidence in your staying power as an athlete. I came home at the end of the week with something in my legs that hadn't been there before.

Earlier that fall, Ian had encouraged me to enjoy this period of my running. It was good advice. In essence, his message was to relax and take things in stride, to work hard, but not to sweat the small stuff. We knew a key for me was going to stay healthy. I started doing heel drop exercises on stairs as a proactive way to keep my Achilles strong.

The spectre of retirement from competitive running loomed as a natural possibility. I was 37. I had had a long, athletic career by most standards. If all went well, Josh and I hoped to compete at the 2016 Paralympics in Rio when I would be 39.

I wrote in a December 2014 blog post about my thoughts on retirement:

> I'm pretty clear on the fact that this is my last serious run at the Paralympics. It's going to be an action-packed year and nine months. If all goes as we hope, we'll have the Para Pan Am in Toronto in August, the IPC Athletics World Championships in Doha, Qatar, in October, and then Rio in September 2016. It's a bit surreal to contemplate the end. Saying that it has been a phenomenal journey would be understating it! After 2016, I could see myself training for a marathon the following year. Beyond that, the thought of spending Saturday mornings at home, evenings relaxing on our deck, or simply focusing on something else has a lot of appeal. How I'll handle retirement from competitive running is another matter, of course. In the meantime, I'm hungry to pursue it to the max.

Then it was Christmas. My brother and I took the train from Ottawa down to Hamilton on Christmas Eve to spend the holidays with our mother and Maurice. Colleen came on Christmas Day, having stayed back to attend a get-together with her dad and brother Shawn, his wife Tanya, and their two girls.

Our mother loved to feed us. She prepared Irish soda bread, potato bread and soup before we even made it to turkey dinner with stuffing, vegetables, a mountain of mashed potatoes, and roasties – always two kinds of potato sides for big meals.

The past can become especially poignant during the holidays. Over the years, I thought a lot about the circumstances surrounding my brother Chris's suicide back in January 2003. He had started to pay back money he had borrowed from me, and I couldn't help but wonder if this might have contributed to the depth of his despair. Although I knew there was much more to his decision, these thoughts sometimes rose to the surface in my quieter moments.

We hardly ever talked about Chris's tragic death in our family. If it crept into the conversation, Maurice would become angry. He saw what it had done to our mother.

That Christmas in Hamilton, my mother and I did talk about Chris outside on their front porch in the unseasonably mild ten-degree weather. I think it was cathartic for her because, for years, she hadn't been able to talk about it with Maurice.

She had spoken with Chris by phone a couple of nights before his death. He had a cold, and she'd told him to take a NeoCitran and go to bed. She felt she should have been there to save him in his darkest hour. He was her son.

She told me never to blame myself for what happened, and I told her the same. When somebody loses their will to live, they are at rock bottom; they're at the mercy of fate, and Chris was destined to reach the end of his path at that time. Talking about it offered us both a way to confront a long-buried trauma and to take a step forward in our journeys of healing.

Maurice was dealing with health issues that year, fighting a blood

24 Continuing the Journey

infection. The intravenous antibiotics he was taking meant he couldn't raise a glass with us. I remember, as kids, he used to let us punch him in the stomach as hard as we could. Back then, we thought he was invincible; however, time has taught me that no one is invincible, but we can be enduring and tough.

In the new year, I picked up a cough, limiting my training for a few days. Fortunately, it didn't last long. Illness often leads us to introspection. I wrote in my blog:

> Success is being able to remain composed and to persevere in light of the possibility that we might fall short. It's reflected in the way we go about trying to succeed. It has to do with commitment and consistency over time, with living and embracing experiences day in and day out, with having faith through the ebbs and flows of training, and with our resiliency when we face adversity, as we inevitably will. It is about bringing one's best self into running, relationships or work.

As runners, we sometimes get seduced into thinking that more is better: more distance, more speed, more sleep. But did we always need more? Maybe we already had what we needed. Maybe it already lived inside us, manifested in our mindset and determination. Maybe it was fed by our enjoyment of the hard work we found so meaningful.

While it is natural to want to do well at the things we put our energy into, the self-sacrifice many runners embrace in the quest to excel could all too easily cross the line into obsession. Often, we joked about it as runners, but what we do involves a streak of extremism. Some of us trained through injuries or illness when, from a health point of view, it made no sense to do so. I had been there. Josh had been there, too.

To be good, you must push beyond your comfort zone. You have to challenge your own limiting beliefs. Sometimes, you have to check your ego and accept that to move forward, it's necessary to take a step back.

Learning how to manage this intensity without letting it manage you was where the sweet spot lay. Our workouts were tough, but we took the rest days very easy. Repeating this cycle of stress and then resting enabled me to come back ready to train hard again, and in this way, it was possible to absorb the training and make incremental improvements over time.

There are non-negotiable components to distance running success, such as good overall health, committed training, and the courage to stay the course even through the inevitable rough patches – especially through the rough patches. Even spells of missed training or sub-par workouts could be managed within the larger arc of a season or a running career.

That February, Josh and I spent another week training in San Diego with a group of mostly able-bodied national team athletes living and training in Victoria, British Columbia. Our camp took place at the United States Olympic Training Centre in Chula Vista, just outside San Diego and close to the border with Mexico. Chula Vista has a network of gravel trails on which you can run for miles, along with fantastic facilities, food, and weather that enable runners and athletes in many other sports to optimize their training.

The Brazilian Olympic 800-metre champion from 1984, Joaquim Cruz, was coaching several athletes there, including blind runners and their guides who were vying for spots on the US Paralympic team. Joaquim had been the US Paralympic head coach for many years. He let me pick his brain about training and what had worked for him during his athletic career. He certainly seemed to know how to get the best out of the athletes he was coaching. That his group included some para-athletes said a lot about his willingness to help anyone ready to work hard and the quality of emerging American athletes with disabilities eager to pursue their competitive potential.

I'd slightly strained my hamstring just before leaving for Chula Vista. As a result, I did mostly easy running, and Josh and I didn't push it in our workouts there. By the time we came home, my hamstring had healed. The sunshine and change of scenery had done us good.

We raced just once together that indoor season, running 9:11 for 3000 metres in January. Josh ran an 8:24 3000 metres on his own. With the hamstring strain and what we knew would be a longer-than-usual outdoor season

24 Continuing the Journey

ahead, we tried to take the long view with our training, not doing too much too early. We figured this would help us later in our season.

On March 7, Colleen and I celebrated the second anniversary of our transplant surgery. That morning, we shared our memories of the day of the surgery, the days of recovery that followed, and our return home from the hospital.

We were fortunate that the surgery had gone well and that we had been able to put it behind us. She thanked me again, but the truth was that donating my kidney to her had given my own life a new sense of meaning. While I never doubted that it was the right thing to do, becoming a kidney donor challenged me to face fear in a way I never had before.

Ahead of our surgery, the doctor told me people can feel a sense of loss after donating their kidney. I never felt that, and if anything, over time, I came to feel even stronger and more whole than before.

Later that month, Josh and I spent a day in Toronto filming with Rick Mercer, the CBC television personality and satirical comedian. We had been invited to appear on The Rick Mercer Show to help promote the upcoming Para Pan Am Games being held in Toronto in August.

Rick briefly interviewed Josh and me on camera about the basics of guide running before he and I set out for a few minutes of jogging. There were jokes and laughter, but we managed to make it around the indoor track and stay on our feet.

25 Championship Preparation

The first of the two international competitions for Josh and me that season was the 2015 Toronto Para Pan American Games, where we would race in front of a home crowd. With the exception of the International Blind Sports Association World Championships in Quebec City back in 2003, each international competition I'd participated in had taken me overseas. At this point in my athletic career, I welcomed the chance to run at home.

These games would be followed by the IPC Athletics World Championships in Doha, Qatar, that October. We knew it would be a long season, facing the challenge of attempting to peak twice.

As the March weather began to warm, we started training mostly outside on the roads, even as the snow melted under our feet. It felt good to be in the fresh air and away from the echo chamber of the stopwatch and lap splits. Our group met for sessions where we ran long hill repeats using the brutal 1200-metre Blair Hill in Ottawa's east end or hard tempos along the gravel river path where I do so much of my running now.

For most of April, Josh and I trained in Flagstaff, Arizona, as participants in a national team training camp. We spent 25 days in the mountains, living and training at 2100 metres above sea level.

Josh and I were in an elite company of athletes. Our group included

25 Championship Preparation

Canada's top middle-distance runners; previous and future Olympians; such world-class American and international athletes as Bernard Lagat, the Athens 2004 Olympic 1500 metre silver medalist; and Mo Farah, the Somali-born athlete who won double gold for Great Britain in 5000 and 10,000 metres at both the London 2012 and Rio 2016 Olympics.

Opportunities such as this, made possible through our connection with the national team, put us in a very privileged position. Few people have the chance to live out their dreams by pursuing their passion, as I was able to do. Yes, it took hard work and dedication, but people work hard in so many areas of their lives, and often nobody notices. Nobody is there to cheer them on or to acknowledge their commitment at the end of a long day.

For me, what has ultimately helped to sustain my determination to work hard, what underlies my intrinsic motivation, is the personal meaning I've found in the challenge of getting the best out of my body in running. Deriving personal meaning adds value to anything we put our best effort into, regardless of whether others see or notice, because each step of each mile matters.

We were with a group of about twenty, mostly able-bodied Canadian athletes. In the evenings, Josh and I made hearty meals in the condo we shared. Occasionally, Josh prepared ugali with stew, eggs, or collard greens. At night, I played guitar with Geoff Harris, an 800-metre runner and 2012 Olympian, and others came to listen or sing with us as the days and weeks passed.

On Saturday mornings, we would drive an hour down the mountain to the little town of Sedona, situated at 1300 metres above sea level, where we could run faster track sessions than at the higher elevation before returning to Flagstaff in the early afternoon. When we had downtime, I did some work for the Active Living Alliance, read, napped, or called Colleen.

We occasionally ventured into town to walk around or drop by the Firecreek Coffee Shop. There were few diversions or distractions.

Josh and I trained well while we were there, slowing down our workout paces and taking more rest than usual between intervals to account for the reduced oxygen, particularly between the longer reps. Even still, I could tell I was tired coming out of the camp. We'd done a lot of running there.

Unlike some other athletes, we didn't race immediately after returning to sea level. But a couple of days after returning to Ottawa, we did a workout on the track consisting of three 1000-metre repeats in 2:55, taking about 2:30 recovery. This was a very good workout for me, and it showed that we'd progressed, but I also knew I was on the edge of fatigue and needed to absorb the training.

Ultimately, our time at altitude set us up for a good summer of training and racing. Josh and I ran 33:54 in the Ottawa Race Weekend 10K about a month after returning home, followed later in the summer by a 15:39 5000 metres, nine flat for 3000 metres, and 4:10 over 1500 metres. We also experimented with switching from running on Josh's right side to his left, which was the inside of the track. While this made more sense in theory since I would run slightly less distance that way, it never felt natural, and eventually, we reverted to me being on Josh's outside.

Our summer of racing culminated in August in Toronto at the Para Pan American Games. The 5000 metres took place in the rain at York University, where the track competition was held. Josh and I took the lead after the first mile and tried to run away from Odair Santos and his guide runner, Antonio Carlos dos Santos. Colleen, her brother and his family, my mother, Maurice, Jon, and Ian were in the crowd. My brother had just missed qualifying for Para Pan Am and had decided to end his track career, as had Stu.

We learned later that Santos was recovering from an Achilles injury when he came to Toronto. This explained why he and his guide hadn't adopted their usual aggressive front-running style.

Josh and I did our best to drop them, but they were tough, and they hung on our heels, eventually moving past us in the final 800 metres. There wasn't a thing I could do. They won in a way that was hauntingly reminiscent of the Paralympic final in 2012 when the Chileans had done the same. Our time of 15:39 was good in the wet conditions, and it was our fastest in three years, but I couldn't pick it up when the real racing started in the final kilometre.

Shortly afterwards, however, we learned that Santos and his guide had been disqualified because of a technical rule violation. The Brazilian coaches

25 Championship Preparation

had inadvertently registered two guides for the race, which was allowed, but Santos only used one. It seemed like an arcane rule, and the Brazilian delegation protested its unfairness.

After hours of waiting for a final decision, their protest was eventually denied, and Josh and I were elevated to the gold medal position. It didn't feel right, and it was certainly not the way we wanted to win. Santos and his guides almost always ran from the front, which takes courage. It was always an honour to compete with them, mostly by trying to hang on to the vicious pace they set.

In the 1500-metre final four nights later, Josh and I ran more conservatively, and the first 1100 metres were tactical and slow. As we approached the bell, we sat right on Santos' shoulder, ready to make our move. Entering the final lap, they took off and got a split-second jump on us. We reacted quickly, but they had a slight advantage, and we couldn't close the gap they had opened, enabling them to win in a time of 4:12. We finished second, a few tenths of a second behind them.

We couldn't rest for very long after the Para Pan American Games because there were only nine weeks before the International Paralympic Committee Athletics World Championships in Doha, Qatar. Josh and I took five days off before getting right back into training. It had been a long season already by then, and we were both in need of a good rest, but we found ourselves doing tempo runs and getting back on the track for 1200-metre repeats in September when we normally would have come back following a proper break.

In mid-September, we raced the Army Run five-kilometre road race in 16:46, affirming what I already knew: that I was running on fumes. I then got a head cold that developed into a cough.

It's difficult to train well when you're coughing because of the effect on your breathing. Despite my need for rest in the weeks leading to Worlds, we couldn't, at least not fully. We ran less and slowed down our workout paces, and I rested as much as I could in between. My cough hung on, though, and it travelled with me to Sharjah, United Arab Emirates, where our team headed in early October to train and acclimatize to the heat before taking the short flight across the Gulf into Doha.

Coming from unseasonably mild Canadian Thanksgiving Day weather, temperatures in the UAE felt oppressively hot as the thermometer predictably climbed into the high 30s each day. I couldn't shake my cold and tried to rest as much as possible, going for light runs and workouts in the park near our hotel or at the track with Josh most days, just enough to keep in touch with our training.

While my teammates explored and took day trips to Dubai, I mostly stayed in the hotel and slept. I had never visited the Middle East before and would have loved to venture out, but I had a job to do and needed to prioritize rest and the little training we were able to do.

Before we left Canada, Ian, who didn't make the trip to the Middle East, had been pragmatic. He told us that while we were short on race fitness, we had our accumulated experience to draw on.

I still had a cold when we arrived in Doha. Josh and I only raced the 5000 metres, which took place in the early evening as the sun was setting. The heat was suffocating, so it seemed improbable that anybody would push the pace. However, our perennial Brazilian rivals, Odair Santos and his guide, ran aggressively right from the start, running their first kilometre in 2:57. The Chileans, Cristiano Valenzuela and his guide, followed them closely, and a team from Turkey also went out hard so that Josh and I found ourselves in a distant fourth place despite running 3:06 for our first kilometre. I felt like I was going flat out.

We had done two small track sessions in the days leading up to the 5000-metre final, but I had little real sense of my race fitness because of the training I'd missed. We'd hoped to be near the front to respond to any moves as the race developed, but the quick pace had changed that.

After 2000 metres, we caught up to the Turkish team and gradually began to edge away from them. A lap or so later, they dropped out. From that point on, Josh and I stayed in third place for most of the race, running essentially on our own.

Ahead, Santos and his guide had opened a big lead over the Chileans, who in turn had a significant gap on us. Josh and I had no one behind us

25 Championship Preparation

within 50 metres. At one point, Josh told me we were closing the gap on the Chileans, but then they surged and pulled away again.

I heard the bell ahead of us as Santos and his guide started their final lap. Josh and I ran the curve before entering the home straight, 150 metres behind them. By that point, Josh and I had slowed to 79- and 80-second laps.

As we reached the end of the home straight and started into our bell lap, rounding the curve and running down the backstretch for the final time, there was a collective gasp in the stadium, and the announcer screamed in English that Santos had fallen.

Josh instantly yelled, "Jay, we've gotta go!" I didn't have much left, but I put everything into it, fully expecting that Santos was too far ahead to catch. However, as it turned out, he had succumbed to heat exhaustion and was unable to stay on his feet. He staggered and, eventually, bravely crawled across the finish line with help from his guide runner, finishing fourth, only to be later disqualified because his guide had assisted him.

I felt mixed emotions running past Santos and his guide on the home stretch and hearing the desperation in his guide's voice as Santos tried to get back on his feet. It felt like we should help them, but there was also a championship at stake, and we had a job to finish.

Odair was ultimately okay. He'd been dehydrated, but fortunately, he recovered quickly. Back at the hotel later that evening, we chatted with him and his guide, Antonio Carlos dos Santos, in halting English and Spanish. The two of them went on to win the 1500 later in the competition.

There were eight starters and only five finishers in our 5000-metre race. Temperatures were in the high 30s, and even Josh complained about the heat. Running 16:11 and finishing a distant second to Cristiano Valenzuela and his guide, Francisco Munoz, wasn't the result we had hoped for, but one I felt sure we could improve upon.

26 Forks in the Road

The Active Living Alliance, where I had worked as a program coordinator for the previous seven years, closed its doors at the end of that summer. Quite apart from being out of work and not knowing what was next, it was sad to feel the life ebb out of a movement with so many committed people behind it. Initiatives we'd hosted, such as the annual Youth Exchange that brought 50 youth with disabilities to Ottawa for several days of activities and leadership training, had been transformational. Many of the youth left empowered to embrace an active lifestyle and advocate for inclusion in their communities. In some cases, these youth become activists and champions for inclusion in government, the private sector, and academia.

With Josh's help – he had worked previously with the Ottawa-based Sport Information Resource Centre (SIRC) before working for the federal government – I picked up part-time work in the fall and winter writing a weekly blog that highlighted sport-related research. It didn't pay much, but I learned a lot. It was something new.

I also continued to receive Sport Canada funding as a national team member. Colleen's job in advertising sales was relatively secure, so while we needed to be careful, we were okay financially.

I had time on my hands heading into winter, and I was running a lot. We took a different approach to training that winter. In previous years, Josh and I did interval sessions on the indoor track two or three times a week from November until March. We had some good workouts but went through periods of illness, injury, and fatigue. Leading into the 2016 Paralympic year, Ian believed that focusing on running higher mileage during the winter but with less intensity could be key to a more linear progression in our fitness and help us avoid the ebbs and flows of other years.

As a result, we mostly stayed away from the indoor track and concentrated on developing a strong aerobic base. I worked up to running consecutive weeks, covering 125 kilometres. It was mostly easy, steady running, with much of it on the treadmill. It was often monotonous, but I kept my eye on the big picture and believed in what we were doing.

We ran two indoor 3000-metre races that winter, running 9:19 in the first and then 9:14. I felt sluggish in both, but this made sense because I hadn't done any faster running. It was still good to race and to be reminded of what hard running felt like.

Finally, in March, we added intensity back into our training, gradually at first through tempo mile repeats, hills, and 200-metre repeats at the end of training runs. We opened our outdoor season in early April by competing in a 5000-metre race at the San Francisco State Distance Carnival, hoping to run under the Paralympic A standard of 16:30.

In San Francisco, Josh and I ran 16:10 in a race where I was tripped on the fifth lap. I bounced up quickly, and we were able to avoid trouble for the rest of the race. It had been hard work to run a time that wasn't especially fast – but good enough to get us under the Paralympic standard, meaning we had a good chance of being selected for the Rio team and what would be our second Paralympics together and my fifth Games.

When it came to team selection, nothing was guaranteed as several factors, such as world rankings and the requirement to prove our fitness at the qualification trials, went into decision-making. Still, our race had put us in a favourable position.

We spent the following week training in Berkeley, where Ian had been a student-athlete in the early 1980's. The iconic campus, a scene of so much history and social upheaval amid student protests against America's participation in the Vietnam War, was buzzing with activity under the April sunshine. Ian took a lot of pride in showing us around his alma mater. We spent a good week training and exploring the city of Berkley, with its great food and many running trails.

Before our trip to California, I was invited to be one of two speakers – along with Paralympic swimmer Camille Berube – at a diversity and inclusion event at Innovation, Science and Economic Development Canada (ISED). Director-General Garima Dwivetti, after learning about my interests and prior work experience, invited me to an informal job interview.

At the interview, which took place after I arrived home from Berkley, Garima was accompanied by Diana Brown, one of her directors, who led a team within ISED's Corporate Facilities and Security Branch. The meeting went well, and I was offered a 90-day casual contract to draft travel briefings, security procedures and other documents.

I worked with a team of 15 people when we were fully staffed. Shera Ozga was my immediate supervisor, and she looked out for me from the start. To do my job, I needed a computer with a program that would speak out what appeared on the screen and a Braille printer to produce Braille documents I could refer to in meetings or follow when delivering presentations. Shera worked to ensure I had these accommodations in place. She also supported and encouraged me to attain the necessary written, reading, and oral French language proficiency, a requirement for many permanent jobs within the public service.

Ultimately, Shera and Diana circulated my curriculum vitae to colleagues working in other branches, advocating for me to be recruited as a full-time federal employee within the Economics and Social Science, or EC stream. Thanks to their efforts, I was offered an indeterminate position within the Corporate Governance Branch at ISED, which I accepted that November. I worked there for the next three years before joining the Accessibility Office at Public Services and Procurement Canada in the fall of 2019.

Meanwhile, through the spring of 2016 and the first part of the summer, Josh and I attempted to solidify our qualification for the Rio Paralympic

26 Forks in the Road

T11 5000 metres with Ian's coaching support. The route we took was a circuitous one. Sport has its moments of poetry and its seasons of dissonance. I felt tired. I knew Josh was too, and I think Ian was as well. The three of us had spent a lot of time together over the preceding five years. The process started to feel like a grind. At times, I found there was little joy in what we were doing. The subtle nuances of conversation and laughter that had flavoured our unity and forward momentum over the years didn't seem to come as easily.

I struggled in our races. We did not qualify for the 5000 metres but we barely squeaked onto the team for the 1500, our goal event. with a run of 4.08, just a few days before the team was to be announced.

The Rio Paralympics came and went in a blur. Josh and I raced to a fifth-place finish in the T11 1500-metre final in a near personal best time of 4:07.98. I remember little about the race and could barely hear a thing in the noisy stadium. I ran purely by feel, and we simply did what our training had prepared us to do.

We ran well, but the real race played out in front of us – Josh and I were never truly in it. In hindsight, I wish we'd gone for it more than we did; I felt detached, almost disembodied.

Ahead of us, our long-time rivals, Odair Santos and his guide Antonio Carlos dos Santos, placed second, behind Samuel Kimani and his guide James Boit, just as in 2012. It would have been poetic for Odair and Antonio to win in their own country. Odair eventually concluded his brilliant athletic career without the Paralympic gold that would have been a fairy tale ending.

At 39, after five Paralympics and 18 years as a member of Canada's national team, it seemed a fitting moment for me to hang up my track spikes. Except when the dust finally settled, my restless spirit awakened to a new, undeniable truth: I was unhappy about the way things had ended. Josh and I had run close to my 1500-metre lifetime personal best. It felt wrong to walk away from competitive sport with the sense that I had still more to give.

For Josh, Ian, and me, it was the end of the road. The three of us had covered a great deal of ground, literally and figuratively. Both had given me so much of their time and support, and both remain, gratefully, good friends.

As I contemplated what the ending of my competitive running might offer me as lessons for the future, I wrote the following in my blog:

> We may never be able to revise the narrative of our sport experiences such that we feel a sense of perfect closure. For better or worse, we bear witness to the emotional footprints of our time as athletes; we study their contours in an attempt to understand where to place our feet on the journey forward, as athletes and as human beings.

Where I would place my feet in the months following the Rio Games was back into a pair of running shoes. I told people who asked that I'd officially retired from the national team but that I was still running a bit and thinking about competing in a few races just for fun.

For many people, retirement from sports means stopping altogether, but I've since come to realize that this doesn't have to be the case. I'd stopped running for a short period following the Rio Games and had felt terrible. Sometimes, we become trapped by the limits of our internal language.

I came to understand that running helped me cope with day-to-day life – a form of meditation that helped me to a deeper inner peace. My blog post from that time said, "I'm running now truly because I want to, because it helps me to feel better, because it grounds me, and because it sets me free."

I also had competitive aspirations, vague as they were, based on exploring what I could do with simple training almost entirely on the treadmill. I was running regularly and feeling great doing it. There was no pressure. I didn't have to worry about chasing a standard or performing on demand. If I felt tired, I could rest or slow down. I was accountable to no one other than myself. It was just me running on the treadmill in our garage. I ran because I wanted to. Some days, I ran twice, and some not at all. Over the winter, I knew I was getting fitter, yet without straining or feeling like I was working very hard.

In April 2017, my 11-year marriage with Colleen ended. It happened at a transitional point in my life. I'd retired from the national team, and in many ways, I know I was trying to find my way.

Years later, and with the benefit of hindsight, I believe I got married because that was what one was supposed to do in one's late 20s. I wanted to believe in the safety of marriage. My parents had failed in their marriage. I'd hoped to break the mould and find stability in mine. I felt Colleen's true heart. I wanted to put down roots and be held in the arc of something lasting and real.

We nurtured a very special togetherness, and that came to mean something important. With Colleen, I felt I had found somebody who could accept me as I was. During our years together, we offered one another a refuge. We shared our 30s in a sort of pseudo honeymoon fog, respectful of one another to a fault, kind, rarely arguing, talking over long dinners at the end of the day, racing through housework to get to bed early, steeped in routine.

Our lives were painted white. I had convinced myself that it was enough to pass a lifetime in this way, but beneath it all, I was deeply lonely. For years, I had told myself I was happy and that we had it all, and in many ways, we did. But I felt there was a part of me that had been repressed and long silenced. I wanted to discover the part of myself that I'd lost touch with.

I couldn't continue as the person Colleen needed me to be, and I couldn't deny the deep longing that pervaded my being. The time we shared was precious, and I treasure the memories we made together. Today, we remain in touch and sometimes have coffee or dinner. I deeply appreciate the relationship we still have. There is a part of me that will always be with her because of the journey we shared. Her kindness and courage represent values I also aspire to reflect on the world.

27 Still Running in Circles

In June 2017, I moved into an 11th-floor, one-bedroom apartment in Ottawa's Lowertown neighbourhood. It had a stunning view overlooking the Ottawa River, as every new visitor pointed out when they first came in. It was a short walk from Ottawa's ByWard Market. I found the apartment through Jane Arkell, my old boss at the Active Living Alliance, and her husband Ed, who worked as a superintendent in the adjacent apartment.

I needed to learn how to get around the neighbourhood. That first weekend, my mother and Maurice drove up to help. They showed me the bus stop right outside the apartment building, so getting to work would be easy. There was a small neighbourhood park behind my building, a corner store a block away, and a coffee shop a block further. Getting familiar with my surroundings helped me feel more rooted in those first days and weeks.

Life was very much in flux, but running remained a constant. Since January, I'd been running consistently around 80 kilometres each week and doing two workouts involving intervals or tempo runs. A lot of it had been on the treadmill. Josh and I had done a couple of workouts on the track together, although he hadn't been running regularly and still had nagging Achilles pain. We participated in Ottawa Race Weekend at the end of May, running 37:36 in the 10K.

In the last few hundred metres, I knew Josh was working hard. There was wonderful crowd support along the course, and as we approached the finish,

27 Still Running in Circles

we even had a little spring in our step, but because of the crowd and the music, I couldn't hear a thing. As we approached the line, though, I could feel Josh's elbow, sure and steady, right there beside mine.

I knew I could count on that elbow. We'd run hundreds of miles together over the last six years, through ups and downs, ebbs and flows. Here we were, crossing another finish line, something we'd done so many times. No matter how Josh was feeling, I trusted that he'd be beside me, the measure of someone you know to be dependable, who is there for you no matter what, the best kind of friend you could have.

Having officially retired from the national team, I was still trying to figure out where running fit in my life. I'd continued running because I enjoyed the training, although it didn't feel like hard training, not like before, and it wasn't driven by any clear competitive aspirations.

Then, one day in early June, I received an email from Athletics Canada asking if I had any interest in being considered for selection to the World Para Athletics Championship team that summer. The Championships would be held in London, in the Olympic Stadium, where Josh and I had competed five years earlier.

Because the period for races to count towards world championship qualification extended back to January 2016, Athletics Canada said that Josh and I could technically be eligible for selection based on the 1500-metre times we had run the previous year. If we could prove our current fitness, we could potentially earn a spot on the team.

Because of injuries and not training a lot in the proceeding months, Josh didn't feel he would be up to it but suggested I reach out to Jérémie Venne, who had trained with our group under Ian's coaching a couple of years earlier. Jérémie was back in Ottawa that summer from Pennsylvania, where he had accepted a track scholarship. He agreed without hesitation to give it a shot.

Everything happened within the space of a weekend. We asked Josh, who had started coaching with the Ottawa Lions and working with a group of high school and university athletes, to coach us. I was happy to have his support, albeit in a much different way than before.

I hadn't competed in a 1500-metre race since the previous September at the Rio Paralympics. Bruce Deacon, a former Canadian Olympic marathoner who would be the Athletics Canada distance coach for the World Championships team, requested that Jérémie and I prove our fitness by running 1500 metres in under 4:18.5 if we wanted to be considered for selection. That worked out to just under 69 seconds for each of the three- and three-quarter laps.

A 1500 metres was being run at the Ottawa Twilight meet that Wednesday. On Monday evening, Josh had Jérémie and me run a short 1500-metre pace workout of 4 x 400 metres at a 68-second pace, taking 2:30 rest between each repetition. It was my first time running at that pace that year, and while my breathing was fine, my legs needed to remember how to run at that intensity.

Going into the race two nights later, I knew that doing those faster 400-metre reps to wake up our legs made an important difference. We ran our first lap in about 66 seconds, feeling relaxed, and reached 800 in 2:14, and I knew then we would be okay.

Jérémie and I were both feeling good, pushing it in the third lap, getting to about 3:06 with 400 metres to go. I knew I was in new territory, but it also felt familiar.

It wasn't until about 200 metres to go that the lactic acid started catching up with me. I just told myself to relax and keep going. Jérémie was able to push me just enough, but not too much. He had been nervous during our warm-up, but for his first time guiding in a race, he did a fantastic job. We finished fourth in a time of 4:14.5, running four seconds faster than we had needed to.

We were fortunate to have good weather, the right kind of race, to be feeling good, and to have the stars align. Almost a year ago, when Josh and I had been training hard, we had run 4:13, just a second faster. There was a lesson there I knew. Sometimes, training harder doesn't necessarily culminate in running faster.

In the race with Jérémie, I'd told myself that regardless of what happened, I'd be at peace with the outcome. I felt incredibly fortunate to have had a long, athletic career. Running owed me nothing. But of course, when it came down to it, I was determined to try hard to make the Worlds team

27 Still Running in Circles

once the door had been opened.

To have the chance to be a part of another Canadian team along with Jérémie and with Josh's coaching support was a scenario I never could have foreseen. A week before, I'd been running mainly for fitness and fun. I still was, but now there was an added purpose.

The Games were in London in mid-July, leaving us six weeks to get ready. Josh had us do some tough workouts in the limited time we had. They included track sessions of 5 x 600 metres at a 1500-metre goal pace, taking about four minutes of recovery between each one.

We also raced at the Canadian Track and Field Championships hosted in Ottawa in early July, where we ran 4:16 in a tactical 1500-metre Para race. We chased Liam Stanley, a young athlete from Victoria coached by Bruce Deacon, who competed in the T37 classification for athletes with a degree of cerebral palsy. Liam was also on the team and would compete in London. Because each disability group had relatively few participants, we competed in multi-disability races at Nationals to fill out the fields.

I never thought I'd have another chance to run in London's Olympic Stadium or revisit the birthplace of a Paralympic movement that has helped illuminate my journey in so many ways. To wear the Canadian singlet and race again in that stadium with Jérémie, a student-athlete born two years before I first represented Canada in 1998, remains a very special memory.

As Josh and I had done in the London 1500-metre Paralympic final five years earlier, Jérémie and I sprinted off the line in our semi-final in hopes of avoiding any early collisions. We led early and maintained our advantage the entire way, winning in 4:15.13 and advancing to the final two nights later.

We would be lining up once again against the Kenyan team of Samwel Mushai Kimani, the 2016 Paralympic T11 1500-metre champion and world record holder, and his guide James Boit. Kimani set his world record of 3:58.37 in the 2012 Paralympic final, in which Josh and I finished third. A few days before the World Para Athletics 1500-metre final in 2017, Kimani and Boit had won 5000-metre gold. In that race, our old rival, Cristiano Valenzuela and his guide, Francisco Munoz, finished second. They would be contesting the 1500-metre final as well.

The final took place at 8:30 in the evening, with barely a breath of wind. It felt like the crowd was on top of us as Jérémie and I walked to the line. That we were there at all was improbable and surreal. Even before proving our fitness and being selected for the team, we told each other that we were going to have fun, no matter the outcome. In the hours before the final, I reminded Jérémie of that promise.

When the gun sounded, we sprinted off the line and took the early lead before Valenzuela and Munoz moved around us on our outside. We sat in second and then third as a Polish runner, Aleksander Kossakowski and his guide, Krzysztof Wasilewski, made a move toward the front. The race was physical, and at one point, I bumped arms with Kossakowski, and all the while, Kimani and Boit ran patiently at the back of the field.

We reached 800 metres in a slow 2:17, and at that point, Jérémie and I, following our pre-race plan, moved to the lead. We wanted to string out the field because we knew the kickers would probably have the advantage over us if the race came down to a late sprint.

We opened up a gap as we rounded the curve and headed into the home stretch with 500 metres to go. We had dealt our hand, and the race was on. Behind us, Kimani and Boit reacted by moving up into second.

We hit the bell and fought to keep our lead. Round the curve and into the backstretch for the final time, and still, we were leading. Then the Kenyans moved up beside us, on our outside. We ran stride for stride together for about ten metres. And then they accelerated, and I couldn't match that aggressive move. Behind us, the Polish runners were also moving.

I strained not to lose ground as we rounded the final curve. Kimani and Boit were well clear and went on to win in 4:11.54. Jérémie and I dug deep over the final 150 metres to finish second in a seasonal best time of 4:13.67, just ahead of the fast-finishing Polish runners, Kossakowski and Wasilewski.

Although we hadn't been able to hold our lead, I was proud of how we had raced. Jérémie was just 21 and still relatively new to guiding, but raced as if he had years of experience.

I had the incredible privilege of competing in international competitions over a 19-year athletic career, but 2017 was among the sweetest because of the spontaneity of coming back after I'd retired from the national team and because, with Josh's coaching support, Jérémie and I had been able to make the most of an improbable opportunity by finishing second in the world. It had been a difficult and painful year with the separation Colleen and I were going through. The experience of competing at Worlds with Jérémie was truly a bright spot in what was otherwise not an easy time.

28 A New Reason

I celebrated my 40th birthday in August. Time was passing, and my life had fundamentally changed. After years of marriage, I needed to learn to face life on my own again. As the summer deepened and its shadows lengthened, I knew I needed to come to terms with how I'd lost my way and figure out who I was.

My father, Peter Dunkerley, had left when I was seven, leaving my mother to raise us. Now, my marriage had broken down. History had repeated itself.

Over the years, I always believed that if I'd had children, I would never have abandoned them. I never knew what was going through my father's head when he walked out on us. In the past, it had never occurred to me that he might have felt disconnected from our mother. It had been easy to blame him. It had been easy to hate him.

Now, I realize that he must have had his reasons, ones I could never understand, yet I no longer judged him in the way I had. I'd learned that love and rejection were emotively powerful forces that worked in unison and opposition. I'd learned that love, with its poetry and, conversely, its risk of inadequacy, could rhyme or dissolve into dissonance and deep pain.

As I became aware of time's reverberations, I felt more attuned to my buried trauma. I felt the sense of abandonment I'd harboured inwardly since my childhood, but I also felt an emerging new awareness deep within me. I

28 A New Reason

wanted my inner child to come out, to feel rooted and secure, to feel loved.

There is a saying that gratitude is an antidote to grief. For me, I knew running would be a remedy for inertia. In that period of deep emotional reckoning, I knew I needed to find a way to begin to look to the future.

I'd never run a marathon before, but it had been in the back of my mind for years. Ray Elrick, my long-time coach, had warned me against it because of the weeks and even months it would take to recover from running 26.2 miles, or 42.2 kilometres. He felt it would hurt my track racing.

I knew I wanted to run a competitive marathon, not just to participate but to finish. At 40, it seemed the time was now.

That fall, I trained for the California International Marathon (CIM), held each year in early December in Sacramento. Targeting a marathon at the end of the Canadian autumn was ideal in terms of training as it would give me time to recover after the summer track season and still allow plenty of time to prepare.

In late August, I reached out to Richard Hunter, a retired US marine who was visually impaired and who, for the previous ten years, had coordinated a visually impaired race at CIM. After talking on the phone, Richard generously extended a free registration, which I gratefully accepted. He also connected me with two Sacramento-based runners, each of whom would guide me for half of the marathon. He even provided me with a bursary to help offset the cost of my flight and accommodation.

In addition, Richard arranged for volunteers to pick up athletes at the airport in Sacramento and shuttle them to the race expo registration. He organized meals and events throughout the weekend. There were so many logistical and other details he took care of for the 51 visually impaired athletes. It felt like all we needed to do was show up and race.

Jérémie returned to school at Saint Francis University in Pennsylvania that fall and had the best cross-country season of his collegiate athletic career, running 32:19 for 10 kilometres in his conference championship meet. Before guiding me at the World Para Athletics Championships, Jérémie had come off what he felt to be a lacklustre collegiate track season. He had even briefly contemplated quitting running, but the spontaneous opportunity to train and race together that summer inspired him to continue.

Following his banner cross-country season, Jérémie returned to Ottawa for Christmas, but something didn't feel right. Athletes are typically well attuned to their bodies. After consulting his doctor and having a series of tests, a tumour was discovered.

It happened so fast. One moment, he was attending a small Christmas party at my place, and the next, he was getting ready for emergency surgery.

Fortunately, his surgery was successful, and after six weeks of recovery at home, he returned to complete his semester in Pennsylvania in the spring of 2018. A year later, he set a 1500-metre personal best of 3:48 at his conference championship. It was a testament to his resiliency. Where others might have counted themselves out, Jérémie remained steadfast in his resolve and worked his way back to running faster than he ever had.

Marathon training was a definite departure from the type of training I'd done in the past. Throughout the fall, I built up to doing regular long runs on Sunday mornings, often with Gilles Gobeil, who had guided Jon in previous years. We used the motivation of a post-run latte to push through the final kilometres of those runs along the Parkway and back towards my apartment.

I also did some long workouts with Alex Berhe. Josh and I had raced against him several years earlier in a 3000-metre indoor race in which we'd run our personal best for that distance. In 2017, Alex was competing in cross country and track for the University of Ottawa varsity team. Josh always kept a special lookout for Alex. They shared the experience of immigrating to Canada from East Africa.

Josh continued to coach me that fall. We did a few runs together along the Ottawa River on Saturday mornings with the young athletes in his group, but I did most of my running on the treadmill. I had some good weeks of training, including two consecutive weeks where I ran over 112 kilometres. There were other weeks, though, where my training was far from optimal. Learning to get to the gym in the neighbouring apartment building, something that should have been so simple, took time and considerable mental energy. Construction was underway between the two buildings. I

28 A New Reason

needed to walk through an underground parking garage, where I got lost more times than I can remember.

In mid-November, two weekends before CIM in Sacramento, I did a 34-kilometre run along the river with Josh and Alex. Josh ran with me for the first 13 kilometres at a steady pace before Alex took over. I took an energy jell, and Alex and I moved into a progressive, 80-minute tempo run that stretched me to my limit.

Flurries of snow began to fall as we got into Alex's car, and he drove me home. In hindsight, that workout prepared me very well.

Then I got sick and didn't run for almost a week. I wondered whether I'd even make it to the start line in Sacramento, but the rest probably did me a lot of good. I still had good training behind me, and going into the marathon, I knew there was nothing to lose.

I was in as good shape as I had ever been at that time of year. Somebody once told me that if you can run 30 kilometres at a good pace and if you are fit, a marathon comes down to rolling the dice. I had run 34 kilometres, and I knew I was reasonably fit. I felt ready to see what I could do.

In Sacramento, I would race with two local guide runners, Greg Bricca and Jacob Huston. The race would begin in Folsom, about 40 minutes from Sacramento by road. Sitting on a bus in the early morning as we drove out to the start along the route we would soon retrace, I thought, this feels far.

I shared a seat with a guide runner who, in each of the previous seven years, had flown to Sacramento to be a guide at CIM. He was in his 60s and had been an avid, lifelong runner. He told me he was recently diagnosed with a serious medical condition – his doctors were monitoring him – but it wasn't going to stop him from running and doing what he loved. That resonated with me. He was making it a priority to help another runner complete a marathon and accomplish something monumental, not dwelling on what-ifs but on making the best of what was.

Speaking with him made me realize that everybody bears a cross, whether blind or sighted, young or old, rich or poor. I met many people during the CIM weekend who had overcome tremendous adversity to be at the race, military veterans who had been shot and lost their eyesight and nearly their lives, and people for whom simply making it to the marathon start line was in itself a victory.

When I started training for CIM back in September, I hoped to run under two hours and 40 minutes. It was an ambitious target because running on the track is very different from a marathon. Because of the days of training I'd missed in my build-up, Josh thought it might make more sense to aim for 2:45. He encouraged me to enjoy the experience and not worry too much about the outcome.

I knew that running a six-minute mile pace was too fast, but that between 6:10 and 6:15 per mile was possible. That worked out to a finish time between 2:42 and 2:44. It was this plan that I talked through with Greg Bricca. He would be guiding me for the first half, and Jacob Huston would then take over. At CIM, the visually impaired runners were given the option of a separate start time, five minutes ahead of the main field, which meant we wouldn't begin with the main pack. We'd start with a clear road ahead.

On the morning of the marathon, the temperature in Sacramento was around seven degrees Celsius, with little wind. We set out, starting on a slight downhill. I could hear one of the other visually impaired marathoners, Don Balcom, who had a marathon personal best of 2:50, running closely behind us with his guide. I felt relaxed and well within myself.

Greg's watch told us we had run our first mile in 6:25, a little slow, but we didn't panic. At that point, we were completely on our own, two men running in rhythm in the early morning silence.

I don't think we consciously increased the pace; we simply started to warm up because our next mile was six minutes, followed by a 5:57, then a 6:05. It felt so easy, as I knew it should, early in the race. We kept reminding each other to hold back. This was a marathon, after all, with so many unknowns ahead.

After about four miles, the elite able-bodied runners, who started five minutes behind us, began to catch up. The eventual race winner would go on to complete the marathon in 2:11. As they passed us, a few said, "Keep it up. You guys are looking great!" This touched me because they were racing hard; such is the generosity of spirit of so many athletes, be they professionals or

28 A New Reason

casual runners, who make the running community a place of belonging for runners of all levels and abilities.

Starting at the six-mile mark, Greg helped me take cups of either water or electrolytes from the aid stations along the course. I had taken an energy jell just before the start and took two more at miles 8 and 16.

Then the sun came out. It felt as if we had a new guiding energy to propel us forward. With the sunrise, my spirits lifted, too.

Greg and I got to 10 miles in 60:50 and reached halfway in exactly an hour 20, and I was feeling great. At that point, Jacob took over. Greg remained in the race and would go on to finish in a time of 2:54.

With Jacob's fresh legs, we ran the risk of going too fast, and I told him I wanted to try to maintain a 6:10 to 6:15 pace for as long as possible. I knew we needed to be careful and that things could change quickly.

At 16 miles, I still felt good but was starting to hurt. Only ten miles to go; just think of it as a tempo run, I told myself.

People always say that in a marathon, the real race begins at 20 miles. Jacob and I reached it in two hours and two minutes. I had done a 21-mile run in training, so I was shortly heading into new territory. I tried to stay as relaxed as I could and let the race come. This was the stage of the race where people started to run out of glycogen. Around us, people were cramping; many were walking.

As Greg Bricca had done, Jacob was telling me everything I needed to know, putting us in the right position with other runners around us, giving me just the right amount of encouragement, and not pushing too hard. I was hurting, and our pace slowed between 18 and 24 miles, with an uphill climb at 21 miles running over the American River Bridge where we ran 6:35, but we also ran a 6:14 and a 6:12, so things could have been much worse.

It wasn't my breathing that was the problem, but my legs, which felt progressively heavier and more difficult to lift as the miles passed. Those last miles seemed interminable – it felt like it would take forever to reach another mile marker.

Finally, we were getting back into Sacramento, and the roadside was lined with spectators. We reached the 25th mile, and the adrenaline from the cheering along the roadside lifted my energy, enabling us to run the next mile in 6:05. We were passing a few people now. I tried to go by them hard each time, trying to forget how much I was hurting. I knew they must be hurting as well.

Eventually, Jacob and I turned into the final straightaway. I thought we had a few hundred metres still to go, but the line came quicker than I had anticipated. We finished in a time of 2:42.09, making us second overall among visually impaired runners, behind Chaz Davis, a US Paralympian who ran 2:38.24.

In a way, it had felt like beginner's luck. I was a track athlete who essentially had rolled the dice in a longer race, but now I saw myself as a marathoner as well. Greg Bricca and Jacob Huston had done a tremendous job guiding me, and Rich Hunter, the coordinator of the visually impaired category at CIM, had been an enabling force, opening a door of opportunity for me to come to Sacramento in the first place.

The California International Marathon was supposed to be a one-off. However, finishing second in the visually impaired category earned me a bursary to join a group called Team with a Vision that would be competing at the Boston Marathon in April 2018. I jumped at the chance to accept the invitation to participate in such an iconic race.

29 Coming to Terms

Winter in Ottawa is a long grind when you're training for a marathon. Maybe I overdid my workouts. Maybe I hadn't rested enough after the CIM. I can acknowledge the telltale signs of fatigue now in retrospect. Athletes are conditioned to ignore tiredness because they believe it will pass.

I knew I was tired leading up to Boston. Alex Berhe and I had been training together that winter, and our workouts had been going well initially. In February, Josh, Alex and I spent a week at an Athletics Canada training camp in Chula Vista, just outside San Diego. One of the workouts Alex and I did that week involved 12 times 1000 metres on the track, averaging 3:15 per kilometre, taking two minutes of rest. It was a confidence-boosting workout, as I'd never done anything like that before.

In early March, Alex and I ran an indoor 5000 metres in Ottawa in a slow time of 16:37, and two weeks later, I travelled to New York City and struggled to run 1:23 in the United Airlines New York City Half Marathon, guided by my friend Paul Thompson. The conditions there were cold, but even still, I knew something wasn't right because there was no spring in my legs.

During the few remaining weeks, I did my best to get ready for the marathon but was in a well of fatigue.

Boston is an experience unto itself, and I was looking forward to running in such a historic event, for which thousands of spectators, Josh among them, showed up despite the miserable weather.

The marathon didn't go well for me. The race was most memorable because of the cold, driving rain. Many of the participants suffered hypothermia or didn't finish.

Yuki Kawauchi from Japan won the men's race. Desiree Linden from the United States claimed the women's title. My guide, Rejean Chiasson, and I finished third in the visually impaired category in three hours and 13 minutes.

Everything that could have conceivably gone wrong did: the weather, fatigue and a stomach that hadn't liked what I'd eaten the night before. At a certain point, our time became irrelevant; the goal was just to finish. When we finally did, Rejean and I sat in one of the tents set up in the finish area and drank endless cups of chicken broth to warm up. I'd never had a broth that tasted so good.

After the Boston Marathon, I wasn't sure what was next, but I was tired: tired of pushing, tired of hurting, and tired of being tired.

In June, I travelled back to New York City again with our Achilles Ottawa group to run in the Achilles Hope and Possibility Race in Central Park, finishing as the first visually impaired athlete and running 23:35 for the four-mile race, guided by Mo'ath Alkhawaldeh, a friend of Paul Thompson. I had met Mo and his wife Maira a few months earlier at the United Airlines half marathon while staying with Paul and his wife Sham that weekend. Originally from Jordan, Mo hoped one day to represent his country in the Olympic marathon. He achieved this at the 2024 Paris Olympics, finishing 65th.

That month, I decided to retire once again from the national team. The Canadian Track and Field Championships were set to occur in Ottawa again, but I felt burned out. I was ready to step back from the national team on my terms.

That summer, I was one of ten recipients of an Athletes in Excellence Award from the Foundation for Global Sports Development, an organization supporting the promotion of fair, accessible, and abuse-free sport for youth

29 Coming to Terms

around the world. I was nominated by Mo, who had received the award himself the previous year. It came as a complete surprise.

I'd always striven to set a positive example through my running, and the Athletes in Excellence award was a call to action for me to do more to help young people thrive through sport, as I had done.

Coincidentally, around this time, Josh had been encouraging me to join him as a volunteer coach with the Ottawa Lions. Initially, I was hesitant to join him, uncertain that I could be of much help as I wouldn't have been able to observe the athletes. But Josh was persuasive, and I agreed to come to practices two nights a week and join him on the long runs with his group each Saturday morning.

Coaching proved to be a deeply gratifying experience, giving me more than I ever could have imagined. We had a small group comprising only ten athletes, so we were able to devote a lot of time and attention to each one, and I came to know them well.

There was Jenna, a brilliant student who unfortunately was injured often but who brought tremendous positive energy and a strong sense of team spirit to our group dynamic. Incredible to me, Jenna had even suggested our athletes wear tiny bells in the laces of their shoes so I could differentiate them from other runners as they passed by.

There was Colin, a former soccer player who cared about nutrition and cooking healthy food and who was the king of long runs. Colin ran two hours and 49 minutes in his first marathon in New York City at only 18 years of age. And there was Harun, a charismatic young man who had immigrated to Canada with his family from Somalia and who made up for his lack of size with an infectious *joie de vivre*. Harun was also absolutely terrified of dogs and hid between other athletes during runs any time a dog came remotely close.

I couldn't check their running form or see whether they were relaxed or straining as they trained, but I got an intuitive sense of how they were doing from our talks before and after a session. I learned to detect whether they were working too hard or not hard enough by listening to their breathing as they ran past.

Over time, Josh and I played off one another. He was demanding and pushed the athletes hard, whereas I was more gentle and ready to listen to their complaints.

The training was inspired in many ways by the workouts Ian had us do. They were long sessions, but the paces were always moderate and controlled. The idea was not to run them into the ground, which is often the downfall of young athletes, culminating in injury or overtraining and eventually leading them to leave the sport too soon. While we prepared them for competition, we also wanted them to connect with the joy of running for its own sake and to develop a love for the sport that would keep them healthy and active as lifelong runners.

We encouraged them to believe consistent and steady training was better than heroic workouts. Training this way wouldn't make them fast overnight. Patience was the key. Within a year, some of them had had big breakthroughs, were able to handle a much higher running volume than before and could compete at or near the front of most competitive fields over distances from 800 metres to ten kilometres.

Although I'd retired from the national team, I had committed to returning to Sacramento in December 2018 to run again in the CIM. It would be my third marathon in the space of a year, and my motivation to train wasn't where it had been. I travelled to Sacramento in early December and ran a time of 2:51.36, finishing second behind Chaz Davis once again. As in the previous year, Greg Bricca and Jacob Huston did a fantastic job guiding me.

There are things in our lives we like to believe are a certainty. Over time, life teaches us that very little is guaranteed. Health is one of the gifts we're not always aware of until it begins to erode.

That fall of 2018, Maurice called one night to tell me that my mother had had a mild heart attack. She was in hospital and likely needed to have an angioplasty, a procedure where a thin tube is inserted to open blocked coronary arteries.

I took an early train to Hamilton the next morning and, by lunchtime, was in her room. Maurice was there with my stepsister Rachael and her partner. By then, Jon was living in Victoria. He'd moved there a year earlier

29 Coming to Terms

to train with the national paratriathlon team.

My mother was stable and a little embarrassed for having caused what she felt was so much trouble. She hadn't been feeling well for a few days and had finally agreed to let Maurice bring her into emergency, where an ECG revealed that she'd had a heart attack without even realizing it.

The angioplasty the following day went well, and by the weekend, she was released from the hospital. She had medication to take and a series of medical follow-ups, but her energy and spirit were good. She even poured a glass of wine, and with Maurice, we raised a glass in gratitude and for her continued recovery and enduring health.

She had been the constant in our lives from the very beginning, and her heart attack came as a wake-up call and a warning sign. Back in Ottawa, I read about how to manage and sometimes reverse coronary disease, for example, by following a vegetarian diet. She was set in her ways, though. She and Maurice ate well, but they enjoyed eggs, meat, and cigarettes. Maurice had stopped smoking at different times over the years; my mother never could.

Doctors advised her to give up smoking, and I believe she did in the beginning. When Jon and I went back at Christmas, however, we knew she'd started again, though at first, she tried to hide it. Her attitude was fatalistic. She said she didn't feel strong enough to stop completely and that we all go when it is our time. It was difficult to hear.

My mother had had a painful journey: uprooted from her home, starting anew in Canada in hopes of giving us a better life. My sister Nicki had chosen to stay behind, and over the years, her resentment and feelings of abandonment had only grown. Our mother wanted to mend their fractured relationship when she and Maurice had visited her years ago, but it did not go well, and they became estranged, which was a source of deep pain for her.

She had endured difficult years with Maurice and lost a cherished son. Perhaps at that Christmas, she knew her reserves of energy were diminishing. Perhaps she recognized just how sick she was.

After the holidays, Jon returned to Victoria, and I took the train back to Ottawa. January 2019 arrived with its typical frigid cold. Still, the group of varsity athletes we coached braved the harsh weather to meet at the Arboretum for long Saturday morning runs, taking refuge indoors at The Dome for our other weekly practices. Slowly, the days started to lengthen.

Then, one late January morning, Maurice called to tell me in a teary voice that doctors had found a mass on my mother's liver, and the world seemed to stop spinning.

A week later, my mother had the first of a series of strokes. I was with Maurice in their apartment when my mother dropped her coffee as she stumbled over her words. We called an ambulance and spent the day and night with her in a hospital corridor before she was finally admitted.

She spent her remaining weeks in the hospital, aside from a brief period of three days at her home. There was cancer in her liver and pancreas, although the origin may have been in her ovaries. We would never know for sure.

I stayed with her during most of her illness. My brother, along with his new guide dog Niesen, stayed for a week, returned to Victoria, and then came back again. I know it brought my mother happiness to see Jon and me together, and I was grateful for the irreplaceable days we had with her.

Although Jon was known for his quirkiness, he could be cerebral and often withdrawn. I'm sure, in his own way, he was trying to process his sense of impending grief. Our mother had been his rock, too, there to encourage him at every turn.

One day, when the three of us were together, our mother said, "Jon, you're a man of many silences!" This struck a chord in me – perhaps an echo of our father's remoteness or my own fear of being trapped in an emotional silo.

Our uncle Alan and his wife Alma flew in from Northern Ireland to be with her. Diane, Maurice's sister, who had first introduced them 29 years earlier, also came. Even Colleen took the train from Ottawa to come and see her. Old work friends of hers from the retirement home where she had been a personal support worker for years stopped by her hospital room, sharing laughs, tears, and old stories.

My mother's health deteriorated quickly. Her illness had laid her bare, but even then, her inner child shone through, playful, subtle, and innocent.

29 Coming to Terms

I wanted to take care of her as she had taken care of us, yet there was so little I could do other than be with her and try to ensure she was comfortable.

Even through her confusion brought about by the strokes and multiple medications, she had moments of lucidity. At one point, she said, "I'm never going to get out of here!" That was painful to hear because I knew in my heart that it was true.

The doctors continued to conduct tests, discuss the possibility of outpatient treatment, and encourage her to get out of bed, if only so we could take her downstairs in a wheelchair to the hospital lobby, but she had little energy or desire to try – heartbreaking because my mother always had energy for everything.

The day before her last stroke, after which she slipped into a coma, it was just the two of us together, waiting for a porter to wheel her back to her room following yet another CAT scan. I said, "Mum, you've got to try to get out of bed, you can't just give up." She told me not to say that. Then, after a moment, she took my hand and said, "Jason, everything will be okay!"

That simple, profound message will never leave me. It's been one I've since turned to for solace and reassurance many times. That day, as we waited together in the hospital basement, I knew she was preparing to let go. While she would no longer be present in our lives, offering us advice and support, she had left me with guiding wisdom, words that would always be the answer.

She slipped away at 10:30 in the morning on March 15. My brother and I were with her, each holding one of her hands. It was just over a month before what would have been her 65th birthday.

In spring, I visited Northern Ireland for two and a half weeks. It was my first time back since Colleen and I had visited after the London Paralympics in 2012. Maurice also made the trip, staying with his sisters while I spent most of the time in Newtownards with my Uncle Alan and Aunt Alma.

My old elementary school friend, Neil McCullough, had invited me to his wedding in Colrain, on the north coast. In addition to meeting Ali, the bride-to-be, I wanted to rediscover my roots during the trip. After attending their small, intimate wedding celebration, I spent three days with them, their blended children, and their friends who had travelled from England, where Neil and Ali were living at the time. We played music and talked and partied late each night. Everybody was a musician, it seemed.

There was something deeply comforting about being back in the place where I came from: the familiar rhythms of language, the smell of coal fires, the freshness of the sea air, the local sense of humour, and the warmth and hospitality. Alan and Alma's door was always opening and closing to admit new guests and let others out.

Yet, I knew I no longer related to my homeland in the way I had before leaving. Canada had changed me. I wasn't the same person. This realization led to a deeper sense of dislocation. Where was home?

Alan took me up to Scrabo Tower and around to our old street, Valetta Park, where Nicki, my brothers and I had lived out our childhoods thirty years earlier. The street was quiet on the afternoon we visited. It felt desolate. My mind drifted to long-ago soccer games, men working outside, the smell of roasting meat or cake in the oven, very often coming from our own house, and our mother telling us not to slam the door because the cake wouldn't rise if we did.

I did some running in Northern Ireland. I had run very little in the months during my mother's illness. Alan, who even in his late 60s still ran a little, took me to a local gym to run on the treadmill any time I felt like it. He also introduced me to Amanda Perry and Norman Mawhinney, two masters athletes who trained with the local running club, Scrabo Striders. They each took me out for a few runs. Norman also guided me in a local ten-kilometre race on Easter Sunday held in Portavogie, a tiny village to the east along the Ards Peninsula. We finished second.

Growing up on the outskirts of Belfast, we rarely travelled into it unless we had to, although the school bus my brothers and I took each morning and afternoon traversed the city. Belfast had not been safe in those days because of the Troubles, which escalated during the 1980s.

The city felt lighter and freer on the day we drove in. It felt vibrant and reborn. We raised a glass of Guinness in my mother's memory at a local pub with Alan, Alma, and my cousin Rebecca.

Still, the memories and the scars of the Troubles remained and many

29 Coming to Terms

who lived through that period harboured vendettas. Occasional violence flared up, triggering corrosive political rhetoric and jeopardizing a fragile peace that hung by a thread.

Returning to Northern Ireland enabled me to connect with the people and places that had formed the bedrock of my early life. My mother's presence felt palpable. She lived in the air, in the smell of the April flowers, in the warmth of the sunshine as it permeated the dampness, and in the sincerity of the people I met who had known her a generation earlier. This was her place of origin and where her essence would remain eternally.

That summer, in the cemetery in Hamilton where Chris's ashes lay, we held a small celebration to commemorate my mother's life. It was an intimate service with about 30 close friends and family. Afterwards, we gathered in a nearby restaurant to toast and share memories.

I remember her in a way that feels tangible because, in many ways, even now, it's difficult to believe she isn't here. Memories of togetherness, the life lessons she imparted to me at a young age and all the way through, her cooking, her love of shopping, her love of laughter, her steadiness, her warmth, her constant encouragement, and unwavering love. She left me with the assurance that everything would be okay.

I wrote a song that my brother and I played at her celebration of life. It was inspired by the Whitney Houston song, "I Wanna Dance with Somebody," one of her favourite songs. Jon played bongos on the recording we made.

One Last Dance

One last dance, with those who knew you most,
In your adopted home, and from your native coast,
Here's to you, whose shadow holds us near,
And to your memory, for you'll always be here.
Troubled island, green and red, gave you breath,
Shifting sands and battle lines, but you walked straight ahead.
We became where the mist and rain falls like tears,

VISIONS OF HOPE

But you kept us dry still the same, through the years.
You made ends meet, you raised your kids by yourself,
You placed your dreams in a box on the shelf,
And you faced the world with a smile all the while.

I hear your voice calling us to come in,
And I feel the heat of our fire warm my skin.
Here's to you, who's carried on the wind,
And here's to true, and the love we knew.
Ocean tide and endless sky brought you west,
Waves that lifted you high on their crest,
New horizons, and he holds you tight next to him,
Maple leaves and winter white touch your skin.
Canada, a place of hopes and dreams,
And echoes of home in the spaces in between,
It gave so much, it took away. Why?
We couldn't keep you anyway, though we tried –
Though we tried.

And I miss you like I can't explain,
Though I know you'll always be near, you who gave us everything.
And you'll always shine, like a beacon in the grey.
I know you'll always be here in your own way.

One last dance, and we hold your hand
By your hospital bed, and we're swimming on dry land.
Here's to you, to your dignity and pride
And to your gentle soul, as you leave this life.
We play a song; it's an ode to you,
And we'll carry on, because I know you'd want us to.
So rest your head, rest your head,
We'll live for you, we'll honour you,
Thank you.

In October 2022, Jon and I planted a commemorative willow tree in Stanley

29 Coming to Terms

Park in honour of our mother. The following spring, I purchased and moved into a house that backs onto the park. It's reassuring to feel that my mother's essence is embodied in the tree growing nearby.

I have always considered myself a closet musician, writing songs to unpack life events. In 2019 and during the ensuing pandemic, Ken Kanwisher, a local musician, recorded and produced an album of my songs in his basement recording studio. He played cello, bass, and percussion on several of the tracks. In June 2023, I released the album Out of the Blue, a compilation of ten acoustic songs exploring themes of love, loss, hope, and renewal. The second track on the album, "This Tree's for You," was inspired by the willow tree in Stanley Park.

This Tree's For You

We plant this tree for you, in the park where we go,
Where the children play, the one the poets know,
Where the river flows, where the wind will set you free,
And hold you in its arms, like you carried me.

We plant this tree for you. Let your roots run deep
In your adopted soil, let your willows weep,
Let your branches sweep, across the autumn sky
And extend their love to you and I.

This tree's for you; it's for our loved one who is gone
Back to the earth which is your home, to the place where you belong.
This tree's for you, and it's in you we'll carry on,
We'll stand with courage on our own, we'll stay connected, we'll never be alone.

We plant this tree for you to project our hopes and dreams,
And to protect us from ourselves, and coming apart at the seams.
We make this plea to you, for we no longer need to grieve,
For what's natural is real, as you nourish the air we

breathe.

This tree's for you, and for the loss that we feel,
And yet we know that in your growth, you can help us to heal.
This dream's for you, as across an ocean of time
A poet offered up a prayer – that hope and history could rhyme.

This tree's for you.
This dream's for you.
And yet we know that in your growth, you can help us to heal.
This dream's for you, as across an ocean of time
A poet offered up a prayer – that hope and history could rhyme.

This tree's for you.
This dream's for you.

Playing guitar for Josh in 2024. (Josh Karanja)

30 Dusting off My Dreams

My mother's death affirmed what I think we each intuitively understand – that life is fleeting and finite. Life passes by so fast. One day, you're in your 20s, full of ambitions and idealism, and the next, you're approaching your mid-40s, and you wonder where time went. What was I chasing? Where did those years go?

For me, running, like life, had been a circuitous journey. At times when I was chasing medals or striving to qualify for national teams, I lost touch with the art of running and the simple joy of it. But when I finally stepped back and appreciated running's special place in my life, I started to understand how much it led me nearer to my inner self. It has imparted so many life lessons, not least that we are recreated with each step forward. Running, I knew, could remake us into a better version of who we are.

Running taught me that pain was something you could get used to; you could learn to live with it. Pain is normal, inevitable, and a natural part of our human experience. Through running, I learned that pain could be embraced as a welcome guest and that it could illuminate a path to healing and growth.

I wanted to run again – not to chase as I might have done when I was younger, but to run empowered by my belief in the ability I knew I still had. That spring of 2019, I'd reached out to Carla Nicholls, Athletics Canada's Para athlete head coach. Carla, ever encouraging, said they would gladly welcome me to rejoin the national team if I wanted to try a comeback.

Losing my mother made me realize that the window of life is before us right now. I still felt I had running left to do. I wanted to run to honour her memory, and I wanted to run for me.

I attended Josh's pre-wedding celebration, a Kenyan tradition, in June. I wasn't able to go to his Canadian wedding, as it had coincided with my mother's celebration of life.

Josh stepped back from coaching after he and his wife Dorothy had a daughter, Serena, in November. As a result, I took on the full coach role with our group, an opportunity I welcomed.

I set my sights that fall on competing in the 2019 California International Marathon. Jérémie was back in Ottawa after completing his degree in Exercise Physiology, and we started doing workouts together. He planned to come to Sacramento to guide me for the first half of the marathon.

The training was going well, but in October, I developed plantar fasciitis on my right foot. Despite having athletic therapy and doing various things at home to try to break up the inflammation, I could barely make it through a run. Even walking became uncomfortable, and it made no sense to continue training.

I took a break for several weeks and tried running again in December, but my foot still wasn't fully healed, and the pain under my heel led me to run even more on my toes than usual. Then, I developed a new pain on the top of my foot early in the new year. A bone scan revealed a stress fracture in my second metatarsal, which runs along the top of the second toe. It was my first, an injury I previously believed I was immune to.

The stress fracture made me realize how depleted I'd become. I'd always felt capable of handling anything that life brought my way, but I started to understand that my resources were finite. I knew I was still grieving. The loss of my mother, the loss of my marriage too – marathon training had probably been the catalyst that took me over the line to injury – the pieces of my life experience were deeply interwoven into everything I did.

I accepted the forced rest from running. I knew I needed it. Jon returned to Ottawa for a few months that winter and lived on my couch. His presence did a lot to lift my spirits. He was training for triathlons, so we spent hours together in the gym in my apartment building, with me riding the stationary bike while he ran on the treadmill. We drank lots of coffee, and I quietly tapped around the apartment after 8:30, his bedtime.

In January 2020, Dave Mather, the father of one of Josh's former high school athletes, joined our group indoor track practices. Mike Mather had trained with Josh a couple of years earlier. Heather Mather, Dave's wife, was also connected with our group through her work as a dietitian. She had come to speak to our athletes previously about the basics of sports nutrition.

Dave had been a national-level middle-distance runner in the late 1980s and early 1990s and had run 3:40 for 1500 metres. He was interested in co-coaching with me, which I welcomed. I knew it would be helpful to have eyes on the athletes and another perspective on training development to bring out the best in them.

Although Dave had been away from the sport for several years, he had an intuitive sense of the type of training that would most benefit each athlete. Low-key, observant, and strategic, he devised workouts that played to their strengths. I valued his perspective and what he brought to our group.

I also came to realize that, given my hopes of trying to make one more Paralympic team, I, too, wanted a person like Dave to help bring out the best in my running. Dave was new to coaching, but I saw this as a benefit and not a limitation, as it meant he'd have new ideas.

We continued to co-coach the group, but he began to oversee my training also. Gradually, he started to craft the weekly workouts for the athletes, taking the coaching lead as I started back to regular running that spring.

Around the same time that Dave Mather and I started coaching together, I delivered a TEDx talk, "Why Not Believe in Hope and Possibility?" organized by students at Ashbury High School in Ottawa. I'd been encouraged to become a speaker by Pippa Kolking, the daughter of Christian Kolking, one of our Achilles Ottawa guide runners and a committed, long-time board member.

In it, I shared the story of how Dick Traum, a middle-aged New Yorker, had challenged himself to complete the New York City Marathon in 1976 as a single-leg amputee. That experience led him to encourage others with disabilities, individuals who may not have run even a mile before, to train for and participate in marathons. Eventually, this culminated in the creation of Achilles International in 1983.

Back in 2010, I had been part of a group that formed our own Achilles Ottawa club, comprising visually impaired runners and volunteer guides, joining an international movement that, at that time, had expanded to 70 countries around the globe. As I explained in the talk, persons with disabilities are often excluded from participating in sports. Still, through the power of connection, a sport like running could become accessible with help from guide runners who selflessly enabled those without sight to run.

I wanted the students to know that each of them was uniquely capable of becoming a guide runner in a metaphorical sense by helping others to discover something hopeful and positive. It didn't have to be running. By supporting those around them through selfless action, they could enable others to identify with something transformational within themselves and, in that way, help to cultivate a better world.

I did my first run following the stress fracture on March 1. It was a sunny, cold, late winter morning. Nancy, a woman whom I had recently started dating; my friend Gilles; and I ran along Sussex Drive in Ottawa, doing three one-minute intervals with one-minute walk breaks between each. The sunshine warmed us and seemed to project a hopeful promise.

A few days afterwards, we went into pandemic lockdown. I joined most other federal public servants in working from home. I was part of a small team within the Accessibility Office at Public Services and Procurement Canada and was working on the development of its interim departmental accessibility plan following the passage of the 2019 Accessible Canada Act legislation, calling for a fully accessible country by 2040.

Our training group wasn't permitted to meet in person during the lockdown, but Dave sent out weekly training plans that we encouraged the athletes to do themselves on the roads. Some did, and others didn't, as each of them attempted to navigate the new reality of the pandemic with its transition to online classes, social distancing, and everything that came with the restrictions.

30 Dusting off My Dreams

Alex drove to my apartment for a run every couple of days, which was courageous and kind at a time when meeting people under any circumstances was strongly discouraged. Running with him enabled me to begin getting back into shape.

Over the weeks, Dave had Alex and I build up our running volume, and by mid-April, we were ready to start back into intervals. With no access to the track because of the lockdown, we did the majority of our running on the gravel path along the Ottawa River.

Canada was the first nation to withdraw from the Tokyo 2020 Olympics and Paralympics only a couple of weeks into the pandemic, and shortly afterwards, the Games were postponed until the following year. For many athletes, this was devastating, as their entire preparation had for years been singularly focused on Tokyo that summer. For Alex and me, it came as a reprieve. Realistically, there would have been very little time for us to get into shape to make the team.

During those first few months of the pandemic, my human interaction was limited to Alex and only a couple of other people. My brother had returned to Victoria by then and was continuing to train in hopes of making the Paralympic triathlon team.

That summer of 2020, as the first series of restrictions loosened, our training group started meeting for sessions at Immaculata High School. It was great seeing everyone again, and many of the athletes who had trained with us previously showed up, along with a few newcomers.

The track at Immaculata was 348 metres, 52 metres short of the standard 400-metre track circumference. Dave did a lot of math to develop workouts that were more or less aligned with standard track sessions, such as 400- or 1000-metre repeats.

In our first Ottawa Twilight race in early August, Alex and I ran 1500 in 4:33. Other than when I'd been injured, I hadn't run that slow since high school. Following that race, I wondered if trying to make another Paralympic team was realistic, but I knew I wanted to try. Only ten days later, Alex and I ran 16:39 for 5000 metres, a big improvement from our 1500 metres the previous week.

That fall, I finally resigned as Achilles Ottawa's president. It had been ten years of working with committed individuals to promote opportunities for blind and visually impaired runners, but I felt it was important not to stay too long in positions of leadership. The club needed fresh energy and ideas. Richard Marsolais, a former national team tandem cyclist and multiple-time marathoner, agreed to step in as president and continues to do excellent work leading the organization, steering it through the closures and re-openings of the pandemic, and keeping the core group of blind runners and guides together. Achilles and its mission of hope and possibility will always be important to me. I continue to serve on its board and remain closely connected with the group.

Alex and I trained throughout that fall, but there were no races on our immediate horizon. Attempting to qualify for the Tokyo Paralympics the following summer was our ultimate target.

31 Chasing Time

In early January 2021, I flew to Victoria, British Columbia, to spend a couple of months living and training with Bruce Deacon, who had been the Athletics Canada middle distance coach at the 2017 World Para Athletics Championships. He was coaching a group of student-athletes. My brother, who was still training in Victoria hoping to qualify for the Tokyo Paralympics in Para Triathlon, lived just a couple of kilometres away. With the impending closures and knowing the challenges of training in an Ottawa winter, it was important to be in a better training environment if I was serious about making the Paralympic team.

I arrived with a minor calf strain, and it took the first two weeks to fully heal. Although I could jog, I needed to be careful in the beginning and avoid faster running.

With guide-running help from Bruce's young athletes, who took to it naturally, and another local runner named Cliff Chiles, I got back to full training and had some good workouts, but I never felt as though I had hit my stride. We had some long, enjoyable Saturday morning group runs in shorts and t-shirt weather along the Goose Trail, trying to keep up with Liam Stanley, Bruce's athlete who had a form of cerebral palsy and was among the best in the world in the T37 category. Many times, I felt like I was hanging on to the back of the group.

VISIONS OF HOPE

The COVID lockdown was in effect throughout my time in Victoria. As athletes, we were permitted to train and use the Pacific Sport Institute of Excellence services, but outside of that, people were discouraged from meeting socially.

Most federal public servants were working virtually, so I rose for work early to be online at six, which was nine in Ottawa.

There were so many uniquely beautiful places to explore on Vancouver Island, and I yearned to walk into nature and lose myself in its magic. I didn't know the suburban area well, though, and I remember a feeling of emotional paralysis, accentuated no doubt by the pandemic, which prevented me from venturing into unknown territory. I even got lost walking one evening to a nearby local restaurant to pick up dinner.

Bruce and his labradoodle Murphy were gracious hosts, and I enjoyed our evening conversations over dinner and a beer. Jon and I met and had pizza on some weekends, and I got together a few times with Jérémie, who had also come out to Victoria to train with Bruce in hopes of improving his 1500-metre personal best of 3:48 and qualifying for the Olympic Trials. We'd walk around Victoria's downtown.

I headed home in early March during a lull in the lockdowns. The 2020 Tokyo Paralympics was rescheduled to late August of 2021. To be considered, Canadian athletes had to be ranked within the top eight in their event, spanning the previous three years. This meant that Alex and I would have to run around 4:16 for 1500 metres, the event we were hoping to qualify for.

As soon as the snow melted that spring in Ottawa, Alex and I returned to the familiar Ottawa River path to run the tempo and interval workouts that Dave emailed to us. Ontario was in yet another lockdown, and we were unable to train on a running track until the May Victoria Day long weekend when restrictions once again started to ease.

By this time, unfortunately, our training group had dissolved. With so many lockdowns, it had been difficult to sustain the previous energy and momentum. As things started to reopen, a few of our athletes drifted away to other groups within the Ottawa Lions to train with faster runners.

31 Chasing Time

Others, such as Harun, the charismatic young 1500-metre runner originally from Somalia, were studying and working to support family members, leaving little time at the end of the day to train.

When we were finally permitted to use the Terry Fox track near the end of May, Dave met Alex and me to time our intervals. Training along the river had given us a good base of aerobic fitness, but 1500-metre training requires specificity, which can only come from spending time on the track.

Alex and I opened our season in Ottawa on the fourth of June with 4:27 for 1500 metres. It wasn't fast, but it represented a six-second improvement from the previous summer. We followed it up by running 4:25 a week later at a meet at York University in Toronto. The week after that, we returned to Toronto and ran 4:19. Suddenly, it felt like we might be able to race ourselves onto the team.

The following week, we drove to St. Laurent, Quebec, and I struggled, running 4:30 in windy conditions. It felt like a step backward, but our workouts and the trajectory of our races gave me every reason to remain positive. Difficult days happen, and I'd known for years that progress in running didn't necessarily follow a linear pattern.

Alex and I ran 4:16.5 in Ottawa ten days after that. This brought us to 11th place in the rankings from the previous three years. We were close to the top eight, but the window for qualification was closing.

We had one more opportunity, once again at York. We led early in the race but faded and ran 4:19.

On the long drive back to Ottawa, neither of us knew what to say. We'd put our hearts into trying to make the team, and it hadn't been enough. It was the first time I'd missed qualifying for a Paralympic team since representing Canada at my first Games in Sydney back in 2000.

Perhaps if we had one or two more races, perhaps if we had been able to start our track training earlier in the season – there were so many what-ifs, but in the end, it wasn't to be.

You never really prepare emotionally for not being selected. Along the way, I'd told myself not to attach too much weight to whatever the outcome might be because running was only one area of my life. I had so much going for me away from the track. As the dust settled in the weeks that followed,

Chris White, a local songwriter, radio host, and community builder, encouraged me to start a radio show. He introduced me to Jacob Shymanski, a young radio producer also with a visual impairment. For the next year, we co-hosted a weekly, 30-minute program, Connection, on CKCU, the Carleton University radio station. The program featured interviews with athletes, musicians, health practitioners, and many others. It was a rewarding experience and allowed me to connect with guests from many interesting walks of life.

Nonetheless, it hurt both Alex and me not to make the team. I knew what the chance to compete in Tokyo would have meant to Alex and how proud his family in Addis Ababa would have been to watch him on television as he guided me in his Canadian singlet.

Representing Canada one more time would have meant a lot to me, too. Participating in the Games would have been an affirmation that I could defy the duress of age and still compete among the best in the world. Instead, I was at home cheering for our team, for athletes like Liam Stanley and Nathan Reich. Nate won in the T38 1500 metres for athletes with cerebral palsy. I felt very proud of the young athletes who were Canada's emerging generation of trailblazers and role models. They were the key to perpetuating the Paralympic ethos in Canada.

I had ambitions of training together with Alex in hopes of competing at the 2024 Paralympic Games. It would have been a poetic ending to my competitive running career. Late in 2023, however, after nearly a year of dealing with a persistent glute hamstring injury, I came to realize that I could let go. I didn't need to run through pain and put it all on the line, as I had done so many times in the past. I could let my body heal and run healthy into old age. I could set myself free.

Now, having just celebrated my 47th birthday but feeling younger, there is no pain when I run. I am incredibly grateful to be healthy and able to enjoy running for its own sake. I'm running strong and honouring my vision of hope, which is really a vision for life and everything the gifts of energy, movement, freedom and vitality have given me.

Acknowledgments

I wouldn't have been able to complete *Visions of Hope* without the care, patience and attention to detail of the people who have worked closely with me on this project. Thank you, Dr. Joannie Halas, for your long-running friendship, committed support, constant encouragement, and gentle nudges to keep writing. My sincerest appreciation to Dr. Bruce Kidd for taking the time to review my initial draft and for penning such a thoughtful and kind forward to this book. Thank you also to my friend Aida Stratas, who I first met through our MA in World Literatures and Cultures program, for encouraging me, in particular, to add key details to the early sections of the manuscript. Thank you, Rosemary Shiller and Ed Shiller at Yorkland Publishing, for believing in this book's potential and for your thoughtful edits and suggestions in ultimately helping to make it better. Thank you also to John Rafferty, Alice Clark, Christen Thomas, David Stinson, and the team at the Canadian National Institute for the Blind for your encouragement and vote of confidence with the development of the audio version of this book.

Above all, I acknowledge my mother, whose vision of hope in search of a better life made all things possible.

To Our Dreams

We talk about our broken dreams
Eroded over time, unmade
They faded, heady hopeful schemes
Betrayed and stymied, stilted, stayed.
We steered away from life's rough seams
And stayed on the beaten track, secure
And set. We dodged the in-betweens.
We settled, grew, advanced, mature
And unsure. Not yet, not today we said
When our dreams came knocking at the door.
Not now, not here. And we plowed ahead,
With a hollow feeling at the core,
Dreaming of more, reliving visions and scenes
Of our youth, from a time of best-laid plans,
Of ambitions obscure behind smoke screens,
Of buried truth under shifting sands.
You speak of languages you knew
Back then, and working at the UN,
Back when the world was set for you,
For you held the key, the brush, the pen
Back then. Me too, I turned away
From words. For practicality
Clouded my vision at the end of the day
And reshaped my reality.
To redefine ambition though
Is to adapt to the forks and grooves
In the road, to come of age, to grow
In our chosen place, on this earth that moves
Through time and space. And so I'll stand
And stir these embers with a pen.
I'll stoke this flame with words, new and
Reclaimed. I'll dare to dream again.

Jason's International Results

2017 World Para Athletics Championships	1500 metres 2nd
2016 Paralympic Games	1500 metres 5th
2015 IPC Athletics World Championships	5000 metres 2nd
2015 Parapan American Games	5000 metres 1st
2015 Parapan American Games	1500 metres 2nd
2012 Paralympic Games	5000 metres 2nd
2012 Paralympic Games	1500 metres 3rd
2011 IPC Athletics World Championships	800 metres 1st
2011 IPC Athletics World Championships	1500 metres 4th
2011 Parapan American Games	1500 metres 2nd
2011 Parapan American Games	5000 metres 3rd
2008 Paralympic Games	1500 metres 3rd
2007 Parapan American Games	1500 metres 1st
2007 Parapan American Games	800 metres 1st
2006 IPC Athletics World Championships	800 metres 1st
2006 IPC Athletics World Championships	1500 metres 1st
2004 Paralympic Games	1500 metres 2nd
2003 IBSA World Championships	1500 metres 1st
2003 IBSA World Championships	800 metres 1st
2002 IPC Athletics World Championships	1500 metres 1st
2001 IBSA Para Pan American Championships	1500 metres 1st
2001 IBSA Para Pan American Championships	800 metres 1st
2000 Paralympic Games	1500 metres 2nd
1998 IBSA World Championships	1500 metres 1st
1998 IBSA World Championships	800 metres 4th

Photo Credits

Cover and page 163: Mark Davidson / Almay Stock Photo
Page 108, 162 (bottom), 233: Copyright Canadian Paralympic Committee
Page 162 (top): Ian Ewing
Page 170: Dan Plouffe
Back Cover Photo: Charlie Pitts

About the Author

Jason Dunkerley never let his lack of sight diminish his drive to live life to the fullest or prevent him from developing his innate athletic talent while also inspiring others, regardless of their abilities, to achieve personal fulfillment through sport. And he never let the demands of his 25-year career as an athlete diminish his devotion to those in need, even to the point of donating a kidney to his ailing wife.

Jason grew up in Northern Ireland during the 1980s with two brothers, who were also visually impaired, and a fully sighted sister. Encouragement from his parents to play outside just like other children, and support from elementary school teachers as he played a variety of sports instilled the love for physical activity that endures as a defining part of his life. When he was thirteen, Jason immigrated with his family to Canada and attended the W. Ross Macdonald School for the Blind in Brantford, Ontario, where students were encouraged to participate in sports. Jason was drawn to middle-distance running.

After graduating from high school, Jason enrolled in the University of Guelph, where the increased level of training enabled him to qualify for his first national team. He graduated with a degree in international development. Years later, while still a high-performing athlete, he earned a master's degree in world literatures and cultures at the University of Ottawa.

Jason now lives in Ottawa. For the past eight years, he has worked for the Canadian government, most recently supporting policy development intended to advance inclusion in sport for persons with a disability. Before this, he spent seven years with the Active Living Alliance for Canadians with a Disability, where he coordinated a national initiative to enhance access to inclusive community recreation opportunities.

www.ingramcontent.com/pod-product-compliance
Lightning Source LLC
Chambersburg PA
CBHW072153070526
44585CB00015B/1120